C000271109

On Revival

A Critical Examination

On Revival

A Critical Examination

PATERNOSTER PRESS

Copyright © 2003 The Editors and Contributors

First published in 2003 by Paternoster Press

09 08 07 06 05 04 03   7 6 5 4 3 2 1

Paternoster Press is an imprint of Authentic Media,
P.O. Box 300, Carlisle, Cumbria, CA3 0QS, UK
and
P.O. Box 1047, Waynesboro, GA 30830-2047, USA

Website: www.paternoster-publishing.com

The right of the Editors and Contributors to be identified as the Author of this
Work has been asserted by them in accordance with the Copyright, Designs and
Patents Act 1988.

*All rights reserved. No part of this publication may be reproduced,
stored in a retrieval system, or transmitted in any form or by any means,
electronic, mechanical, photocopying, recording or otherwise, without the
prior permission of the publisher or a licence permitting restricted copying.
In the UK such licences are issued by the Copyright Licensing Agency,
90 Tottenham Court Road, London W1P 9HE.*

British Library Cataloguing in Publication Data
A catalogue record for this book is available from the British Library

ISBN 1-84227-201-2

Unless otherwise stated, Scripture quotations are taken from the
NEW REVISED STANDARD VERSION BIBLE,
copyright 1989, Division of Christian Education of the National Council
of the Churches of Christ in the United States of America.
Used by permission. All rights reserved

Cover Design by FourNineZero and Tom Walker
Typeset by WestKey Ltd, Falmouth, Cornwall
Printed in Great Britain by Bell & Bain Ltd, Glasgow

'There are some Christians who never get more excited than when "revival" is mentioned. But is it any more than a fad, fashion or even a fantasy? Here is a significant collection of articles – not all speaking with a single voice – to guide us in our thinking about revival biblically, theologically, historically and pragmatically. The papers are written by scholars, but scholars who are engaged in the realities of the contemporary church scene. This is simply the most helpful and honest introduction to the subject of revival I have seen.'

Derek Tidball,
Principal of London Bible College.

'These authoritative essays offer a comprehensive overview of what is meant by revival and revivalism. They survey the various forms revival may take at different times and in different places. They also offer important material on – and keys to – the modern situation, especially in the United Kingdom.'

David Martin,
Emeritus Professor of Sociology,
London School of Economics.

'All Christians want revival but few of us want to think about it. *On Revival* helps us think about what we all want. This collection of essays offers us an intelligent profile of the theology, nature, history and sociology of revival.'

Joel Edwards,
General Director,
Evangelical Alliance.

Contents

Foreword

Roger Forster

It was a privilege and a great delight to be a very willing participant
in the two-day conference on revival called by Professor Andrew
Walker of the Centre for Theology and Culture at King's College,
London in 2002 and run jointly with Kristin Aune. Not only did
I hear as many of the papers as was physically possible, but I have
since eagerly read them all, this further encounter being even more
enlightening and stimulating. The high level of research, scholarship and its objective integrity will make this volume a standard
work on revival for years to come. Occasionally, it is true, the
authors' predispositions show through and most chapters glow with
some excitement, anticipating 'revival fire', but these elements in
no way detract from the careful academic assessments; rather they
add to the richness of the papers. Nearly all the writers address the
problem of definition – what is revival? Most note the evangelical
church's persistent interest in revival, and some question the desir-
ability of certain types of renewal and their final results. Clearly then
there are a number of reasons why this book should be read.

First, and perhaps above all else, those of us who have sought to
live in the flow of the church's mission – and is there such a thing as
church without a missionary calling? – will want to investigate every
aspect of church deepening and evangelising known and experienced
in history. Whether such aspects are called 'Revival', 'Awakening',
'Evangelistic Movements', 'Cross-Cultural Missions', or by a host of
other names, the eschatological rose of 'blessing all the families of
the earth' will smell just as sweet to those of us who are longing
that God's goodness should be preached in all the world and that
the eschaton might come. Those wanting to fulfil the mission of the

church more effectively, intelligently, genuinely and authentically will be grateful for this timely book. Revival can only be of value to the degree in which it finally contributes to fulfilling the purpose of God.

Second, since some of us have experienced preachers who without doubt are sincere proponents of revival, but whose major objectives seem to have been to promote the phenomena and accompaniments of revival, it is important for us to be able to identify what is truly God at work, albeit mediated through human agency, and avoid unnecessary concentration on spiritual red herrings, time-wastings, peddlings, and even prostitutions of the holy engracings of God. Much spiritual wisdom born of experience as well as the formal disciplines of the Academy is contained in these pages with holy warnings not to root out the tares of the natural and 'soulish' in revival while campaigning against the demonic. These pages will help us discern: 'trying the spirits' has not been overly heeded in our current plethora of prophets, but sadly also, too many 'despise prophesyings' as a consequence. It is still God's word: 'You may all prophesy.'

Third, the historical research here is enlightening and invaluable. No revivalist or period of revival is eulogised as if we were erecting a mausoleum – which is warned against by our Lord. All of us who love history are tempted to live in an unreal dream past and thereby ignore God's calling in the present. Nonetheless, this book will help us to know where we come from and, in doing so, help us find our way into the future. Whatever our ecclesiastic tradition, or prophetic mother's milk, or eschatological hope – from 'the church in ruins' to 'end time harvest' – to be aware of our roots will help us to respect and honour those of different revivalist expressions while adjusting our own appropriately. For instance, despite the apparent diversity of two of our contributors, Mark Stibbe and Meic Pearse, their approaches are really complementary. On the one hand, Mark inspires us for future revival by introducing us, with 'a great affection', to a little known Norwegian revival and revivalist Hans Neilsen Hauge, whose perseverance, sacrifice and labour in his most difficult of situations sound heroic. On the other hand, Meic Pearse's more cautionary lesson for the future reminds us of the need for persistent hard work in leading the flock of God if we are looking for current growth and permanent fruit.

Whether revival is defined as normal or abnormal Christianity, whether God given or sought by us through faith, whether essential, optional or even unnecessary, we can all benefit from the contributions of these papers for a comprehensive and stimulating presentation of the God of revival.

Finally, on a personal note, I have found my own heart, after nearly 48 years of Christian ministry, revived with this inquiry into revival. It has shown me a fresh vision of Jesus the source and objective of revival. May it do the same for all its readers. Thank you, Andrew and Kristin, for bringing about this collection of essays which will be a spiritual resource for God's kingdom.

Acknowledgements

We would like to thank Jill Morris, Lucy Atherton and Robin Parry of Paternoster Press for their sterling support for this project, from helping in the preparation of the King's Conference in 2002, through to the final preparations for this book.

Contributors

David Bebbington is Professor of History at the University of Stirling. He was an undergraduate and postgraduate at Jesus College, Cambridge, and a research fellow at Fitzwilliam College, Cambridge, before taking up a post at Stirling, where he has taught since 1976. He has also taught at the University of Alabama, Birmingham, at Regent College, Vancouver, at Notre Dame University, Indiana, and at the University of Pretoria. His books include *Patterns in History: A Christian Perspective on Historical Thought* (Downers Grove: IVP, 1979), *The Nonconformist Conscience: Chapel and Politics, 1870–1914* (London: George Allen & Unwin, 1982), *Evangelicalism in Modern Britain: A History from the 1730s to the 1980s* (London: Unwin Hyman, 1989), *William Ewart Gladstone: Faith and Politics in Victorian Britain* (Grand Rapids: Eerdmans, 1993) and *Holiness in Nineteenth-Century England* (Carlisle: Paternoster, 2000).

Neil Hudson is the Director of Undergraduate Studies at Regent's Theological College, Nantwich, Cheshire, the national training college for the Elim Pentecostal churches. He has been a minister with the church for seventeen years and alongside his teaching activities leads a church in Salford, Manchester. His areas of interest include the history and development of British Pentecostalism and the challenges facing churches in contemporary society. He is the consultant editor of the *Journal of the European Pentecostal Association*, in which the article 'The Earliest Days of British Pentecostalism' appeared in 2001. He has contributed to *Pentecostal Perspectives* (ed. K. Warrington, Carlisle: Paternoster, 1998) and the *Encyclopaedia of Christianity* (ed. J. G. Melton, forthcoming).

Kenneth S. Jeffrey was born in Northern Ireland and studied history at Stirling University. After two years teaching in Malawi, he returned to Aberdeen to study theology, where he gained a first-class honours degree. He undertook further postgraduate studies by researching the 1859 Revival in the north-east of Scotland. He is currently the parish minister of Cupar Old and St Michael of Tarvit in Fife.

William Kay is Senior Lecturer in Religious and Theological Education at King's College, London and Director of the Centre for Pentecostal and Charismatic Studies at the University of Wales, Bangor. He has been associated with the Pentecostal and charismatic movements for more than thirty years. He was educated at Oxford and worked as a Religious Education teacher and in a Pentecostal church during the 1970s. After completing a PhD in education, he did research on collective worship at the University of Southampton, before spending ten years in ministerial training. In 1989 he completed a PhD in theology, which told the story of Assemblies of God in Britain. Subsequently, he wrote *Pentecostals in Britain* (Carlisle: Paternoster, 2000), which broadens the field of focus to other Pentecostal denominations. He continues to pursue both interests – religious education and the Pentecostal and charismatic movements – and has written numerous academic papers in both fields.

Steve Latham pastors an inner-city Baptist church in Paddington, London. His PhD thesis analysed the phenomenon of contemporary prophecy.

Graham McFarlane read theology at London Bible College and then trained to teach Religious Education. After four years of teaching he returned to LBC for the MA before taking a year out with L'Abri Fellowship. Subsequently, he took his PhD at King's College, London. He joined London Bible College in January 1990 as Lecturer in Systematic Theology and has a passion for teaching people to think in relation to their faith. He has written two books on the Scottish theologian Edward Irving, *Christ and the Spirit: The Doctrine of the Incarnation according to Edward Irving* (Carlisle: Paternoster, 1996) and *Edward Irving: The Trinitarian Face of God* (Edinburgh: St Andrew Press, 1996), and has launched the popular Paternoster *Why Do You Believe?* series with *Why Do You Believe What You Believe about the Holy Spirit?*

(Carlisle: Paternoster, 1998) and *Why Do You Believe What You Believe about Jesus?* (Carlisle: Paternoster, 2000). He is Theological Adviser to the Christian Medical Fellowship and Course Tutor for the Institute of Counselling (Glasgow).

Mark Patterson is currently Senior Pastor of Community Presbyterian Church, a congregation of 900 in Ventura, California. He did undergraduate studies in theology and biblical studies at Whitworth College in Spokane, Washington, and theological training at Princeton Theological Seminary, Princeton, New Jersey. He completed a PhD in theology at King's College, London, writing a thesis entitled *Designing the Last Days: Edward Irving, the Albury Circle, and the Theology of The Morning Watch.*

Meic Pearse obtained his doctorate in ecclesiastical history from Oxford for his research into mid-sixteenth-century English religious radicals. He is Lecturer in Church History and BA Course Leader at London Bible College, and Associate Professor of Church History at the Evangelical Theological Seminary, Osijek, Croatia. He is author of four books, including *The Great Restoration* (Carlisle: Paternoster, 1998), about British and European religious radicalism in the sixteenth and seventeenth centuries, and (with Chris Matthews) *We Must Stop Meeting Like This* (Eastbourne: Kingsway, 1999), about being church in a postmodern culture.

Tom Smail studied philosophy and theology in Glasgow, Edinburgh and Basel. He was ordained into the Church of Scotland and served in parishes in West Calder, Irvine and Wishaw. He became involved in the early charismatic renewal in the mid 1960s and later joined and then succeeded Michael Harper in the leadership of the Fountain Trust, which was then engaged in promoting charismatic renewal in the mainline churches. In 1979 he became Vice-Principal and Lecturer in Doctrine at St John's College, Nottingham and was ordained into the Anglican ministry. In 1985 he became Team Rector of All Saints, Sanderstead in Croydon, from which he retired in 1994. He is Senior Visiting Research Fellow of King's College, London and was Visiting Professor of Preaching at Fuller Theological Seminary in California in 2000. His books are *Reflected Glory* (Grand Rapids: Eerdmans, 1975), *The Forgotten Father* (Grand Rapids: Eerdmans, 1980), *The Giving Gift* (London: Hodder & Stoughton, 1988), *Windows on the Cross* (London: Darton, Longman & Todd, 1995) and *Once* *and For All: A Confession of the Cross* (London: Darton, Longman & Todd, 1998).

Ian Stackhouse was Leading Pastor of the King's Church, Amersham, Buckinghamshire – a charismatic-Evangelical House Church in the Chilterns – for the last ten years. During this time he completed an MTh on the subject of immediacy in charismatic worship and is currently finishing a PhD on the subject of revivalism before returning to the pastorate.

Mark Stibbe is Vicar of St Andrew's Church, Chorleywood, and a visiting lecturer at London Bible College, as well as a research fellow. He is author of fourteen books, including *Thinking Clearly about Revival* (Crowborough: Monarch, 1998).

Max Turner is Professor of New Testament Studies and Vice-Principal at London Bible College. Some of his main writings engage various aspects of the New Testament views of the Holy Spirit, and their relevance for today. He is also a Baptist minister, engaged in the broader charismatic renewal movement and in regular dialogue with the academic leaders of the Pentecostal debates.

Pete Ward is Lecturer in Youth Ministry and Theological Education at King's College, London. He was formerly the Archbishop of Canterbury's Adviser for Youth Ministry. His publications include *Liquid Church* (Carlisle: Paternoster, 2002), *Mass Culture* (Oxford: BRF, 2000) and *Youth Work and the Mission of God* (London: SPCK, 1999).

Rob Warner has degrees in English and theology from York and Oxford universities. He was previously editor in chief of religious books at Hodder & Stoughton, and now leads an experimental church in Wimbledon. He has preached at many conferences, including Spring Harvest, Easter People, Keswick and Lee Abbey, and is asked to speak in many denominational settings on the re-imagining of the church. A broadcaster and journalist, he is the author of more than a dozen books, mainly on missiology, spirituality and discipleship. He is a trustee of the Evangelical Alliance, Renovare and Rebuild and a former trustee of Scripture Union and the Shaftesbury Society. His current research project at King's College, London examines the reconstruction of English Evangelicalism, 1980–2000.

Nigel G. Wright is Principal of Spurgeon's College, London, and President of the Baptist Union of Great Britain 2002–3. An ordained Baptist minister, he has had a dual career as a local church pastor and as an academic. He is the author of a number of books, including *The Fair Face of Evil* (London: Marshall Pickering, 1989), *Charismatic Renewal: The Search for a Theology* (with Andrew Walker and Tom Smail, London: SPCK, 1993, 1995^2), *The Radical Evangelical* (London: SPCK, 1996), *Disavowing Constantine* (Carlisle: Paternoster, 2000) and most recently *New Baptists, New Agenda* (Carlisle: Paternoster, 2002).

Introduction

Andrew Walker and Kristin Aune

'Revival' is an exhilarating word for a Christian: it evokes visions of new life, the power of the Spirit, renewal, restoration, the restitution of hope. And yet on examination, whether by scholars or Christian activists, it is clear that there exists no consensus as to the meaning of the word. Some think revival refers to the spiritual revivification of individual Christians. Others view it as renewal of the church through the sovereign act of the Spirit of God. An alternative way of looking at revival, much favoured by historians and social scientists, is to consider it as a proper noun to describe religious movements of enthusiasm. This raises a separate yet important secondary issue – how to distinguish between revival and revivalism?

Revivals as enthusiastic movements can themselves be delineated in terms of a hierarchy of significance. The Evangelical Great Awakenings of the eighteenth and early nineteenth centuries, for example, are often cited as the pre-eminent revivals because they are thought to have had a major impact not only on the church but also on the society at large. Religious movements that lead to social transformation, however, are rare. A more common use of the term revival that is still important, although lower down in the hierarchy than Awakenings, is to apply the noun as a description of those periods in church history of intense religious experience accompanied by a rapid increase in new converts. The Welsh Revival at the beginning of the twentieth century is often evoked as the paradigm example of this kind of enthusiasm. Some observers of religious movements, and also some revivalist practitioners (notably Pentecostals), have an augmented and extended understanding of this kind of revival, seeing it as successful evangelism enhanced by miraculous signs and wonders.

But if we think of revival in terms of a descending scale from Awakenings, charismatic outpourings of the Spirit, to intense periods of evangelism, then lower still would come revivalist forms that may be just as spiritually authentic as those higher up the scale, but are altogether more routinised and formatted affairs. Typical examples would be the urban revivals pioneered by D.L. Moody in the late nineteenth century, which were continued in more flamboyant vein by Billy Sunday and Aimee Semple McPherson in the first half of the twentieth century. Revival thought of as a successful evangelistic mission or campaign will always be associated in the last half of that century with its most respectable, successful and spiritually gifted proponent, Billy Graham.

At the bottom of the scale we should not ignore the vestigial remains of former intense and successful revivals. In the United States, for example, residual revivalism can still be found in the United Methodist Church, where the legendary banner of 'revival' heralds a special speaker for a weekend engagement. People do not expect the event to measure up to the excitement and fervour of the old camp meetings, but it is still hoped that God will do something out of the ordinary. And in Britain one can think of the tradition in the 1950s and 1960s in the Elim Pentecostal Church of holding locally advertised 'Great Revival and Divine Healing Crusades', which were no doubt genuine heartfelt 'times of blessing', but which were usually minor affairs couched in the revivalist language of successful past evangelistic campaigns.

Beyond the language of enthusiasms there is an even more radical way of thinking about revival: the reversal of what sociologists call secularisation. Imagine what a revival it would be if there was a turnaround in Europe of the seemingly inexorable decline of church attendance. And revival would be a perfectly appropriate epithet should religion regain its authority in what Richard Neuhaus has memorably called the 'public square'. At the moment, however, there seems to be no prospect of these two things happening, and should they do so, we do not at the present time have adequate conceptual tools to account for such a sea change in Christianity's fortune. It would not be enough, therefore, simply to cling to the older language of revival without a concomitant reconceptualisation of the term. This would need to include such reviving features of European religion as the reappropriation of Christian tradition, institutional reconstruction, and the regeneration of national and regional spiritual life.

Furthermore, in the light of an expanding Europe, particularly with the prospect of a mainly Islamic Turkey joining the European Union, we might have to ask whether revival, as a term mainly associated with Protestant Evangelicalism, will need to be reconfigured to include the regeneration of all religions. Clearly that remains an issue for the future, but even now, within Christianity, the extended uses of the word revival, and the complexity of revivalist phenomena associated with movements of enthusiasm, indicate that before we can declare that we are in favour of revival, or perhaps even be opposed to it, we need to understand what we mean by the term.

It was in the light of the conceptual uncertainty surrounding revival that The Centre for Theology and Culture at King's College, London held a symposium over two days in the summer of 2002 to tease out its nuances and highlight its ambiguities. The distinguished contributors to the revival debate presented papers to an audience that included church leaders, lay members of denominations, academics from a variety of disciplines, College students and revivalist practitioners. The symposium was one of those occasions that was not only felt to be a success because it was well attended and enjoyable, but because it was also a salutary occasion: the intellectual and moral thrust of the two days, through the process of clarifying the meanings and usages of revival, was to help today's church face up to its potential foibles and disadvantages as well as its spiritual benefits.

The chapters that make up this book are the full published proceedings of the King's Conference. Written by practising Christians from a wide range of theological traditions and academic disciplines, they are intended, in the spirit of the King's weekend, to be an open, frank, and critical examination of the nature of Revival. Yet each chapter seeks to discern the spiritual realities at the heart of revival as well as provide substantive information and a range of theoretical perspectives.

We have divided the book into three parts to help capture and order the multifaceted features of this important topic. Part 1, Theological Perspectives, begins appropriately, in Chapter 1, with a biblical understanding of revival by Max Turner. He focuses on Luke–Acts, noting that the gift of the Spirit to the church should not be interpreted as an elitist or atypical experience for Christians. Turner also demonstrates that there is, strictly speaking, no Greek equivalent for the English term 'revival'. He suggests that the New Testament understanding of what it is to be revived by

God's Spirit is a broader and deeper reality, more akin to 'salvation' and the empowerment for mission, than many of the modern and restricted uses of the word revival.

In Chapter 2, Mark Stibbe, utilising narrative theology and a grammatical theory of stories, draws on the events of the Norwegian Great Awakening to help us understand the nature of revival and present us with an *apologia*. Echoing Jonathan Edwards' predilection for adopting the Pietist use of the term 'affections', Stibbe translates this popular spiritual vocabulary of eighteenth-century revivals into a more contemporary concern with the notion of intimacy: revival is, Stibbe declares, a 'falling in love' with Christ. Graham McFarlane, in Chapter 3, also believes that revival must be Christ-centred. Engaging with recent debates on the Trinity within systematic theology, he presents a view of the Spirit whose primary function is to focus attention on Christ, while acting as something analogous to a force field in his own right. McFarlane also asserts that the Spirit's reviving activity is not intended for a spiritual elite, but for the whole of humanity, especially the poor, the overlooked and the marginalised.

Part 1 ends with Chapter 4, in which Tom Smail throws down the gauntlet to triumphalist religion and misplaced Christian optimism. Reacting to an exposition of the Book of Jeremiah by Walter Brueggemann, Smail offers a sober appraisal of the Christian situation in the contemporary West. He asks whether European church decline should perhaps be better understood in terms of God's judgement than human failure, and whether the future of the church may turn out to be not success or revival (though Smail prefers the language of resurrection) but exile. Exile, however, can be a time of reflection and repentance and is in itself a means whereby God revives his church.

Part 2, Historical Perspectives, presents both case studies and theoretical approaches to revival defined as movements of enthusiasm. David Bebbington, in Chapter 5, building on his seminal work *Evangelicalism in Modern Britain*, begins at the point where modern revivalist movements are usually thought to have begun: the eighteenth century. Bebbington shows that the Evangelical revivals of the period, far from being opposed to the philosophical Age of Enlightenment, actually embodied its rationalism, empiricism, individualism and optimism, and that the Holy Spirit, despite certain antagonisms, was able to work through the spirit of the age.

But by the early nineteenth century, Mark Patterson argues in Chapter 6, after the French Revolution and the collapse of feudal

Europe, a deep-seated pessimism influenced English Christianity. Using original research based on the prophetic journal *The Morning Watch*, he shows how the movement associated with Edward Irving and the Albury Circle interpreted these events as God's wrath upon an apostate Europe. The authors of *The Morning Watch* were convinced that the end of the world was imminent, and that only a tiny remnant would be saved from the disaster that would overtake the world.

Despite what the late Arthur Wallis called the 'eschatology of disaster' that stemmed from Albury (and also the Brethren conferences at Powerscourt in Ireland), the idea of the imminent Second Coming of Christ in time acted as a spur to revivals. The nineteenth century, if anything, witnessed an acceleration and proliferation of enthusiastic movements, both in the United States and Europe. One that is not so well known as, say, the 1801 Cane Ridge Revival in Kentucky, or the Holiness movements associated with Keswick in the last quarter of the nineteenth century in England, was the 1859 Aberdeenshire Revival in Scotland. In Chapter 7, in a carefully researched and well-argued historiography, Kenneth Jeffrey shows us that the revival was not uniform or all of a piece, but subject to the quite different variables associated with urban and rural life. A 'season of grace' there may have been, but in fact the revival of the settled farming community, the emotional enthusiasm of the fisher folk, and the more sophisticated and modern experience of revival in the city of Aberdeen cannot be understood in an homogenous way.

In Chapter 8, Nigel Wright compares the 1904 Welsh Revival and the ministry of John Wimber in the 1980s and 1990s, and in so doing makes an important contribution to the distinction between revival and revivalism. He contends that revival should be understood as a divine gift, whereas revivalism is the human effort to help bring it to realisation. Wright shows that in practice revival is ambiguous, for it reflects the divine presence of the Spirit of God, human ingenuity and, because of our fallen condition, folly. He observes, for example, that the Welsh Revival in fact presaged spiritual decline rather than religious renewal, and that the Wimber phenomenon was negatively bound up with 'consumption-driven promotionalism', as well as positively being a blessing to many. Wright makes a plea for seeing ecstatic experience as intrinsic to our human condition, and argues against both excessive credulity in the face of the miraculous and the witch-hunting approach that seeks to discredit spiritual experience whenever it appears.

Neil Hudson and Andrew Walker, in Chapter 9, pick up on Wright's theme of ambiguity in a careful re-evaluation of the founder of the Elim Church, George Jeffreys. Jeffreys, they argue, was probably the most successful revivalist in Britain in the twentieth century, but they also demonstrate that, as a reformer of the church he founded, he was a disaster. Even as a revivalist, they assert, his legacy was a mixed blessing for the denomination, as they found it hard to survive without a revivalist figurehead. Nevertheless, Hudson and Walker claim that it is time Jeffreys was recognised as the great evangelist he undoubtedly was, and note in conclusion that in the Elim Church, sixty years after he left it to found a rival denomination, he is being rediscovered.

This historical section ends with Chapter 10, in which Meic Pearse, who considers revival primarily to be an Evangelical phenomenon, questions whether the revivals of the past are indeed paradigmatic events for the future. His own view is that revivals are historically situated. He looks at the Britain of the twenty-first century, where he sees a lack of familiarity with the Christian message, as it is no longer embedded in the culture at large. Consequently, there is disinclination by ordinary men and women to attend and be influenced by preacher-led campaigns. He has no doubt that God can generate pulpit-led revivalist campaigns if he wishes, but he observes that he does not. Pearse favours the prayer and hard work of the many as the way forward rather than relying on the high-profile preaching of the few.

The essays in Part 3, The Contemporary Scene and Multi-disciplinary Approaches, encompass on-the-ground observation of (mainly) contemporary charismatic Evangelicalism with insights from psychology, sociology and cultural studies, as well as theology. Steve Latham, in Chapter 11, makes perhaps the major contribution of the book in terms of the conceptual clarification necessary to understand revival. He suggests a typology of six distinctive forms of revival – including the slide into revivalism. In a survey of recent forms of revivalism, ranging from John Wimber, the Kansas City Prophets and the prophecy connected to Princess Diana's death, Latham sets such events in sociological and political context. He is committed to revival as a genuine visitation of the Spirit of God but, like a number of our authors, he also highlights the ambiguity of revivalist endeavours.

William Kay, in Chapter 12, compares and contrasts two revivals – the mainly rural Welsh Revival of 1904–5 and the mainly urban Azusa Street Revival of Los Angeles in 1906–7 – by submitting them to modern social scientific analyses. Reflecting on the revivals' empirical aspects with the aid of sociological and psychological models, he argues that the classical sociological understandings of religious life stemming from Durkheim, Marx and Weber are no more successful in fully accounting for such revivals than psychological analyses. It is not that Kay believes such approaches are useless, but that he believes that on their own they are too reductionist fully to comprehend and encapsulate such profoundly religious events.

Adopting a cultural studies approach, Pete Ward in Chapter 13 shows a marked shift in Evangelical practices of revivalism in the last twenty years. He suggests that revivalism can be viewed as a product, which traditionally Evangelicals marketed as the gospel for an unbelieving audience. He argues that both the product and the audience have changed. The product is now worship, and the audience Christian believers. Ward details how this shift in the 'culture of production' from evangelism to worship and from conversion to intimacy has occurred from the 1980s, concentrating particularly on the collapse of Music Gospel Outreach (MGO), the success of *Come Together* and the impact of Spring Harvest.

There are parallels with Ward's argument in Chapter 14. Rob Warner asks why the mid-1990s charismatic events associated with the religious experience known as the 'Toronto Blessing' were so successful. Warner claims that this can be understood in part by realising that the secular entrepreneurial drive of the 1980s generated an Evangelical culture of success. He shows also how 'Toronto' reveals a specific life cycle of ecstatic spirituality that Warner understands as the search for 'ultimacy'. British charismatics, however, Warner argues, accustomed to filtering out American excesses as they are, ultimately filtered out the 'Toronto Blessing' itself.

Ian Stackhouse ends the collection in Chapter 15 by arguing that the common yet unhelpful use of the term revival has been responsible for the current malaise of the British Evangelical charismatic movement. Revival, he maintains, has been wrongly understood as a kind of 'package' involving large-scale conversions. In a tone that echoes Smail's disenchantment with revivalist excesses and exaggerated claims, Stackhouse believes that the disappointment and failure experienced by Christians who expected rapid and expanded church growth has led to substitute or misplaced revivalism, which he calls 'faddism'. Faddism embraces those human attempts to make revival happen that Wright talks of in Chapter 8. Fads may include turning to American prophets, restoring New

Testament apostles, establishing cell groups as the way forward to church growth, or putting one's faith in 'seeker-sensitive' services. This faddism, Stackhouse believes, has contributed to the demise of Christian identity and to a general loss of faith in the gospel. Ironically, says Stackhouse, only when the church places its faith in the gospel again and concentrates on the messy but necessary business of spiritual formation in a 'cruciformed' ecclesia open to the world, yet fed on the regular diet of word and sacrament, will revival occur.

Part 1

Theological Perspectives

Chapter 1

'Revival' in the New Testament?

Max Turner

1. What on Earth are we Talking *About*? Some Initial Linguistic/Semantic Considerations

Unlike the words 'renewal' and 'refreshment' (see below), the word 'revival' has no obvious Greek equivalent in the New Testament (hereafter NT). That itself does not mean that NT scholars need maintain a holy silence on the issue. We can cope with responding to what the NT teaches on 'Trinity' or 'personhood', even though there are no corresponding *terms*, as such.

In such situations the procedure is usually relatively simple. We first attempt to define in *our* language the 'concept' we are attempting to investigate; then, armed with the definition, we seek to explore any NT material that looks relevant to the concept in question. Thus we might define 'Trinitarianism' as standing for some form of the view that 'the God of Israel coexists distinctly as Father, Son and Spirit, yet related in such a way that they are one God, not three gods (which would be tritheism, instead)'. And with the search for that conceptual entity in mind, we walk confidently, spade in hand, into the NT dig, knowing that there is plenty of relevant evidence to unearth.

It is a bit different with 'revival', because (as Steve Latham's essay, see Chapter 11, ably demonstrates) we may not be sure which of several 'concepts' of revival are most important within our contemporary theological horizon, and consequently we are uncertain as to which we wish to use as a lens through which to examine the NT contribution. In terms of his typology, if we were to examine what the NT has to say about R1 – 'a spiritual quickening of the individual believer' – there would be an impracticably great amount of NT evidence to review. At the other extreme, it could be argued that the NT has little, if anything, to say concerning Latham's R5 and R6 ('cultural "awakenings"' and the 'possible reversal of secularisation and "revival" of Christianity as such').

At this point, linguistic semantics may help us prioritise the issues for investigation. In semantics, we distinguish between the 'stereotypical' use of a word, and what is called its 'extension'.

The 'stereotype' of a word is a list of those characteristic and distinguishing aspects of the sense of a word that would be regarded as linguistically 'normal' to its use. For example, the stereotype of a 'stool' (used as a noun, and speaking of artefacts) would include that it is:

(1) an item of furniture for sitting on (in contrast to 'table', 'wardrobe', 'bed', etc.);
(2) a seat for *one* person (in contrast to 'bench', 'sofa', etc.);
(3) a seat of hard material and without back or arms (contrast 'chair', *'chaise-longue'*, etc.);
(4) the seat being a somewhat thin slab or disk, supported by three to four relatively long legs.

The stereotype of a 'stool' is transparently related to what we also mean by the 'concept' of a stool.

By contrast, the 'extension' of the word 'stool' is the total class of entities in the world that we would refer to by such a name, even though that would include many items that do not exactly fit the 'stereotype'. I have sat on items I would call a 'stool' that only had one pedestal leg, and some had a small back and arms. Some 'stools' have also been soft rather than hard. The 'extension' of a word always shows that the 'stereotypical' sense has 'fuzzy borders'. And some words have fuzzier borders than others. Words that usually denote concrete entities in the world, like chairs, pencils and cars, are much less hazy than essentially relative lexemes like 'middle aged', 'bald', 'short', or, for that matter, 'revival'.[1]

I suggest that a 'stereotypical' sense of the word 'revival', in broadly Christian ideolect, is as follows. 'Revival' essentially *means*

---

[1] In 1978 *Expository Times* published a series on 'slippery words' ('Apocalyptic', 'Eschatology', 'Gnosis', 'Myth' and 'Wisdom): 'Revival' would surely be a prime candidate for inclusion.

a powerful re-intensification of God's comprehensive saving work[2] in and through his people:

(1) experienced at *community*, not merely individual, level;
(2) experienced over a relatively prolonged period of time (at least months, more probably years);
(3) with positive transformative effects on the holiness, 'life' and worship of the original community (with strong connotations of passing from 'moribund' [even 'dead'] to a 'live/living' state);
(4) extending to and including outsiders, in significant numbers.

We can use this to tease out a little further Latham's helpful typology.

(a) In agreement with him, we would not wish to use 'revival' for his R1, because it seems to exclude *the main stereotypical trait* (1). As such, it is surely semantically anomalous. A sentence such as 'Revival came to Watford, but only Peter experienced it!' would be regarded as *linguistically* odd by most Christian English-language users. It would appear to be a denial of what we all mean by the word 'revival'.
(b) Again, basically agreeing with Latham, we should not include R2 within the 'extension' of this sense of 'revival'. R2 actually marks a totally different 'sense' of the (polysemous) lexeme 'revival': it means 'a human event organised in the hope of promoting some form of what we stereotypically mean by "revival" '.
(c) R3–R5, I suggest, are not actually distinct linguistic/semantic senses at all. They all cohere with our stereotypical sense. The only difference between them is in respect of the geographical/cultural extent of the community in consideration.[3]

---

[2] I use 'saving work' here in its comprehensively inclusive sense – embracing regeneration, communion, sanctification, etc.

[3] Again, the key test is possible linguistic anomaly. Consider the two following utterances:

(1) 'The revival in Stirling spread to the whole of Scotland.'
(2) 'It wasn't really "revival" in Stirling until it had spread to the rest of Scotland.'

The linguistic normality of the first utterance shows that the lexeme 'revival' *normally* includes local *and broader* horizons. The linguistic 'abnormality' of the second utterance is clear – especially, as here, when the word 'revival' is in quotation marks.

(d) R6 – 'the possible reversal of secularisation and "revival" of Christianity as such'. It is clear from the very form of this sentence fragment that 'reversal of secularisation' is at best a possible *consequence* of revival. We may hope for it, but it is *not* part of the linguistic/semantic 'meaning' of the word 'revival' as such.

Before we return to the NT and examine what it has to say about our stereotypical sense (or 'concept') of the word 'revival', we must now give a brief account of the partial synonyms 'renewal' and 'refreshment'.

'*Renewal*'

While the English versions use 'renew' cognates in their translations of a handful of NT texts, brief examination shows that there is a degree of semantic gap between the NT use and the contemporary. In the NT we have to do with essentially two verbs and one verbal noun.

The verbs are *anakainoô*, at 2 Corinthians 4:16 and Colossians 3:10 (with no LXX 'background' examples), and *ananeoô*, at Ephesians 4:23 (with 10 LXX examples; but mainly in 1 Macc. 12–14, and there always with the sense of 'renewal of political friendship/brotherhood').

The 'renewal' in question in 2 Corinthians 4:16 is the daily strengthening of the believer's 'inner (and eschatological) man', in contrast to the wasting away of the 'outer', physical and Adamic man. In Colossians 3:10, the contrast is between the 'old [Adamic] humanity' of the erstwhile unbeliever, and the 'new man' in Christ that is being 'renewed in knowledge after the image of its creator'. While Ephesians 4:23 uses a different verb form, the contrast is essentially a slightly differently nuanced version of what Paul had said in the parallel Colossians passage.

The noun *anakainôsis* is only found in Romans 12:2 and Titus 3:5 (and again without LXXal parallels). In the Romans passage the challenge is that we should not be conformed to the world, but be transformed by the 'renewal' of the mind (and the co-text implies a parallel sense to Col. 3:10/Eph. 4:23). In Titus, the phrase 'renewal in the Holy Spirit' is most probably a parallel amplification of the phrase 'the water/washing of regeneration/ rebirth' – and the allusion is to a Christianised version of Ezekiel 36:25–27. Here, 'renewal' is a partial synonym for 'regeneration':

the latter being primarily inceptive in force, the former more durative.[4]

The point of all these passages is that they have to do with that 'renewal' which consists in the discarding of unbelieving, alienated, rebellious existence, and the embracing of the new-creation, relational, humanity, in the image of the eschatological Adam, i.e., Christ.

All this means that the NT language of 'renewal' is not closely related to our contemporary religious use – as in such labels as 'the charismatic renewal movement', where 'renewal' essentially denotes the recovery of certain spiritual gifts, and the dynamic impact of them on the life of the church. And if speakers today deliberately choose the word 'renewal', *rather than* 'revival', to describe some contemporary work of God, the implied contrasts are usually these:

(1) the *intensity* of God's work is less dramatic than what we would like to use 'revival' to denote; and/or

(2) the work of God in question is comparatively more focused on the revival of the internal life of the individual believer, and on significant changes in the life and worship of the church, than it is on the extension of the gospel to outsiders;

(3) 'renewal' connotes 'continuity' with, and 'strengthening of' what went before,[5] while 'revival' tends to stress 'discontinuity' by connoting some 'dead' (or exceedingly weak) existence brought back to vigorous life and health.

'*Refreshment*'

It has become common to appeal to Peter's preaching in Acts 3 to justify the view that God may be expected to provide occasional/periodic 'times of refreshment' (Acts 3:19 [Greek 3:20]). Within *current* usage, the phrase 'times of refreshment' is sufficiently ambiguous to include 'revival', but is more often used in mild contrast with the latter, in a way that makes it a much closer synonym to 'renewal'. For example, it is quite regular to refer to the so-called 'Toronto Blessing' as a 'renewal' or (even more often) a

---

[4] See the discussion in Dunn (1970: 165–70) and Fee (1994: 777–84).

[5] This is certainly the emphasis intended by the Catholic writer, Peter Hocken, in his choice of the title *Streams of Renewal* for his study of the charismatic movement in Great Britain (Hocken 1986).

'time of refreshment' (cf. Stibbe 1995: 62–65), while relatively few United Kingdom Christian English-users would adorn it with the title 'revival'.

Once again, however, there is a gulf between the NT term and the contemporary use. The word translated 'refreshment' (Greek *anapsychsis*) is represented only here (in the NT) and at Exodus 8:11 (LXX).[6] In Peter's speech, the plural 'times of refreshment' promised to Israel, should she repent, matches the plural 'times of restoration' to follow the Messiah's return (3:21). Neither of the terms denotes a periodic *cycle* of decline and restitution, as is clear from the latter. The plurals denote rather a more-or-less extensive period. From Peter's perspective, the *whole* future of the church envisaged (not just segments of it) is that of 'times of refreshment', or of 'release from oppression/affliction', and this is simply one of several metaphors for what we might otherwise call the 'messianic age'.[7]

It follows that contemporary uses of 'times of refreshment' to denote what *we* may regard as *special* periods of grace within the church – that is, to cover anything from the Great Awakening to the emergence of the Pentecostal movement, or even the 'Toronto Blessing' – are liable to prove hermeneutical attempts to ride a bucking pony. The original use of the metaphor simply does not match, but rather subverts, its modern reappropriation.

In conclusion, neither the word 'renewal' nor the phrase 'times of refreshing' help us towards a NT understanding of the modern phenomenon of 'revival'.

2. 'Revival' in the New Testament? Introductory and Methodological Issues

We may now return to what we have defined as the stereotypical sense of 'revival', and explore how the NT relates to that concept.

---

[6] The cognate verb *anapsycheô* is used at 2 Timothy 1:16 for personal refreshment brought to Paul by the visit of Onesiphorus; more usually the verb used for such refreshment through fellowship is *anapauô* or cognates (Rom. 15:32; 1 Cor. 16:18; Philem. 7,20).

[7] Danker (2000) appropriately offers as the sense of *anapsychsis* 'experience of relief from obligation or trouble', and the translation equivalents 'breathing space', 'relaxation' or 'relief'. The entry correctly glosses Acts 3:20 as 'fig., of the Messianic age ... *times of rest*' (75).

As Stuart Piggin notes, 'some find it difficult to find revival in the New Testament'. As it happens, he does not count himself in that group, but immediately continues: 'fundamentally, I think, because it is everywhere. The entire New Testament is really an account of revival' (Piggin 2000: 37). In part 3, we shall concentrate primarily on Luke–Acts, because that has been the main NT hunting ground in such discussions, and raises the most relevant questions: indeed, it is not uncommon to interpret Acts 2 as providing the archetype for all revivals (cf. Ortlund 2000: ch. 4, Piggin 2000: 39–43, Stibbe 1995: 49). In part 4, we turn to broader NT perspectives.

3. Luke–Acts as Prototypical of 'Revival'?

Many in the Jewish Christian communities described in the early chapters of Acts might indeed have regarded the happenings amongst them as 'revival' – more particularly as Israel's New Exodus and the Spirit-given restoration of her true vocation as a 'light to the world', as depicted especially (not uniquely) in Isaiah 40–55. It has become increasingly recognised that Luke himself shares key elements of such a perspective.[8] But, as we shall see, he regards most aspects of this as inherently *normative* to what he means by the 'life of salvation', not as extraordinary re-intensifications of 'salvation' such as mark 'special periods' of 'revival'. Let us first (in 3.1 – 3.3) remind ourselves of the main plotline[9] before asking more specifically to what extent Luke–Acts provides a paradigm of 'revival' (in 3.4).

3.1 Luke 1–4 and the Promise of Israel's Salvation/the Kingdom of God

In these chapters Luke sets up the interpretive framework for the whole of what follows. A whistle-stop tour readily confirms the centrality of the New Exodus hopes of Isaiah 40–55.

---

[8] For the major arguments, see Turner (1996) and Pao (2000) and the extensive literature they cite. For the view that such a perspective was cardinal to the historical Jesus' own understanding, see Wright (1996).

[9] Aspects of the description below are controversial: see the ongoing debates (in monographs and articles) between R.P. Menzies and M. Turner.

In 1:8–23, an angel announces to elderly Zechariah that he will have a son, John the Baptist, who will turn Israel back to the Lord, in the Spirit and power of Elijah (1:16–17; cf. Mal. 4:5), and in preparation for God's own return to Zion in glorious rule. In 1:26–38, the angel announces the birth of Jesus to Mary (in a scene that reminds every Jewish reader of Isa. 7:14), and explains: 'He will be great, and will be called the Son of the Most High, and the Lord God will give to him the throne of his ancestor David. He will reign over the house of Jacob forever, and of his kingdom there will be no end' (1:32–33). Clearly, the reader at this point will be expecting Jesus to restore Israel. In 1:46–55, Mary responds with the prophetic hymn of praise, 'My soul magnifies the Lord ...', essentially a song about the reversal of forlorn Israel's sad condition (as is especially clear from v. 50 onwards). In 1:57–69, after the birth of John the Baptist, his father Zechariah exclaims a prophetic 'blessing', which identifies the *content* of the salvation awaited. God will return to reign in Israel and act decisively through these two holy children to reverse Israel's fate. The outcome will be a liberated community that can live and serve God fearlessly, fully and righteously. It will be like the relief and peace of dawn breaking upon the fearful benighted.

In 2:25–49, Simeon sees the baby Jesus in the Temple, and bursts out with the prophetic hymn: 'Master, now you are dismissing your servant in peace, according to your word; for my eyes have seen your salvation, which you have prepared in the presence of all peoples [2:29, alluding to Isa. 40:5], a light for revelation to the Gentiles and for glory to your people Israel [alluding to Isa. 42:6; 49:9,6].'

Next, at the outset of Jesus' ministry, John the Baptist explains his own role in the words of Isaiah 40:3–5 (Lk. 3:4–6) – the key opening words of Isaiah 40–55 about Israel's hoped-for return from exile – and Luke deliberately adds the concluding sentence of Isaiah 40:5, 'and all flesh shall see the salvation of God', to the quote he has received from Mark. And the Baptist then goes on to promise that Jesus will 'baptise' (= 'cleanse') Israel in the fiery power of the Spirit (3:16–17). He will undoubtedly have been thinking of a figure such as the Servant of Isaiah 42:1–2 and 61:1–2, and for the reader the divine voice at Jesus' baptism confirms the former (3:22), while Jesus' own sermon in Nazareth (especially 4:18–21) emphatically and paradigmatically confirms the latter.

So, we have seen what the hopes were for God's return to reign in Zion. But we must now face the question: '*What did Luke think became of these hopes?*' Did Luke think they were fulfilled?

Or did Israel's disbelief and rejection of Jesus' message result in tragic failure of the promise?

3.2 Were the Promises Fulfilled in the Ministry?

Having read so far, what would we expect to read next? If we did not *already* know the story, the reader would expect:

(1) a vigorous campaign, with Jesus taking the country by storm, and the masses jubilantly following him;
(2) a deep awareness of revival breaking in around Jesus as the people sense God's reign through him in the power of the Spirit;
(3) a truly triumphant entry to Jerusalem, with the city's leaders coming out to pay reverence to him and to welcome him in;
(4) Jesus enthroned in the Temple, and the messianic reign beginning in earnest, precipitating deep revival of the nation;
(5) the Romans, seeing the measure, nobility and power of him, readily deposing Herod Antipas and Philip, and gladly handing back the land to one they could hail as a prince of peace;
(6) Israel thus to become a light to the nations.

But, as we know, that is not how it happened (little wonder John the Baptist doubted, and from prison sent his disciples to Jesus, asking: 'Are you the one who is to come, or are we to wait for another?' [Lk. 7:19]). The point is that Jesus had relatively little impact on the nation during his own lifetime. (And John the Baptist, languishing in Herod's dungeon, knew that better than most!) There were certainly some startling evidences of God's reign breaking out around Jesus, and healing, liberating and transforming some individual lives (cf., for example, Lk. 5:12–14; 7:11–17, 21–23, 36–50; 13:10–17; 19:1–9, etc.), and these are in a sense 'typical' stories, representing to hearers a taste of what Jesus' ministry was like for many others. But we do *not* see transformed *communities* of fervent supporters, regularly thanking God for what he has done in his messianic Son, and seeking to export the good news.

So there are glimmers of the kingdom in Jesus' ministry, but it is more promise than reality. The Kingdom of God or Israel's 'salvation' may be present, but weakly – more like the seed growing secretly in the soil than the magnificent harvest Luke 1–4 seem to promise! And no one is clearer about that than Jesus himself. Hence the 'Lord's Prayer' (Let your kingdom come!): from the perspective of his ministry, the centre of gravity of the 'kingdom' hopes he speaks of lies in the future – the imminent future.

And, of course, then there is the Cross, which might at first seem to put an end to such hopes (as Cleopas laments in 24:20–21). But Luke has carefully prepared his reader to think otherwise. Jesus' death will be the blood of the new covenant (22:20); the passover is soon to be fulfilled in the Kingdom of God (22:14–16); the twelve are soon to rule over the twelve tribes of the restored Israel (22:30); as the co-crucified criminal sees, Jesus is soon to come into his kingdom (23:42); and Jesus' death/resurrection is nothing less than his (prophesied) 'entry into glory' (24:26). What can all this mean? Acts explains.

3.3 *The Promise Fulfilled in Acts? Paradigmatic Issues in Acts 1–2*

1. *The all-important preface (1:1–11) alerts the reader to the following essential points:*

(a) The main theme is still the 'Kingdom of God' (1:3), and this is interpreted in terms of the disciples being 'baptized with Holy Spirit' (Acts 1:5), or of their receiving the Spirit 'poured out' as 'power from on high' (Lk. 24:49). If the first takes up the Baptist's promise, the second takes up its Isaianic New-Exodus hinterland of Isaiah 32:15 and 44:3. Both are New-Exodus promises, concerned with the Spirit being given to restore the nation.

> [Israel will remain like a desert] until a spirit from on high is poured out on us, and the wilderness becomes a fruitful field, and the fruitful field is deemed a forest. Then justice will dwell in the wilderness, and righteousness abide in the fruitful field (Isa. 32:15 ff.).
>
> For I will pour water on the thirsty land, and streams on the dry ground; I will pour my spirit upon your descendants, and my blessing on your offspring. They shall spring up like a green tamarisk, like willows by flowing streams. This one will say, 'I am the Lord's,' another will be called by the name of Jacob, yet another will write on the hand, 'The Lord's,' and adopt the name of Israel (Isa. 44:3–5).

(b) The disciples are to become the Isaianic Servant 'to the end of the earth' (Acts 1:8, NKJV). The last phrase is strikingly unusual. We would expect a plural 'ends' of the earth (and many translations provide that). But it is singular, and any Jew would recognise it as a quotation from Isaiah 49:6. There, God says to the remnant of Israel, 'It is too light a thing that you should be my servant to raise up the tribes of Jacob and to restore the survivors of Israel; I will give you as a light to the nations, that my salvation may reach to the end of the earth.'

The implications should be clear. Through their witness, the disciples and the church gathered around them will act as the remnant Israel. The implication is that restoring the rest of *Israel* will be the first part of their work; but then they will bring salvation to the nations.[10]

2. *The Promises to Israel in the Narrative of the Pentecost Account*

By the first century, Pentecost had begun to be celebrated as the feast of the giving of the covenant to Israel. As Jews remembered that event, Moses had ascended on high to God (at Sinai), there was wind, smoke, fire, a shaking of the mountain, and then Moses had returned to the assembled people with a gift that was constitutive for Israel (the tablets with God's covenant words inscribed), while also intended to reach the nations.

The Pentecost narrative in Acts is essentially a deliberate contrast: Jesus ascends even higher than Moses, again there is noise of wind, and tongues of fire, again there is a mighty and constitutive gift (the Spirit) given to God's assembled people, and his word immediately goes to the nations. In all this, Luke is telling us that Pentecost is the beginning of the *new* covenant – and the Spirit is the power thereof.

3. *Peter's Sermon as the Key to Interpreting Acts*

The heart of this speech comes in 2:32–36, and it is rightly regarded as the lynchpin or pivot of the whole of Luke–Acts.

> This Jesus God raised up, and of that all of us are witnesses. Being therefore exalted at the right hand of God, and having received from the Father the promise of the Holy Spirit, he has poured out this that you both see and hear. For David did not ascend into the heavens, but he himself says, 'The Lord said to my Lord, "Sit at my right hand, until I make your enemies your footstool."' Therefore let the entire house of Israel know with certainty that God has made him both Lord and Messiah, this Jesus whom you crucified.

---

[10] Paul later explicitly quotes the verse (Acts 13:47): 'For so the Lord has commanded us, saying, "I have set you to be a light for the Gentiles, so that you may bring salvation to the end[s] of the earth."'

Here, at last, we see the fulfilment of Luke 1:32–33, but on a more glorious throne than David's in Jerusalem – the one at God's right hand, as promised in Psalm 110! And at last, too, Jesus begins to reign over Israel, through the Spirit with which he 'baptizes/cleanses' his people.

4. The Church of Acts 2:43–47 is portrayed as the Restored Israel – the 'Israel of fulfilment'

If we go back to Zechariah's prophetic hymn (Lk. 1:68–79) with which we started, and ask if the community in Acts fulfils the vision for Israel which it announces, I think we should agree it does. It is a community of the profound and empowering *presence* of God, one that meets the ethic of the beatitudes, and the Sermon on the Plain, a community of love and joyful worship. And while they still have some oppressive enemies, they do not live in the *fear* of their enemies, but with boldness and thanksgiving. 'Salvation' is far more richly present in this community than in the time of Jesus.

This picture is confirmed in Acts 3–8, notably in the other 'summaries' in 4:32–35 and 5:12–16. And it is especially re-inforced in James' crucial interpretation of Amos 9:11–12 (Acts 15:15–17) in the centrally important council of Jerusalem. There, James equates the rebuilding of the broken down 'cabin of David' with the restoration of Davidic rule in God's Israel, and draws the conclusion that, with Israel restored, it is now at last appropriate for the 'rest' of humankind – the Gentiles – to be admitted to God's people.[11]

3.4 Luke–Acts as a Paradigm of 'Revival'? A Loud 'No!' – with a mild echo of 'Yes!'

The first and most important answer must be a theological and categorical 'No!' Pentecost is *not* a story about the revitalisation – or re-intensification – of God's saving work in a moribund church. *It is fundamentally* about the eschatological and Christological work of God, which first *creates* that total transformation of God's people, which *begins to make them the 'church' of Christ.* Points one and two below elaborate this cardinal 'No!' before we turn to the muted 'Yes' in point three.

---

[11] See Turner (1996) chapters 10 – 14 for support, especially chapter 14.

1. *No!, because Acts 2 represents not merely a dramatic*
   re-intensification of the experience of the Kingdom of God,
   but the only possible way of its continuation at all

If the Kingdom of God had been made present to Israel through
Jesus' ministry, it was precisely by his work in the power of the
Spirit. With his 'removal', through death and resurrection/ascen-
sion, the only way of God's 'reign' *continuing*, as a dynamic presence, is through Jesus' outpouring of the Spirit as the Lord reigning
from God's right hand (so Acts 2:33–36).

2. *No!, because the gift of the Spirit promised is a Christocentric*
   version of Joel's 'Spirit of prophecy', and this is essential to
   the very existence of the church and of its experience of the
   'salvation' that Luke depicts in the opening chapters of his
   Gospel

It is precisely through such stereotypical gifts of the 'Spirit of prophecy' as revelation, charismatic wisdom, invasive prophecy/praise
and acts of power that the Spirit *becomes God's self-manifesting,*
transforming and empowering presence to the community, giving it
the decisive 'shape' and 'dynamics' announced in Luke 1–2. In this
sense, Luke actually offers a *challenge*, rather than a support, to
the Classical Pentecostal paradigm, which reduces the Spirit to a
'second-blessing' of empowering for mission (Turner 1997 and
2001). *On any account it is clear*:

(a) Luke includes the 'gift of the Spirit' within the broader concept
    of Jesus' baptising with Holy Spirit, and he only knows of *one*
    gift of the Spirit, not two. Put the other way, Luke does *not*
    suggest that believers first receive the Spirit for 'salvation', and
    are then only later baptised in Holy Spirit, in revival fashion, for
    mission.

    That is agreed by *all* NT Lukan specialists, *including* the Pent-
    ecostal ones (e.g. Stronstad, Menzies, etc.).[12] In fact, as Menzies
    agrees, Luke does not expect any chronologically significant
    degree of what classical Pentecostals call 'subsequence'. Rather,
    the gift of the Spirit is expected to be given at conversion-initiation,
    and Luke himself regards any departure from that anticipated
    time line as extraordinary. On closer analysis, the apparent excep-
    tions (Acts 8:16 and 19:2–7) demonstrate such.

---

[12] See Turner (2001) for details of the debate.

(b) Luke knows of regular 'reactivations' of the Spirit's presence in charismatic events, some more powerful than others, for which he regularly uses the language of 'filling' with the Spirit. But these he would largely regard as part and parcel of 'the normal Christian life', and (more importantly) as the expected and *characteristic* expressions of Joel's 'Spirit of prophecy', promised to all who repent and believe (Acts 2:38–39), not some special 'revival' phenomenon.

(c) Equally certainly, and by the same token, Luke does *not* view Pentecost, or any of the other notable occasions of the giving of the Spirit (Acts 8, 10, 19), as 'revival' of a church that is emerging on the positive side of a cycle from rebellion, through repentance and prayer. Nor is there any clear evidence he thinks other churches received such 'revival-type' regular dramatic interventions. It is clear that the churches of *Syrian* Antioch were very committed, 'charismatic', and had evangelistic impact (cf. Acts 11:19–30; 13:1–3): but is that what we mean by 'revival'? The situation in *Pisidian* Antioch (Acts 14) is somewhat less clear, but still essentially positive, as (in lesser degree) is that of Iconium, Lystra and Derbe. Luke's accounts of Philippi, Thessalonica, Borea and Athens (Acts 16–17) leave little information about the churches in those cities, the last being perhaps especially restrained. Hearty 'mission' there may have been in those cities, but clearly there was no 'revival' in Athens (and how far back through the list should we go before we could say, with clear head, 'Yes, there was "revival" there'?).

In short, at the heart of the problem of deciding in what way the language of 'revival' might apply to what Luke–Acts describes stands this all-important question: '*What counts as the "normal" experience of life, salvation and mission through the Spirit, and what counts as "extraordinary powerful intensification or re-intensification of that"?*'

If we put the question that way it becomes clear not merely from Luke, but from Paul and John too, that both 'normal' reception of the Spirit and 'normal' ongoing activity of the Spirit in the believer were deeply experiential. These were foundational matters of immediate perception. People simply *know* whether or not they have received the Spirit (as is testified in Acts 2; 8:14–19; 10:45–46; 19:1–6; Gal. 3:3,5; 1 Thess. 1:5, etc.).

And what is more, the Spirit is widely experienced as God's self-revealing, empowering and transforming presence in the *whole* of

Christian life (1 Thess. 1:5–6; 4:8; 1 Cor. 6:11; 2 Cor. 3:17–18; Tit. 3:5–7, etc.), flooding the heart with the love of God (Rom. 5:3), inspiring spontaneous joy, worship and praise, even in difficult circumstances (Lk. 10:21; Acts 2:4; 10:45–46; 13:52; 1 Thess. 1:6; Rom. 14:17; 15:13; Col. 3:16–17; Eph. 5:18–20, etc.), interceding through the believer in charismatic prayer (Rom. 8:26–27; 1 Cor. 14:14–15), bringing the believer to deep and liberating existential understanding of the truths of the kerygma (cf. Eph. 1:17–23; 3:16–19; Jn. 14–16), actively leading the Christian in the fight against sin and 'the flesh' (Gal. 5; 2 Cor. 3; Rom. 8), and so forth.[13]

For all three writers, these things are not special 'revival' manifestations and graces; rather, for them such experiences of the Spirit belong to the heart of what 'salvation' *means. Take these things away from the community, and all three writers would be asking whether the Kingdom of God or salvation was present in and to that community at all!* From a Johannine perspective, a group that did not experience communion with the self-revealing presence of the Father and the Son, in and through the Spirit, would simply be left in darkness and in death (Turner forthcoming).

3. *'Yes!' It is very probable that Luke considered the events of Pentecost and its duplications at Samaria and amongst Cornelius' household as especially intense, and so a possible 'example' for further 'revival' situations*

Unique phenomena and intensity would certainly be appropriate for the occasion that initiates the new covenant, and for those that mark its initial progress to Samaria (the religious relics of the northern kingdom, expected to be restored with the southern, according to Ezek. 37) and to Gentiles. Luke also sees the experience of the apostles, and of some others he calls people 'full of Holy Spirit', as untypical: for him, they are the elite of the movement, not the average troopers. He is aware, too, that even by Paul's standards, the Ephesus ministry (of Acts 19) was one of special intensity of God's grace and power, and it is there that God even works 'out-of-the-ordinary' miracles through the hands of the apostle (19:11).

Similarly, Luke almost certainly regarded the little incident in Acts 4:30–31 as unusual. There, a (small) group around Peter and John pray for boldness to carry on preaching, despite the Jewish council's intimidation. Luke tells us: 'When they had prayed, the place in which they were gathered together was shaken; and they

---

[13] See especially Dunn (1975), Fee (1994) and Turner (1999).

were all filled with the Holy Spirit and spoke the word of God with boldness.' It is doubtful that the shaking of houses was common-place. So this too is an exceptional event, and perhaps comes nearest to our stereotypical definition of 'revival', as it is indeed a dramatic re-intensification of the Spirit's work – though clearly not a case where the group were being brought back from a cycle of rebellion or a period of moribund Christian existence.

All these cases of relatively exceptional intensity of the Spirit's working might be encouragement to pray for what we mean by 'revival'. They show how dramatically God has indeed been occa-sionally pleased to intensify his saving work. And some of them have proved archetypal for the type and quality of divine interven-tion that are associated with great revivals from the eighteenth century to the present day.[14]

But the importance of Luke–Acts does not lie in any provision it might make for understanding such periodic and episodic workings of God. *The real importance of Luke–Acts is its implied call to what it regards as the 'normal' character of the experience of salvation in the church* – and, at least to some observers, that looks more like what they see in the Pentecostal and charismatic renewal move-ments, or in the historically occasional phenomenon of 'revival', than in what they find (or sometimes do not find) in some more historic–traditional churches.

Believers may not necessarily be *expected* to be able to pray with confidence that God will send the remarkable phenomenon of revival. But, where the church is in decline or even moribund, arguably believers *should* pray – with repentance, faith and expec-tation – that God will renew his church in what the NT Scriptures regard as the 'normal Christian life and experience of salvation'.

4. Revival in the New Testament: Broader Perspectives

Space only allows the briefest of comments: in a notable paragraph in an article on the Spirit's role in 'revival', David Smith suggests:

> Central though the Pentecostal narrative unquestionably is for our understanding of the church and its mission, it is important to remember

---

[14] See, most recently, Ortland (2000) and Piggin (2000) for examples of 'revival' phenomena similar to those of Acts 2.

that the picture provided by the book of Acts forms part of the narrative of the progress of the church in the New Testament, not the whole. Indeed, by the close of the apostolic period we are looking at a very different picture: the revival fires have cooled, the love of many has grown cold, and Christians seem to be increasingly at home in a world dominated by Roman idolatry and materialism. Certainly, the Holy Spirit is not absent from this picture, but he comes now not with the sound of ... rushing wind, but with a searching critical voice, seeking for those, evidently a minority, who are still able to 'hear what the Spirit is saying to the churches'. These texts need to be read alongside the Pentecostal story because ... they furnish us with the material for a theology of the Holy Spirit which enable[s] ... us to account for *decline* as well as advance, placing such periods of recession and struggle firmly within the divine purpose (Smith 2001: 23).

Sensitive as this is to important issues, I consider the dualism between Acts and the later period to be overdrawn.

(1) As we have noted, the 'revival fires' are sometimes pretty weak (if there at all) in parts of Acts, while the only passage that looks forward explicitly to Luke's own day – the Miletus speech (Acts 20:17–35) – expects problems with false teaching, but not with diminution of the Spirit's presence.

(2) While there is evidence that *some* congregations came under the prophetic censure and judgement of Christ, in Revelation 2–3, there is little evidence for the wider picture of decline that Dr Smith suggests, and sub-apostolic writings, including especially Didache, Shepherd of Hermas, and the Ignatian letters, suggest otherwise.

(3) In any case, the same mix that we find in Revelation 2–3 may be found in the church in Corinth. The Corinthians' divisive handling of the Lord's Supper (we are told in 1 Cor. 11) was bringing God's judgement upon them in the form of illness and even death, yet chapters 12–14 witness an abundance of the Spirit's presence and charismatic activity, which would be suggestive to some of 'revival' conditions, if encountered today. The evidence of periodic decline and revival in the NT period is wanting.

(4) Certainly at the close of the Pauline mission, if not beyond it, Titus 3:5 can still refer to the church's 'renewal' by the Holy Spirit, and expand that by saying this Spirit has been 'poured out on us richly through Jesus Christ our Saviour'. Clearly, the

Spirit was still an 'immediate presence' to the writer and his congregations.

5. Conclusion

The NT sets a deeply experiential and evidentially 'charismatic' norm for what is meant by 'salvation'. In the Pauline and Johannine writings this clearly centres on what John describes as a deeply renewing and transforming communion with the Father and the Son that the Spirit brings. Luke's message is essentially the same. The gift of the Spirit in Acts 2 is much more about what Luke–Acts means by 'salvation' (including empowerment for mission) than what he might be construed to mean about our understanding of 'revival'.

References

Danker, F.W. (ed.) (2000). *A Greek–English Lexicon of the New Testament and Other Early Christian Literature*. Chicago: Chicago University Press.

Dunn, J.D.G. (1970). *Baptism in the Holy Spirit*. London: SCM.

Dunn, J.D.G. (1975). *Jesus and the Spirit*. London: SCM.

Fee, G.D. (1994). *God's Empowering Presence*. Peabody: Hendrickson.

Hocken, P. (1986). *Streams of Renewal*. Exeter: Paternoster.

Menzies, R.P. (1994). *Empowered for Witness: The Spirit in Luke–Acts*. Sheffield: Sheffield Academic Press.

Menzies, W.W. and Menzies, R.P. (2000). *Spirit and Power: Foundations of Pentecostal Experience*. Grand Rapids: Zondervan.

Ortlund, R.C. (2000). *Revival Sent from God*. Leicester: IVP.

Pao, D.W. (2000). *Acts and the Isaianic New Exodus*. Tübingen: Mohr.

Piggin, S. (2000). *Firestorm of the Lord*. Carlisle: Paternoster.

Smith, D. (2001). The Work of the Holy Spirit in Revival and Renewal. *Foundations* 47: 20–31.

Stibbe, M. (1995). *Times of Refreshing*. London: Marshall Pickering.

Turner, M. (1996). *Power from on High: The Spirit in Israel's Restoration and Witness in Luke–Acts*. Sheffield: Sheffield Academic Press.

Turner, M. (1997). The Spirit in Luke–Acts: A Support or a Challenge to Classical Pentecostal Paradigms? *Vox Evangelica* 27: 75–101.

Turner, M. (1999). *The Holy Spirit and Spiritual Gifts: Then and Now*. Carlisle: Paternoster.

Turner, M. (2001). Interpreting the Samaritans of Acts 8: The Waterloo of Pentecostal Soteriology and Pneumatology? *Pneuma* 23: 265–86.

Turner, M. (forthcoming). 'The Churches of the Johannine Letters as Communities of "Trinitarian" *koinônia*'. In Menzies, R. and Ma, W. (eds) *The Spirit and Spirituality: Essays in Honor of Russell P. Spittler*. Forthcoming, publisher unknown.

Wright, N.T. (1996). *Jesus and the Victory of God*. London: SPCK.

Chapter 2

'Seized by the Power of a Great Affection': A Narrative Theology of Revival

Mark Stibbe

Writing in a detached way about revival is like writing a doctoral thesis on love. If the writer has ever experienced what it is to fall in love, and indeed to stay in love, this is no easy matter. How do you write cognitively about something that has impacted you so affectively?

This is exactly the dilemma I find myself in here. My task is to contribute to a collection of papers that looks at the phenomenon of revival objectively. My problem is that I have actually experienced Christian revival. My conversion to Christianity took place in an extraordinary outpouring of the Holy Spirit at Winchester College in the mid to late 1970s. In 1977, I was one of well over 100 pupils whose lives were transformed by the power of God. Since then, I have visited and ministered in various churches around the globe that have been visited by something looking very like revival. Today, I find myself the vicar of a church, St Andrew's, Chorleywood, that has grown significantly as a result of various visitations of God's Holy Spirit. This has occurred on at least two occasions in its history: firstly in the 1960s under John Perry's leadership; secondly in the 1980s under David Pytches.[1] Today, St Andrew's Church is expecting more of the same, affecting our community and beyond.

So writing in an objective way about the phenomenon of revival is for me as challenging as writing analytically about love. Having

---

[1] For a rather pedestrian but thoroughly researched history of St Andrew's, I recommend Alex Twells' book (1998).

fallen in love with my wife, and remained in love, there are some things that I could say in a technical way about this wonderful yet sometimes costly experience. Yet at the same time, I would find myself straining beyond pedestrian prose to the more multivalent language of poetry. The same is true as I write about revival. Christian revival calls for more than analytical description. It calls for the language of the heart as well as the head.

The Miracle of Revival

With this caveat in mind, I would like to start by providing a brief definition of Christian revival. To revive something is to bring it back to life. The word is usually used in contexts where the subject under scrutiny is in a state of decline or near death. So, people speak about the revival of British cinema, or the English national cricket team. In common parlance the noun 'revival' is used of almost anything that has been given a new vitality after a period of what looked like decay. To revive something is to cause it to flourish again.

In the context of Christian revival, the object of the verb 'revive' is the church. This is an important point, because the word is sometimes used about places where a church has never existed. So it might be used of a very successful mission in which hundreds are converted in a very short time, and in a place where the Christian message has never been heard. But this, I would submit, is a false use of the term. Strictly speaking, the word 'revival' should only be used in contexts where the church has already been at work. You cannot revive something that did not formerly exist. That would be to create something *de novo*, and this only occurs where the church begins its missionary activity in territory it has hitherto untouched. Revival, if it is to make any sense in a Christian context, must and can only refer to the revivifying of a moribund church or churches.

If the object of the verb 'revive' is the church, the subject is always God. At this point, we enter the classic argument about the divine and human initiative in revival. On the one hand, we have those who follow Jonathan Edwards and regard revival as the sovereign work of God. On the other, we have those who follow Charles Finney and regard revival as humanly orchestrated by 'special means'.

I have written about this elsewhere (M. Stibbe 1998: 13–28), so a few comments will have to do at this point. My own perspective is that true revival has God as its subject. Unlike the revival of British cinema or the England cricket team, Christian revival is not the result of a fresh injection of finance or the new impetus of dynamic leadership. It is the result of God's sovereign and loving initiative. To say that we can create a revival (through evangelistic 'crusades', as they are somewhat insensitively known) is a mistake. That would be 'revivalism', not 'revival'. An authentic Christian revival is not subject to a purely human initiative or a purely humanistic interpretation. Although much can be learned using other disciplines (such as history, psychology, sociology and the like), none of these methods, not even the combination of them, can fully explain the phenomenon of Christian revival. Christian revival is *a divinely initiated process in which a dying church is revitalised through the power of the Holy Spirit, leading to a new love affair with Jesus Christ, which in turn transforms the community, region and even nation in which that church is situated.* Put this way, we can see that Christian revival is very much like love: it is a mystical, even miraculous, phenomenon requiring more than a merely cerebral explanation. Anything less ends up in reductionism.

The Prototype of Revival

There are few topics more vulnerable to experientialism than revival. There have been many preachers and writers who have started with their experience of a move of what they sensed was God's Spirit and then created a theology out of it. Although the relationship between experience and Scripture is a complex one, it is safer to begin with what the Scriptures say about revival and then reflect theologically on past and present history that stands in continuity with that fixed revelation. That way we avoid the pitfalls of subjectivism as well as experientialism.

When looking at what the Bible has to say on this subject, we need to focus on the New Testament. This is not to indulge in some kind of neo-Marcionite dismissal of the Old Testament, as if the Hebrew Scriptures have nothing to say about the phenomenon of revival. As I have shown elsewhere, the Old Testament contains indirect teaching on the subject and contains instances of the verb 'revive' (M. Stibbe 1998: 104–7). However, if revival means revitalising the church of Jesus Christ, then we have to make the New Testament the focus of our attention. Though the Christian church stands in continuity with the people of God in the Old Testament (engrafted as it is on to the cultivated olive tree of biblical Israel), the church as the bride and body of Jesus Christ is of course a post-Pentecost phenomenon.

As we scan the pages of the New Testament, the place where many revival theologians tend to begin is Acts 2.[2] In other words, Luke's narrative description of the outpouring of the Holy Spirit on the Day of Pentecost, with its subsequent spiritual harvest and miracles, is most often regarded as the prototype of revival. While I am in sympathy with this perspective, there are at least some grounds for saying that Pentecost marked the creation of the church, rather than its revitalisation. What we do not have in Acts 2 is a church on the edge of death being revivified. Instead, Luke's portrayal of events suggests that the 120 believers who received the tongues of heavenly fire were united in prayerful expectancy after the revelation (both seen and heard) of the risen and ascended Lord. They were not a moribund band of defeatists. They already had a living faith.

So where do we look for a biblical prototype of revival? If we are to be consistent with the nuance of revitalisation, then the most obvious port of call is the letter to the church in Ephesus (Rev. 2). This is the first of the seven letters of the ascended Lord and sets the scene for the rest:

> To the angel of the church in Ephesus write: These are the words of him who holds the seven stars in his right hand, who walks among the seven golden lampstands: I know your works, your toil and your patient endurance. I know that you cannot tolerate evildoers; you have tested those who claim to be apostles but are not, and have found them to be false. I also know that you are enduring patiently and bearing up for the sake of my name, and that you have not grown weary. But I have this against you, that you have abandoned the love you had at first. Remember then from what you have fallen; repent, and do the works you did at first. If not, I will come to you and remove your lampstand from its place, unless you repent. Yet this is to your credit: you hate the works of

---

[2] Evident often from only the titles of various books on revival, for example Iain Murray's excellent study *Pentecost Today: The Biblical Basis for Understanding Revival* (1998). I do not mean to deny that the Pentecost narrative sheds at least some light on revival (see M. Stibbe 1998: chapter 5). However, I would now be less strong than I was in insisting that Acts 2 forms the 'prototype' of authentic Christian revival.

the Nicolaitans, which I also hate. Let anyone who has an ear listen to what the Spirit is saying to the churches. To everyone who conquers, I will give permission to eat from the tree of life that is in the paradise of God (Rev. 2:1–7).

Here, more than anywhere else in the New Testament, we see the biblical prototype of revival. In Ephesus, during the second half of the first century AD, we find a church that had begun well. When the apostle Paul visited Ephesus he found twelve believers who had only been baptised with the baptism of John, not the baptism of Jesus. He quickly resolved the situation by immersing them in water in the name of the Lord Jesus, and Luke records that 'When Paul had laid his hands on them, the Holy Spirit came upon them, and they spoke in tongues and prophesied' (Acts 19:6). A strong church was born in the fire of God's love, a church that became known in heaven for its hard work, its perseverance under pressure, and its intolerance of doctrinal aberrations.

Then comes the word 'But'. '*But I have this against you, that you have abandoned the love you had at first.*' There has been a lot of ink spilled on the meaning of the phrase '*proten agapen*', first love. One thing seems to me to be certain, however: the reference is to the fervent passion for Jesus that characterised the church in Ephesus 'at first', that is, in its earliest days. As a result of their charismatic beginnings, the twelve (who must have grown quickly in numbers) became ardent lovers of God as the fire of the Spirit burned continuously in their hearts. There was no holding these people back. No mountain was too high for them to climb. They worked hard, and they did so because they were in love, not because they had to.

However, in the course of time the fire began to dim. The church in Ephesus, pictured symbolically as a menorah – a seven-branched lampstand – began to lose its radiance as the light began to fade in people's hearts. Instead of continuing in the law of love, this community turned to the love of law. Instead of worshipping a lover, this church began to worship a law giver. Instead of being a community serving the Lord out of joy, it became a place where duty was the primary motivation. Servile fear replaced filial love. While the church excelled in hard work and doctrinal purity, it did not excel in the most excellent gift of love: love for the Lord, love for each other, love for the lost. It had become a cold place. The flames on the seven candlesticks were barely flickering.

And so the word of prophecy comes from heaven in the form of a letter from Jesus. His word amounts to a great challenge:

You have abandoned your early passion for me. Remember how it was. Recall how you attained great heights of heavenly love on the wings of the Spirit. Repent of your lack of spiritual fervour. Experience true godly sorrow as you realise how far you have fallen. Come back to me. Service is no substitute for a love affair.

History does not record how the Ephesian believers responded to the voice of prophecy. But the ascended Lord warned the church that he would remove the lampstand from its place in heaven if there they did not repent. In other words, the church would not be revitalised but be removed. The oil of the Spirit would stop flowing. The lights would go out. The menorah would be gone.

From all this we can see something of the prototype of revival in Scripture. The church's destiny is to be a bridal community charac-terised by an affective, not just a cognitive, knowledge of the divine lover. When the church loses her passion for the Son of God, there is lamentation in heaven. Even if the church is doing well in issues of behaviour and belief, it is already on the road to death if holy affection has become a thing of the past. Christianity, as Jonathan Edwards often used to say, is a religion of the heart. God is after our affections, not just our works. Christian revival is *a divinely initi-ated process in which a dying church is revitalised through the power of the Holy Spirit, leading to a new love affair with Jesus Christ, which in turn transforms the community, region and even nation in which that church is situated.* While revival often involves a challenge to the church's doctrinal and behavioural impurities, it is primarily focused on whether the church is in love or not. From a loving heart there flows a living faith and a holy life.

The Story of Revival

Church history records many instances over two millennia in which this kind of divine romancing of the church has taken place. John Gillies' book *Historical Collections of Accounts of Revival* was first published in 1754. It contained over 600 pages in small print by the time Horatius Bonar re-edited it. In his preface to the 1854 edition, Bonar commented that there had never been an age in which the Holy Spirit has not caused a church to be revived or 're-awakened':

Never has there been an age when it could be said there is not one awake. The multitude has always slept, but there has always been a little flock awake. Even in the world's deepest midnight there have always been children of the light and of the day. In the midst of a slumbering world some have been in every age awake. God's voice has reached them, and His mighty power has raised them, and they walked the earth, awake among the sleepers, the living among the dead (Gillies 1981: v).

Gillies' book is a heartwarming record of countless episodes in which churches have experienced a divine awakening.

Looking at these and many other instances of revivals, it is possible to see in them a kind of archetypal story. In other words, many of the accounts of revival (written up in the form of narrative history) share a similar 'emplotment'. On the one hand, there is undoubtedly a genre to this kind of storytelling, a set of hagiographical literary conventions that the reporters consciously or unconsciously adhere to. On the other hand, the basic similarities between the stories (often drawn from very different and disconnected situations) suggest something larger than these conventions, a kind of transcendent 'grammar' of revival. While every revival account has its own set of distinctives (and these should not be obliterated), it is also true that each one seems to be the expression of a kind of archetypal storyline. To use structuralist terminology, every individual revival is like a speech utterance that obeys a larger grammatical system. It is like a *'parole'* that conforms, consciously or unconsciously, to a bigger *'langue'*. What we confront in any authentic Christian revival is the retelling of a divine story. It is the story of what happened to the church in Ephesus being revisited in a new and different context.

In my work on John's Gospel I have used A.J. Greimas' grammatical theory of stories in order to analyse more effectively the plot of the fourth gospel (M. Stibbe 1994: ch. 2).[3] Greimas, in his book *Semantique Structurale* (1966), proposed what he called an 'actantial' analysis of stories. In other words, he discovered a grammar of storytelling focused on various recurrent 'actants', or characters, in a story. These he identified as the Sender or Originator, the Receiver, the Opponent and the Helper.

In addition, Greimas discovered that these actants related to each other in archetypal ways. So, the Sender relates to the Receiver

---

[3] Other scholars, such as David Tolmie and Andrew Lincoln, have subsequently followed suit and applied Greimas' structuralist methodology to aspects of John's Gospel. This should show that the method itself is regarded as highly useful in the analysis of plot and characterisation in storytelling.

(and vice versa) along an axis of commission. In other words, the Sender commissions a Receiver to perform a task (the task being identified as 'the Object'). In addition, the Helper and the Opponent relate to the subject (the hero of the story) along an axis of 'power' (i.e. conflict).

Finally, the subject relates to the object along an axis of volition. In other words, the hero desires to perform the task or quest given by the Sender and obstructed by the Opponent. In diagrammatical form, Greimas' transcendent grammar of stories looks like this:

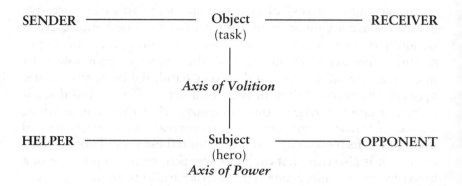

Applying these categories to revival is helpful in highlighting some of the salient features of its fundamental story.

In authentic revival, the Sender or Originator is God. True revival is not worked up on earth, but sent down from heaven. It is a miraculous and mystical phenomenon in which the whole of the Triune God plays the leading role – the Father initiating the process, the Spirit empowering and revivifying the church, the Son revealed and glorified afresh in the community of faith.

The Receiver is accordingly made up of those Christian believers who are open to the restoration of divine intimacy through the empowering, personal presence of God. This can be on a small or large scale.

The Object is simply a revival of living faith in the Lord Jesus Christ, characterised by a fresh obedience to the Great Commandment – loving God, loving one's neighbour, loving oneself (the worship, mission and community dimension of the church's life).

In the archetypal story of revival, the Opponent is the person or group of people who oppose the revitalising work of the Holy Spirit. Very often this antagonism comes from the institutional church, intimidated by the re-emergence of emancipating charisma.

The Subject of the story is confronted by this institutional oppression. The Subject can be an individual charismatic leader, usually surrounded and followed by a group of like-minded disciples. It can be a whole church or a group of churches. Whatever the case, these people are usually at the epicentre of God's revivifying work, and their quest is often characterised by fervent prayer and zealous evangelism. These people simply cannot resist giving away what they have freely received, and do so usually at great cost.

The Helper is the Holy Spirit. Though human helpers often emerge in revival episodes (and often from the most unlikely quarters), it is the Holy Spirit who constitutes the primary Helper for the Subject of revival. It is the Holy Spirit who causes the fire of God to burn in the hearts of those who carry the message of revival (Rom. 5:5). It is the Spirit of God who empowers both the Subject of revival, and those affected by this Subject.

This, then, is the classic, archetypal story of revival. While for some people this may be too rigid, for others it will be a great aid to identifying the main plot of revival. Some may argue that I have contradicted myself by using this model. I stated at the beginning that I wanted to highlight the *romance* of revival, and here I am now proposing a descriptive, formalist model! My response to this is quite simple. The genre of the story I have just told is that of romance. The story of revival is a love story. It is the stuff of spring and summer, not of autumn and winter. It is the story of Jesus himself played out again in his body, the church. It is the story of Ephesus all over again – the story of a divine lover wooing his bride into a renewed and unquenchable passion. For this reason, it should come as no surprise that in revival one of the most quoted books of the Bible is the Song of Songs. It is as if the church hears once again the bridegroom's voice:

> My beloved speaks and says to me: 'Arise, my love, my fair one, and come away; for now the winter is past, the rain is over and gone. The flowers appear on the earth; the time of singing has come, and the voice of the turtledove is heard in our land. The fig tree puts forth its figs, and the vines are in blossom; they give forth fragrance. Arise, my love, my fair one, and come away' (Song 2:10–13).

An Illustration of Revival

As an example of the way in which individual revivals mirror this deeper story I propose to take the Great Awakening in Norway,

beginning in 1796. I choose this example because Hans Nielsen
Hauge was the central figure of this revival movement and his life
and teaching are instructive for our own time. More than that, my
extensive travelling and ministry in Norway has given me a great
admiration for this man and a desire to see his story made more
familiar outside of Scandinavia. Indeed, one British writer has
described Hauge as 'Norway's Wesley' (Pilcher 1930). The English-
speaking world has yet to appreciate the importance of this individual, especially in Northern European church history.

Hauge's impact on Norway was immense (M. Stibbe 2001:
140–5). From 1796 onwards he travelled the length and breadth of
Norway (and parts of Denmark) preaching the gospel and establishing small businesses. The eight years from 1796–1804 were his
most productive in terms of preaching and writing. He made eight
major journeys, covering thousands of miles, on foot and by ski,
four from Tune (south-east Norway) and four from Bergen. He
often knitted gloves and socks for the poor as he walked. Hauge
wrote or translated over thirty books, nineteen of them in this
eight-year period.

It is no exaggeration to say that Hauge's preaching led to the
conversion of thousands of Norwegians, especially among the
bondestand, or poorer farming community. In fact, his ministry
led to national transformation. As Joseph Shaw has written:
'Hauge is remembered today as the man who revitalised religious
life in Norway in the early nineteenth century and gave Norway a
Christianity marked by intense personal faith and upright
personal and social conduct' (Shaw 1955: 5).

In the remaining part of this paper I want to map the story of
Hauge's ministry against the archetypal revival story already
discussed.

(a) The Sender

Looking at the Sender or Originator under Hauge, it quickly becomes
clear that Hauge's story is one of revival rather than revivalism.
Hauge's ministry was not launched out of a purely social agenda, or
out of any psychological need on his part, or as the result of a humanly
orchestrated missions strategy. Rather, Hauge was launched into
his ministry of revitalising Norwegian Christianity by an intense
experience of God. Many have tried to reduce this transformational
experience to a secular explanation, but in the end this will not suffice
(Dale 1942, Danbolt 1971: 241–53, Gundersen 2001: 116 ff.,

Kornerup 1937: 552–67). For those familiar with twentieth-century Pentecostal and charismatic spirituality, not to mention the great heritage of Christian mysticism and Pietism, Hauge's experience in 1796 is patient of only one plausible explanation – that he was visited by the fire of God in a dramatic and life-changing way.

On the 5 April 1796, Hauge was ploughing a field on his father's farmland. He was singing a Norwegian hymn, 'Jesus, I Long for Thy Blessed Communion', containing the lines: 'Mightily strengthen my spirit within me / that I may learn what Thy Spirit can do.' Hauge had been seeking a deeper walk with God. He had been praying:

> If Thou, my Father, wilt give me power, create Thy love in my heart and preserve me in humility, then I will serve Thee with all my strength. I will sacrifice everything, even my own life, as did the early martyrs, rather than depart from Thy commandments (Hauge 1954: 40–41).

Hauge's great longing was to know God as Father and to have an intense heart-knowledge that he was God's child. As Hauge was ploughing the field he came to the end of the second verse of the hymn. Twenty years later, in his book *Religious Experiences*, Hauge described what happened next:

> At this point my mind became so exalted that I was not myself aware of, nor can I express, what took place in my soul. For I was beside myself. As soon as I came to my senses, I was filled with regret that I had not served this loving transcendently good God. Now it seemed to me that nothing in this world was worthy of any regard. That my soul experienced something supernatural, divine, and blessed; that there was a glory that no tongue can utter – that I remember as clearly as if it happened only a few days ago (Hauge 1954: 41–2).

From that day on, everything changed. Hauge had a deep burning love for God and his neighbour. He experienced a sorrow over sin and a desire that others should know God's grace. He was given a special desire to read the Scriptures and new ability to understand them. The focus of his life became the gospel, the good news that Jesus Christ came to save sinners and that men and women must repent of sin and believe in Christ. Hauge saw the whole world as submerged in a great, dark ocean of evil and sensed the urgency of the task of rescuing his fellow human beings from disaster. He asked God what he should do and sensed the Holy Spirit impressing on him the following:

You shall confess My name before the people; exhort them to repent and seek Me while I may be found and call upon Me while I am near; and touch their hearts that they may turn from darkness to light' (Hauge 1954: 42–3).

From that day forth, Hauge surrendered himself to this grand quest.

The Sender of revival in Norway was very clearly God. Hauge's heart was suddenly and marvellously seized by the power of a great affection. This was God's doing and was not the result of any special methods. Indeed, we should note that the use of revivalist meetings (under Finney's leadership) was still thirty years away in America.

(b) The Receiver

The farming community of Norway (of which Hauge himself was a part) formed 96 per cent of the population at the time. The other 4 per cent was made up of government officials and administrators (Dyrvik 1979: 131). This included the clergy, because the Dano-Norwegian church was state governed.

In Hauge's time there was a great gap between the ordinary people of Norway and the clergy. The clergy had been impacted by eighteenth-century rationalism, and spoke a language that was not easily understood. The people, when religious, opted for their Pietistic roots from the mid 1700s. Furthermore, many clergy lived lives that seemed wholly at odds with the moral code of the Kingdom of God. Many ordinary people in Norway had what Sverre Steen calls 'a burning religious compulsion' (Steen 1951: 67), but the gap between their need and the teaching of the clergy was too great.

When we look at the chief recipients of the revival from 1796 onwards, the primary candidates are the farming community, for which Hans Nielsen Hauge became the charismatic leader and chief spokesperson. When revival came to Norway at the end of the eighteenth century, God's power emancipated these people in an unprecedented way. While force of arms was being used to bring liberation in Revolutionary France, the love of God was achieving similarly emancipating effects in Norway.

(c) The Object

The purpose for which revival was sent was the restoration of what Hauge was constantly to refer to as 'a living faith'.[4] In contrast to

---

[4] Andreas Aarflot says of Hauge's teaching: 'The surest sign that faith is

the dead orthodoxy of the past and the soul-destroying rationalism of the present, Hauge preached an unadorned message of the Cross given in the power of the Spirit. In *Religious Experiences*, Hauge describes his 'simplicity of faith' and how God's Spirit empowered his gospel preaching:

> I was surprised that when I talked with people and was in a happy mood, those who listened wept and cried out with longing to be even as I. For I felt that what I said was so simple. But I discovered that there was a power of God in the foolishness of preaching, as Paul says in 1 Corinthians 1.31 (Hauge 1954: 47).

In contrast to the dead rationalism of the clergy, Hauge proclaimed the importance of a living faith in Jesus. This does not mean that Hauge was anti-rationalistic; in fact, he insisted: 'I have learned more and more to respect knowledge and learning in every field' (Hauge 1954: 70). Furthermore, there is strong evidence to suggest that some of Hauge's methods were based on Enlightenment principles, even if his message was a very simple one. Hauge stressed the need for heat in the heart as well as light in the head. This was the key to a living faith.

(d) The Subject

Hans Nielsen Hauge and his immediate followers (the Haugianere or Haugians) were the subject of the story of Norway's revival. It was through them that this living faith was disseminated throughout Scandinavia. They were the ones who were responsible for massive spiritual and social change in the final years of the eighteenth century and the opening decades of the nineteenth (A.H. Stibbe 2001). It was Hauge and the Haugians who pioneered lasting national transformation. As Alv Magnus puts it:

> Hauge worked through his followers; it was through them that his work had an effect on history. Small colonies of faithful and industrious Haugians all over the land must have represented an enormous potential for effecting a change in attitude that introduced improved agricultural techniques to the farmer's advantage (Magnus 1996: 199).

---

[4] (*continued*) living is that the believer has a burning desire to win others for Christ' (Aarflot 1979: 8).

(e) *The Helper*

Hauge relied throughout his life and ministry on the help of the Holy Spirit. In preaching he had tried to use a more prepared, reasoned approach, but it had failed him. More and more he relied on the empowering of the Spirit. As he wrote:

> I was singularly driven by the power of the Spirit of God to speak to people. For even though at times I was tempted to remain silent for fear of persecution by wicked men, still that was only to bring upon myself the experience and cry of the prophet in Jeremiah 20.9. It was as if a fire burned within me and I could not keep still, especially when many people were present (Hauge 1954: 63).

He also commented:

> I called then on the Lord for power, acknowledged my own impotence and dependence on God's grace; and when I merely yielded to him, prayed that He would guide my tongue, and believed that He would give me what I need in that hour ... then it was always easy for me to speak about the way of life on every occasion (Hauge 1954: 63–4).

Hauge was truly a man of the word and the Spirit. His preaching was Bible based and entirely reliant on the help of God's Spirit. This same Spirit who helped him to deliver the message helped his hearers to receive it, often with demonstrations of power (such as godly sorrow and substantial conversions).

(f) *The Opponent*

The state church and secular authorities of Norway quickly rose up against Hauge, and he was arrested and imprisoned. Hauge spent much of the period 1800–14 imprisoned. Shaw identifies four reasons why the state church opposed Hauge (Shaw 1955: 66–7).

Firstly, *unlawful vagrancy*. The 1741 Conventicle Act forbade any itinerant preachers from performing their ministry without proper licence. The act itself had been created to ensure that only legitimate church-controlled conventicles or gatherings took place, and that 'fanatics' like the Zinzendorfians and Anabaptists were suppressed. The refined version of the Act was used against Hauge and he was imprisoned as a vagrant (i.e. an itinerant without official government passes).

Secondly, *unskilled preaching*. Hauge and his followers were charged with being untrained preachers, unable to read the Bible in its original languages, and incapable of understanding, let alone expounding, the Scriptures.

Thirdly, *unattractive mannerisms*. Hauge and his followers were persecuted for their 'whining voices, distorted eyes and hanging heads'. This caricature was concocted to accuse the Haugians of lacking the Enlightenment value of refined dignity and respectability.

Fourthly, *unpalatable theology*. Hauge preached that people were saved not by their own noble efforts but by God's grace alone, and that even the most virtuous Enlightenment men and women were under God's judgement until they repented of sin and believed in the Lord Jesus Christ.

When Hauge was eventually formally charged, it was for violating the 1741 Conventicle Act, for uttering insulting remarks about the Norwegian clergy, and for misappropriating the funds of his followers.

(g) Summary

Even a brief (and somewhat superficial) look at the story of the Haugian revival demonstrates its conformity to the narrative grammar of revival. The model described above can be applied in this way:

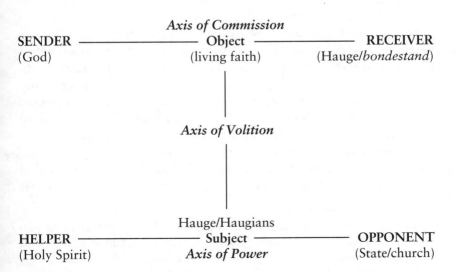

Axis of Commission

SENDER ———————— Object ———————— RECEIVER
(God)   (living faith)   (Hauge/*bondestand*)

Axis of Volition

Hauge/Haugians
HELPER ———————— Subject ———————— OPPONENT
(Holy Spirit)   *Axis of Power*   (State/church)

The Power of a Great Affection

Christian revival is *a divinely initiated process in which a dying church is revitalised through the power of the Holy Spirit, leading to a new love affair with Jesus Christ, which in turn transforms the community, region and even nation in which that church is situated.*

Through Hauge and his followers, Norwegian Christianity was transformed in a lasting way. It all began when Hauge was 'seized with the power of a great affection'. This beautiful phrase was commonplace in the deep south of the United States a hundred or so years ago. Caught up in a revival atmosphere, people would not ask one another, 'Are you born again?' Instead, they would ask, 'Have you been seized by the power of a great affection?' This phrase describes what happened to Hauge. The nature of Hauge's experience is undoubtedly rich and complex. Andreas Aarflot says that Hauge formulated some of his views 'in a manner closer to medieval Catholic mysticism than to Lutheran doctrine', pointing to Hauge's use of phrases like 'heat from the fire of God's love' (Aarflot 1979: 142).[5] The influence of Pietism should also not be neglected; nor should the Pentecostal interpretation of Hauge's experience as 'Spirit baptism'. Whatever terminology one chooses to employ, the fact remains: a great revitalisation of the Norwegian church began when Hauge fell in love with God.

This, I would submit, is the key to understanding authentic Christian revival. Of course, the *holiness* of God is a vital feature of revival. This cannot be denied, and in other places I have given this aspect of God's nature and our response ample treatment.[6] There is absolutely no doubt that revival brings a sense of the judgement of God and an awful realisation of his purity and our compromises. In revival times, one of the primary works of the Spirit is certainly conviction and repentance, as people cry out for mercy and come to the Cross for salvation and forgiveness. None of this should be forgotten, lest we will fall into the trap of crass sentimentality, emphasising intimacy at the expense of purity.

Yet at the same time I cannot help thinking that the love of God has found far too little emphasis in revival theology. Howel Harris

---

[5] Aarflot calls this 'the terminology of mysticism'. This insightful connection with Catholic theology should prevent us from seeing Christian revival as a purely Protestant, let alone Pentecostal/charismatic, phenomenon.

[6] See M. Stibbe 1998: chapter 2 and M. Stibbe 2001: chapter 4, where I deal with the *ordo salutis*.

wrote: 'Love fell in showers on my soul, that I could scarcely contain myself. I had no fear, or any doubt of my salvation … I felt I was all love – so full of it that I could not ask for more' (quoted in Bennett 1962: 30–31). He added that his heart had melted within him like wax before a fire. John Wesley, of course, talked about how his heart had been 'strangely warmed'. When Charles Wesley met William Grimshaw he said of him that 'his love was full of triumphant love' (quoted in Laycock 1909: 46). Grimshaw himself concluded a letter to Charles Wesley with the words: 'my desire and hope is to love God with all my heart, mind, soul and strength to the last gasp of my life' (Miles 1813: 188). Sarah Edwards said of George Whitefield that 'he speaks from a heart all aglow with love' (quoted in Murray 1972: 162).[7] Jonathan Edwards spoke of the true gospel minister as someone whose 'heart burns with love to Christ … and also with ardent love to the souls of men, and desires for their salvation' (Edwards 1974: 957). Time and again, we find this kind of godly love language in eighteenth-century revivals. If this fact had been more widely recognised, there might have been less cynicism about the Toronto Blessing, where a theology of the love of God has always been central.[8]

In the final analysis, the ministry of the Holy Spirit is not monochrome, but multi-faceted. He can do many things in the same place at the same time: convicting, saving, empowering, revealing, healing, and so on. However, I profoundly believe that one of the priorities of the Spirit of God in revival times is the reawakening of love. The apostle Paul recognised the profound relationship between the *dunamis* of the Spirit and the revelation of God's love. His prayer in Ephesians 3 highlights the importance of praying for more of God's power in our lives so that we may comprehend better the limitless ocean of God's love. In an increasingly secular society, the church of Jesus Christ – especially in the West – needs to pray this prayer with fervour once again. 'Lord, seize our hearts with the power of a great affection.' Or, as St Paul puts it (Eph. 3:18–19):

May your roots go down deep into the soil of God's marvellous love. And may you have the power to understand, as all God's people should, how wide, how long, how high, and how deep his love really is. May you experience the love of Christ, though it is so great you will never

---

[7] Whitefield's own prayer at the start of his ministry was: 'Unloose my stammering tongue to tell / Thy love immense, immeasurable.'

[8] See, for example, John Arnott's book *Catch the Fire* (1994).

fully understand it. Then you will be filled with the fullness of life and power that comes from God.[9]

---

[9] Eugene Petersen's paraphrase in *The Message* (Petersen 1993: 405).

References

Aarflot, A. (1979). *Hans Nielsen Hauge: His Life and Message.* Minneapolis: Augsburg.

Arnott, J. (1994). *Catch the Fire.* London: Hodder & Stoughton.

Bennett, R. (1962). *The Early Life of Howel Harris.* London: Banner of Truth.

Dale, K. (1942). *Hans Nielsen Hauges åndelige gjennombrud.* Norsk Teologisk Tidsskrift: 44–60.

Danbolt, E. (1971). *Kallopplevelsens betydning for Hans Nielsen Hauges kallbevissthet.* Tidsskrift for Teologi og Kirke.

Dyrvik, S. (1979). *Befolkningsutviklinga 1700–1850.* Oslo: Universitetsforlaget.

Edwards, J. (1974). *Works of Jonathan Edwards* Vol. 2. Edinburgh: Banner of Truth.

Gillies, J. (1981). *Historical Collections of Accounts of Revival.* Edinburgh: Banner of Truth.

Greimas, A.J. (1966). *Semantique Structurale.* Paris: Larousse.

Gundersen, T.R. (2001). *Om å ta Ordet – retorikk og utsigelse i den unge Hans Nielsen Hauges forfatterskap.* Norsk sakprosa (3).

Hauge, H.N. (1954). *Religious Experiences* in *Autobiographical Writings of Hans Nielsen Hauge* trans. J.M. Njus. Minneapolis: Augsburg.

Kornerup, B. (1937). *Hans Nielsen Hauges religiøse udvikling.* Kirke og Kultur.

Laycock, J.W. (1909). *Methodist Heroes in the Great Haworth Round.* Keighley: Rydal Press.

Magnus, A.J. (1996). *Veirydder med gnagsår: Hans Nielsen Hauge og vekkelsen som forandret Norge.* 2312 Ottestad, Norway: ProklaMedia. (Quote trans. A.H. Stibbe).

Miles, W. (1813). *Life and Writings of William Grimshaw.* London.

Murray, I. (1972). *Jonathan Edwards: A New Biography.* Edinburgh: Banner of Truth.

Murray, I. (1998). Pentecost Today: The Biblical Basis for Understanding Revival. *Edinburgh: Banner of Truth.*

Petersen, E. (1993). *The Message.* Colarado Springs: NavPress.

Pilcher, C.V. (1930). *Hans Nielsen Hauge – Norway's Wesley.* Theological Forum 2(1): 44–52.

Shaw, J. (1955). *Pulpit Under the Sky: A Life of Hans Nielsen Hauge.* Connecticut: Greenwood Press.

Steen, S. (1951). *Det frie Norge 1814.* Oslo.

Stibbe, A.H. (2001). *Hans Nielsen Hauge: Religious Revival and Modernisation in Nineteenth Century Norway.* Unpublished dissertation, Department of Scandinavian Studies, University College, London.

Stibbe, M. (1994). *John's Gospel.* London and New York: Routledge.

Stibbe, M. (1998). *Thinking Clearly About Revival*. Crowborough: Monarch.

Stibbe, M. (2001). *Fire and Blood: The Work of the Spirit, the Work of the Cross*. Crowborough: Monarch.

Twells, A. (1998). *Standing on His Promises: A History of St Andrew's Church, Chorleywood – A Story of Sustained Renewal*. Wimbledon: Clifford Frost.

Chapter 3

The Role of the Holy Spirit in Revival

Graham McFarlane

The subject of the Holy Spirit and his relation to anything, let alone revival or revivalism, comes with a strange imperative, a not-of-this-world health warning. It risks horribly self-inflicted consequences, for one must be ready to grapple with what Brueggemann describes as the irascible, evasive and polyvalent nature of the (biblical) subject (Brueggemann 1998: 198–9). Implicit to the subject in hand is the categorical warning of Jesus Christ himself, expressed in typically Johannine form: 'The wind blows where it chooses, and you hear the sound of it, but you do not know where it comes from or where it goes. So it is with everyone who is born of the Spirit' (John 3:8).

Inherent, then, to the subject of pneumatology as it engages with the human condition are intrenchable difficulties. We might describe them blandly as to do with form and content. On the one hand, the evasive nature of the subject creates a methodological warning we ignore at our peril. This subject, put bluntly, is not easily grasped. As such, we must be more careful than others in terms of how we handle the stuff and matter of the Spirit. On the other hand, however, the very content itself defies ultimate control. Even the briefest of encounters with biblical and sociological scholarship testifies to this fact, as Max Turner's paper so admirably illustrates. The sheer evasiveness of the subject substantiates its subsequent irascible nature: love it or hate it, this subject gets us all going! Small wonder, then, that when we come to the general subject of pneumatology we expose ourselves to a polyvalent rather than ubiquitous set of voices: there is, it appears, more than one take on the subject.

Part of the reason for this has to do with the fact that both biblically and theologically, dogmatically and credally, the subject of the
Holy Spirit has no one point of location. Perhaps if we compare and
contrast our opinions concerning the Spirit with those concerning
Christ, the illustration will become more clear. That is, there is no
pneumatological parallel to Christology. Quite the reverse. Whereas, biblically, the word became flesh and dwelt among us, the Spirit
has no such incarnation within history. Theologically, then, the
issues that dominated Christological discussion in the patristic era,
namely, how two different natures could coexist together in the one
historical reality, form no basis for any Spirit talk. As such, then,
dogmatically, the focus of the early church and its successors was
Christologically not pneumatologically driven. It is no surprise,
then, that when we turn to the credal, very little is said concerning
the Spirit, since at that time the Spirit was not a problem. He simply
existed! Indeed, when Nicaea comes to its statement of faith
concerning the Spirit, after several tortuous caveats regarding the
Son, the confessing simply state 'and in the Holy Spirit'.

If only things remained that simple! Things tend to change over
the odd millennium or two! It would certainly appear that the Spirit
has come of age today, in an era of unprecedented communication.
As a result, the churches of the twenty-first century no longer confess
one *credo* concerning the person and work of the Spirit. Thus, whilst
Eastern and Roman Christendoms maintain some sense of decorum
through their allegiance to ancient statements of faith, this has not
been the case as regards their Western counterparts.

Part 1: A Problem to be Aired

Western society with its cultural individualism impacts contemporary pneumatology significantly, and on two counts:

Firstly, from Hegel onwards, we have been experiencing what
has been described as the secularisation of the Spirit (Gunton
1996: 107–8). That is, the Spirit has been removed from the
confines of the church and scattered amidst the wider milieu.
Spirit, as an abstract noun, dominates our culture. In addition, the
notion of and need for God as Spirit has been hijacked by modern
markets and media, which provide secular alternatives to what the
Spirit traditionally provides, whether placebo or counterfeit.

Secondly, Western Christendom has developed highly individu-
alised doctrines of the Spirit that are incommensurate with one

another. Unfortunately, as Western churches face controversy, and no more so than with the subject of revival, these independent and autonomous communities inevitably offer abstracted and sometimes conflicting presentations of the Spirit.

Perhaps this is where the particularity of systematic theology might offer some help on the subject. Admittedly, in the past systematic theology was the prerogative of theological pharmacists, that is, scholars who provided prescriptions to be taken as and when, whatever the time, culture or place. Today, however, contemporary systematics concerns itself with a more open-ended agenda. On the one hand, it seeks to work in tandem with Scripture. It is an appeal, according to New Testament scholar Joel Green, to ' "Rules of faith", narrative summaries of the kerygma … shaped before and alongside the formation of the Christian canon' (Green 2002: 12). On the other hand, the systematician works within that space, as Gunton puts it, where 'theological thought seeks, in obedience to the gospel, to find those words best suited to express the limited truth that is granted of the ways of God toward and in the world' (Gunton 1998: 42). As such, the systematician seeks to develop a 'rule of faith' for the believing community as it engages with specific issues, drawing from Scripture and subsequent theological tradition and contemporary imagination.

It is the contention of this paper that the systematician does indeed have something of importance to contribute to a theology of the Spirit in relation to revivalism. It will do so both in terms of the emerging relationship between Scripture and theological development and in its practical engagement with a problematic requiring some kind of dogmatic resolution. In order to do so, one must first locate the problem.

Touching on the Problem

The problem can be easily located between two clear loci. On the one hand, we can identify the problem as the Western proclivity towards amnesia regarding things of the Spirit – *Geistvergessenheit* (Spirit forgetting). We confront here, as it were, a pneumatological parallel to the Christological danger stated in Matthew 7:32 – that one can experience 'Jesus things' but not actually know Jesus. So too with the Spirit: in being caught up with various forms of revivalist evidentialism it is possible to lose sight of and connection with the Spirit.

A good example of this is to be found in the inviting book entitled *Elusive Present* by S. Terrien (1978). Here, the author seeks to delineate the 'reality of the presence of God' that 'stands at the centre of biblical faith'. Terrien goes on to add that 'This presence, however, is always elusive' (1978: xxvii). And so it is. Indeed, over the subsequent 500 pages, the author manages to discuss the biblical and dogmatic presence of God with only one allusion to the Spirit in the main text. *Geistvergessenheit* indeed: others would simply describe it for what it is – blatant binitarianism.

The alternative, on the other hand, is quite the opposite. Here, the Spirit is very much centre stage. With the reification of Trinitarian theology being currently experienced in the West, there is a plethora of offerings concerning the Spirit. Whilst it is neither the intention nor purpose of this paper to deliberate on such august contributions, it is pertinent to our subject matter to point out one fault line when the subject matter turns to the subject of charismatic revival. We might describe it as pneumatological evidentialism. Here, the spectacle of divine inbreaking is identified in terms of both the phenomena it produces and the means by which these charismatic phenomena may be induced.

Unfortunately, the problem here is that such revivalistic pneumatologies inevitably collapse into various forms of evidentialism. That is, revival is deemed to have occurred on the grounds that certain phenomena, usually charismatic, are evidenced. The problem with this, put bluntly, is that the phenomena inevitably become ends in themselves. In time, a vicious circle of cause and effect emerges, somewhat similar to the revivalist dog repeatedly chasing its own tail. In such instances, 'revivalism' becomes simply a catchword for the more insidious 'human technology for producing "revival" ' (Piggin 2000: 1).

One recent attempt at avoiding such 'revivalistic' tendencies is Piggin's *Firestorm of the Lord*. Here, the author seeks to develop a more balanced theological approach to the subject. However, in offering his own definition of revival as well as criteria for identifying what the next great revival will be, he falls prey to the pitfalls mentioned above.

Firstly, his definition:

> Revival is a sovereign work of God the Father, consisting of a powerful
> intensification by Jesus of the Holy Spirit's normal activity of testifying
> to the Saviour, accentuating the doctrines of grace, and convicting,
> converting, regenerating, sanctifying and empowering large numbers

of people at the same time, and is therefore a community experience. It is occasionally preceded by an expectation that God is about to do something exceptional; it is usually preceded by an extraordinary unity and prayerfulness among Christians; and it is always accompanied by the revitalisation of the church, the conversion of large numbers of unbelievers and the diminution of sinful practices in the community (Piggin 2000: 11).

Secondly, Piggin offers six hallmarks of the next great revival. There will be:

1. a revived concentration by the church on the centrality of Christ and his gospel;
2. a revived Trinitarian theology;
3. a revived spiritual agenda within the church fellowship;
4. a revived leadership;
5. a revived confidence in God's word;
6. a revived involvement of Christians with the community and nation (Piggin 2000: 210–17).

Admittedly, there is nothing evasive here. The diagnostic criteria offered by Piggin are clearly set out. As a descriptive and explanatory exercise, Piggin offers the reader a robust framework within which to exercise expectation and hope. However, has he correctly identified the mechanisms of revival? The working definition is certainly clear, but is it not misdirected? Perhaps so, for it could be argued convincingly that Piggin is guilty here of a category mistake: that is, of confusing one reality for another. Perhaps this is essentially due to the evasive nature of the Spirit's work within and for the church, but Piggin, and those he represents, confuses here revival and revivalism with the Kingdom of God. That is, with this kind of definition, Piggin does not describe revival so much as articulate the expectations that centre on the Kingdom of God. The only caveat here might be that this kind of definition expects large numbers. And yet, even this expectation may be an ecclesial example of our wider cultural (and male) obsessions with size.

More significantly, however, it is what is missing from the diagnostic test offered here concerning any future great awakening that reflects both a thoroughly Western and thus culture-conditioned set of expectations. Bluntly put, there is little here that smacks of the quirky and odd that so characterises the Isaianic and synoptic declarations of what to expect when God 'does his stuff'. Certainly, there is no disposition towards the objects of God's intentions that so epitomises Jesus' own orientation towards the lame, blind, disadvantaged, marginalised, disenfranchised. Contrary to the revivalism outlined above, with its inevitable familiarity from overexposure to the divine, whether charismatic or rationalistic, the central biblical insight remains. It is expressed well when Brueggemann says: 'The utterance of the primitive God of Scripture is an utterance that is in an unfamiliar mode' (Brueggemann 1998: 197). Unfortunately for us, our expectation is no longer tempered by such discontinuity.

The reason for this, as Plascher persuasively argues, is not too hard to locate: we suffer from what he calls the 'domestication of transcendence' (Plascher 1996). God no longer comes to us strangely. The God and Father of our Lord Jesus Christ is no longer a startling figure. He is benign, friendly, overly familiar. Consequently, the Spirit who raised our Lord Jesus from the dead is no longer a Holy Spirit, that is, other, transcendent, different, or, to use Brueggemann again, evasive, irascible, polyvalent. Rather, this Spirit is a terribly familiar Spirit, whom we have made into our own family likeness: the evasive has been captured; the irascible has been broken and controlled; the polyvalent has been reduced to a single theological economy.

Part 2: Towards a Solution

I have deliberately laboured the problems facing a contemporary discussion concerning the Spirit and revival for clear personal and methodological reasons. Firstly, on a personal level, I speak into an ongoing dialogue concerning the Spirit and revivalism as one who earns his bread and butter for doing so. But my interests are not those vested in the purely economical or professional. At a deeper level, I come to the dialogue as one who has himself been addressed by the Spirit's revivification; as one who has drunk from the well of revival and known its horizon-expanding matrix. Consequently, I speak as a dialogue partner, not as cynic or abstracted commentator.

Secondly, however, there are also methodological reasons. As stated above, it is the peculiar task of the systematician to identify a given problem and then proffer a solution. This has been the aim of theology, whether that offered within the canon itself, or by the church Fathers, the Reformers or theologians of the last century. Unless we can articulate the problem, all we can offer are abstracted propositions that rarely release the church into further service.

The problem here is well put by Welker, who points out that when looked at biblically, 'the Spirit does not have an abstract self-reference like the human person, but that a "public personality" can be attributed to the Spirit' (Welker 1997: 31, see also 1994: 312). I believe this offers a vital clue to unlocking some neglected aspects of a doctrine of the Holy Spirit, due to our own 'forgetting the Spirit'.

Put simply, the issue centres around the problem of *identification*. This identification, in turn, can be located at three points.

Firstly, and perhaps a trenchant warning for any revivalistic tendencies, the Spirit is not to be understood in terms of his own independent personality. Whilst danger bells may well be ringing at this point, the issue needs to be stated unequivocally: the Spirit never comes to us in his own name but in the name of another, whether Father and/or Son. As such, then, to focus attention on either the Spirit himself or on his effects is to miss the whole point. Whoever or whatever the Spirit is and does, it is for another. He is never an end in himself.

We can tease this further in suggesting that the hallmarks of spiritual maturity consist of two things. Firstly, that the faithful become more and more conformed to the image of Christ. There is no room for abstracted, otherworldly spiritualities here. To be like Christ is to be earthed in the same *modus vivendi* that characterised Jesus Christ's own ministry. Put simply, its hallmark is one predisposed to those who require the gospel, not those who are entertained by it. Secondly, the virtues that come about as a result of the Spirit's agency in our lives are typically those that deflect attention from the individual ego, from what Merton describes as the false external self to the true internal self that is focused on the will and therefore love of God (Merton 1972: 7). Thus compassion, kindness, lowliness, meekness, patience, forbearance, forgiveness and love become the church's advertisements of the Spirit (Col. 3:12–14).

Interestingly, such virtues are earthed clearly in relation not to the Spirit, but to both the believers themselves and to the Lord of the church. It is only a specifically bourgeois church that perceives the Spirit's action as being achieved outside the common matrix of struggle, pain and self-denial. Indeed, more trenchantly, only an indulgent church would attempt to dumb down the Spirit's testimony to impersonal phenomena in its attempt to subvert the true purpose of charismata.

The second aspect of identification concerns the nature of the Spirit's activity within and for creation. This can be identified in terms of power. This agency requires the unpacking of a particular metaphysic or view of reality before the Spirit's place within it can be identified. Put simply, the world in which the God of Abram, Israel and Jesus operates is one where there is no direct contact between the Creator and the created. Creation, as it were, is of a completely different order of things from the Creator. Creation is not the actualisation of idealised forms in the mind of the Creator, as in Greek philosophy. As Gunton reminds us, there is 'an ontological homogeneity' about the created realm that originates in the fact that it simply is different from the Creator. It is a creation *ex nihilo*, and as such one that differs from its Creator, who has no beginning or end (Gunton 1998: 71–3).

Now, this is an extremely important point to make, for with it we are able to articulate the notion of mediation. As Barth reminds us, it is the nature of an idol to be accessed directly. However, not so with the living God. He cannot be accessed as if he were a divine PC: double click on the right creed or prayer, and in you go! Rather, he is accessed only in terms of mediation. The reason for this lies at the very core of the Judaeo-Christian creation stories: the Creator creates through his word and Spirit – not directly. This is the golden thread that runs throughout Scripture: a genesis of creation that requires mediation; a story of redemption peppered by salvific figures that culminates in the great mediator himself, Jesus Christ, whose Father always comes to us through his Son and Spirit; and, finally, a goal where the one mediated promises to make his home with us. Indeed, without this sense of apartness, otherness, transcendence, the final promise of the Father is awkwardly anticlimactic.

The bottom line remains: the Spirit's primary significance is as the One who actualises the intentions of God both in creation and recreation, in the cosmos and in the church. He is God's power both to create and to recreate, to sustain and to fulfil. The Spirit brings creation and church into being, holds them together, separately and corporately, and preserves them from the powers that would otherwise lead to their respective destruction. To state otherwise is to run contrary to the grain of Scripture.

The third aspect of identification, then, centres on this issue of mediation and power. If the Spirit is God's power, then we need to ask questions concerning the nature of that power. It is here that two contemporary systematicians' understandings of the Spirit impact with meaning. Wolfhart Pannenberg has opened discussion concerning the Spirit in terms of a field of force (1991: 382–3). Using the analogy of cosmic fields and physics, and in particular

Michael Farady's idea of a universal force field, Pannenberg argues that the biblical presentation of the Spirit is better understood in terms of a unifying force field, as one who unites both the Father and the Son, and that the force field be identified in terms of love.

Michael Welker takes this a little further. He seeks to safeguard the Spirit's identity from reductionistic interpretations as an individual person and presents an alternative model for the Spirit. For Welker, the centre of divine action is not the Spirit, but the one upon whom he rests, the Messiah of God, Jesus Christ. As such, then, Jesus Christ is the centre of action. The Spirit is better understood as the domain of resonance, the realm within which Jesus operates. Again, the notion of mediation is present, and whilst we must take on board Gunton's criticism of this notion of the Spirit as a field of force (Gunton 1998: 160–61), namely, that it affords the Spirit only an impersonal identity, there is much to commend in both understandings of the Spirit. Indeed, it may be that, seen from a specifically pneumatological perspective, it is not our understanding of the Spirit that requires modification, but rather our notion of what it means to be a person.

What is of importance here is how we understand the nature of this power. If there is a problem inherent to the phenomenon of revival it centres on this point. It has to do with the notion of means and ends, form and content. Whilst the means of revival is quite categorically the Spirit, the purpose of such is not to focus attention on the Spirit: it is to elevate Jesus Christ. Thus, the nature of this power takes on a much more Christological than pneumatological face.

It is for this reason that Paul affirms both the creational and ecclesial, that is, the cosmos and the church in relation to Christ. Whilst the power at work in creation and re-creation is that of the Spirit, the one in whom and for whom all things were created and have their being is Christ (Col. 1:16). Or, as John proclaims in his prologue, without him was not anything made that was made (1:3). All this is so that the Father of our Lord Jesus Christ may have his 'style', his way of doing things, his hallmark, his glory displayed to all and sundry. Thus it is that the wisdom of God is so marvellously displayed in creation and finds its apex in Jesus Christ. Indeed, and because of this, a notion of pre-existence inevitably emerges out of any Jesus-talk, for it is the same wisdom we see at work in salvation that was at work in creation. But the point remains: this power takes on a Christological identity even though it comes from the Spirit.

Of course, there is a basic sociological point being dressed up here in theological garb. It is this – that (as Schweiker helpfully puts it): 'Only through access to power do agents or communities endow their world with meaning' (Schweiker 1995: 214). This is a profoundly important point: one that Welker has sought to make, albeit in unconventional language; and one that enables us to rediscover a lost plot within the narrative of Scripture. It is this – that revival or any work of the kingdom finds its ultimate meaning, delivers its greatest punch, only to the degree it understands the nature or identity of the power that makes anything happen.

My contention is, therefore, that it is only as we understand the nature of the power made available to us that we, in turn, will endow our communities and wider world with any meaning. Such endowment is not ultimately of a holy-spiritual distinction. It is completely Christological. And, thus, once again, the Spirit fulfils and affirms his own way of doing things – of pointing away from himself to the one in whom the glory of God is perfected. Perhaps this is what Paul is getting at in his exhortation to the believers at Ephesus (1:15–23) that they may be found within the Spirit's domain of resonance. Interestingly, too, here also the end is not a focus on revival or specifically Spiritual gifting, but on Christ. Once again, pneumatological agency has a Christological goal.

Part 3: Conclusion

The thesis of this chapter centres on the proper identification of the Spirit, the true nature of his power and thus the kind of communities who have access to such power. The central contention has been that in properly identifying the Spirit we access, surprisingly, another: the Christ of God, the crucified, resurrected and ascended Jesus. It is also the contention of this chapter, in accordance with true Scottish Common Sense, that true encounter with this Spirit is conditional upon inevitable internal transformation that is externally evidenced: the removal of tired and defeatist modes of being and the cultivation of transforming characteristics that constitute the very Kingdom of God. To touch the Spirit's domain of resonance, to be transformed within his force field, is to become transformed into the image of Christ, the very Son of God. And this is no flight from that which resonates of the fallen, the graceless corruption of what is good. Rather, true revival, if it has anything to do with the Spirit of Jesus Christ, must surely impact the political and economic foundations of any given group, for this is where real human power operates. Only in revival, as in any kingdom extension, such power is transformed by the Spirit's presence: it is *divine* power manifesting itself through human media. As such, a reconfiguration occurs, one we describe in terms of the Kingdom of God, and inevitably so because it comes about as a result of *God's* Spirit, and not any other.

Thus far, I have remained within the contours of the relation between the biblical and the dogmatic. However, for us correctly to dialogue with revival and revivalism, we must also engage with what Ricoeur describes as a 'transformed imagination' (Reagan and Stewart 1979: especially chs 15–16).

For too long the caricature of revival and revivalism has drawn from the spectacular, the transcendent, the downright dotty. But in real terms, the power of revival is most empowering at the level of the mundane, the routine. This, if you think about it, makes sense. For, as Gunton reminds us, it is the Spirit who gives direction to the created order (Gunton 1998: 86). As the Spirit recreates the divine intention for creation, it is in the slight, the insignificant, the menial and mundane that the true nature of God's power is revealed. The transcendent power remains God's and as such cannot be confused with the 'earthen jar' within which it operates (2 Cor. 4:7). Such a blueprint is taken from the most mundane of deaths, that of the crucified one. Therefore, should we not be too surprised to discover that this is the stuff and matter of the Spirit's domain of resonance? For if, as Edward Irving so famously presented things, the Son of God takes to himself a humanity that is earthy, fallen, prone to the vicissitudes of humanity (Irving 1830: 4–5), it is a fallen, alienated humanity in which the Son lives out the Father's will. It is humanity at the margins that experiences the Spirit's revivification, not humanity at the heights of its own glory. Otherwise, are we not guilty of reading the conclusion before the main text has been written?

There are significant benefits from discussing revival and revivalism from within a matrix that builds upon the biblical and dogmatic and yet allows for contemporary imagination to ask and answer questions either unasked or ignored. The biblical and dogmatic earth us within the tried and tested and allow for what Lindbeck describes as a social embodiment (Lindbeck 1996) that prevents us from losing the text (or plot) (Brueggemann 2002: 536), whilst latitude is given by means of the transformed or baptised imagination that seeks to give answers that cannot be read from the text of Scripture.

Ultimately, however, it has been the contention of this chapter that the only forms of revival or revivalism that warrant proper Christian analysis and respect are those that are characterised by two clear criteria. Firstly, that 'revival' or 'revivalism' brings about internal transformation that bears the hallmark of Jesus Christ, that is, transformation brought about by divine rather than human fiat. Secondly, that it brings about external consideration for those most predisposed to the Kingdom of God, namely, those for whom divine grace works – the disempowered, disenfranchised, marginalised and overlooked. Such are the characteristics, the virtues, of those who enter into the Spirit's domain of resonance.

References

Brueggemann, W. (1998). Preaching a Sub-Version. *Theology Today* 55 (2): 195–212.

Brueggemann, W. (2002). A Text That Redescribes. *Theology Today* 58 (4): 526–40.

Green, J.B. (2002). Scripture and Theology: Failed Experiments, Fresh Perspectives. *Interpretation* 56 (1): 5–20.

Gunton, C.E. (1996). *Theology Through the Theologians*. Edinburgh: T&T Clark.

Gunton, C.E. (1998). *Triune Creator*. Edinburgh: Edinburgh University Press.

Irving, E. (1830). *The Orthodox and Catholic Doctrine of Our Lord's Human Nature, Tried by the Westminster Confession of Faith. Set in Four Parts*. London: Baldwin & Craddock.

Lindbeck, G. (1996). Atonement and the Hermeneutics of Social Embodiment. *Pro Ecclesia* 5 (2): 144–60.

Merton, T. (1972). *New Seeds of Contemplation*. New York: New Directions.

Pannenberg, W. (1991). *Systematic Theology*, Volume 1. Edinburgh: T&T Clark.

Piggin, S. (2000). *Firestorm of the Lord*. Carlisle: Paternoster.

Plascher, W.C. (1996). *The Domestication of Transcendence*. Louisville: Westminster John Knox Press.

Reagan, C.E. and Stewart, D. (eds) (1979). *The Philosophy of Paul Ricoeur*. Boston: Beacon Press.

Schweiker, W. (1995). Power and the Agency of God. *Theology Today* 52 (2): 204–24.

Terrien, S. (1978). *Elusive Present*. San Fransisco: Harper & Row.

Welker, M. (1994). *God the Spirit*. Minneapolis: Fortress Press.

Welker, M. (1997). Spirit Topics: Trinity, Personhood, Mystery and Tongues. *Journal of Pentecostal Theology* 10: 29–33.

Chapter 4

The Ethics of Exile and the Rhythm of Resurrection

Tom Smail

My main preparation for this essay has been an extended study of the Book of Jeremiah with the help of Walter Brueggemann's commentary (Brueggemann 1998). This commentary to a remarkable degree captures and conveys the prophetic quality of the book itself. It offers us a biblical paradigm in terms of which we can begin to make some sense of the Christian situation in the contemporary West and gain theological perspective on the issues of decline and renewal that are the concerns of this book. I almost called this chapter a 'concluding Jeremiad', not in the sense of a lugubrious lamentation, because I hope it is not that, but because the message of Jeremiah permeates what I shall have to say from first to last.

The central thrust of Jeremiah's ministry is defined from the moment of his calling and is sustained to the end. It is 'to pluck up and to pull down, to destroy and to overthrow, to build and to plant' (1:10). That is what the prophet is about, because it is what Yahweh is about in his dealings with his people. The God of Jeremiah is both a destroyer and a builder; he is both attacking the status quo in church and state in order to remove it and, having cleared the ground of what is old and effete and finished, is going in his sovereign purpose to replace it with something that will move his people on towards a fulfilment that it can never reach on its own, but is his undeserved and gracious gift to it.

The negative of judgement and the positive of renewal are both constitutive for Jeremiah, but they live in very uneasy relationship with each other; there is no easy or prescribed path from the one to the other, no ten easily treadable steps from failure to success, from decline to growth, from withering to flourishing. Yahweh's judgement will not be deflected by prevailing prayer or by a too-long-postponed and now impossible repentance. More than once Jeremiah contemplates a cancelled covenant, a finality of rejection, the utterance of an ultimate 'No' that will mean the unalterable dissolution of God's relationship with Israel. In the mercy of God that 'No' in the end remains penultimate and not ultimate. Nevertheless, that the 'Yes' of renewal should follow the 'No' of rejection is never a foregone or indeed calculable conclusion, but always a creative and sovereign act of God. As Brueggemann himself puts it, what can follow judgement can only be 'a new relationship wrought not out of Judah's repentance but out of Yahweh's resolve' (Brueggemann 1998: 147). The positive can follow the negative only by the same miracle by which resurrection can follow death.

Jeremiah reminds us that it is on these deep and stormy waters that we are sailing when we explore the theological dimension of the decline and renewal of churches and societies, that we live all the time between the threat of death and the hope of life. Both national and Christian institutions have times of stability when everything seems fixed and immovable, but they also have times when what seems an acquiescent providence moves into negative mode. The seemingly solid foundations are shaken and broken and the future becomes ambiguous and indeed threatening because, in the last resort, everything turns on what is happening in terms of our relationship with the living God, who holds all the issues of that, to us, uncertain future in his hands.

The basic connection between Jeremiah and us is that he lived in one such critical situation and we live in another. He invites us in the name of Yahweh to see our situation in the ultimate terms I have been describing, a matter of death and life, of no future or new future for God's people. Of course, such a destabilising diagnosis did not go unchallenged then, as it does not go unchallenged now. In the central chapters of the book we see Jeremiah in debate with, and indeed under attack from, a Jerusalem establishment for whom it was inconceivable that Yahweh should jettison his people either into exile or to death, who affirmed the Davidic throne and the Jerusalem Temple as the unalterable pledges of Yahweh's perpetual presence and protection, and who saw invading Babylon at the gates as the enemy whom Yahweh would quickly overthrow, reviving royal authority and priestly power.

Even after the royal family and the elite of Judah had been deported to Babylon and the Temple had been despoiled, there were prophets in Jerusalem claiming to speak just as Jeremiah did, with divine authority. Not without support from the Scriptures and the history of Israel, they held out hopes that a great reversal of fortunes was just around the corner; that Nebuchadnezzar would be overthrown; that the city would get back its king and the Temple its treasures; that what was amiss would be reformed; that sin would be rooted out by repentance; and that the old order, rejuvenated and reinvigorated, would resume its divinely guaranteed sway.

I have described that scenario because I find it strangely familiar. Like Jeremiah, I also have lived and ministered through nearly fifty years of institutional decline in the life of the people of God in this country. These have been years in which the churches have not only lost huge numbers of adherents, but in which for so many people religious practice, whether in terms of ritual observance or emotional highs, has become a leisure activity in very uncertain relationships to the rest of life. Many church people, including those ever so orthodox in their faith and ever so charismatic in their experience, have looked very much like everybody else. They have surrendered as much as everybody else to the idols of consumerism and self-fulfilment and so have been unable to make a decisive impact on a culture that has been becoming increasingly distanced from the knowledge and understanding of the gospel.

As in Israel, there have been establishment voices assuring us that it is not as bad as that, and that with a few adjustments we can get back to where we were, but also – and more germane to our present purpose – there have been prophetic voices telling us that the decline and the decay were about to be miraculously reversed and a revival to take place that would get us back to where we had been before.

Now, I have to say that the only revivals that I have had anything to do with are the ones that did not happen. By saying that, I do not, of course, intend to cast doubt on the reality or authenticity of these eras of Christian regeneration, which in these days we have been trying to understand. I am simply saying that the prophecies of such a revival that we have been hearing over the forty years of charismatic renewal have been false prophecies, by the simple test that what they promised has not happened. Because of this, one is bound to approach still more prophecies of the same kind with a considerable degree of caution, to say the least.

I have no doubt at all that the long procession of panaceas that have been swept on to our shores by the transatlantic swells have been real blessings from God to many people. Yet every one of them has been oversold and has proved inadequate to the claims made on its behalf. Speaking in tongues, praising God for everything, asking God for anything, having your memories healed or your personal demons exorcised, to name but a few of the recipes, may have done much good to many individuals, but they have neither revived the church nor been the spearheads of large-scale evangelistic penetration into the world around. The decline they were supposed to arrest has continued unabated, and many who grew up, and indeed entered into ministry, with that sort of promise ringing in their ears have reached their forties and their fifties in the grip of a disillusionment which can be either the threshold of a deeper and more realistic grasp of what God is really doing in our world, or else the gateway to despair.

As it has developed, the movement of the Spirit that was at the heart of the renewal movements of the 1960s and 1970s has been emasculated, and to a degree corrupted, by Pietistic individualism, sensationalistic superficiality, its preoccupation with a relatively few spiritual gifts. Perhaps most of all, it has been corrupted by its subordination to the search for personal self-fulfilment, which is the overarching paradigm of a great deal of secular counselling.

For all that, the renewal movements of the second half of the twentieth century, of which the charismatic renewal is the most obvious manifestation, have been the means by which in a time of decline and decay God has given his people a reassuring sign that he is not dead but alive, not passive to the principalities and powers in control of our culture but active and sovereignly pursuing his purposes among them. The renewal movement has therefore been a sustaining source of hope and energy in a situation where there was little reason to maintain either.

To return to Jeremiah, I see the renewal movement in terms of God's promise to the prophet as he enters into the era of the great plucking up and pulling down, the destroying and the overthrowing that is to have its way before the building and planting can begin. 'Do not be afraid of them, for I am with you to deliver you, says the Lord' (1:8). In other words, the charismatic renewal is to be seen as an energising preparation for prophecy rather than an induction into revival. It gives first and foremost the insight and confidence to address decline and to discern what God is saying and doing in and through that decline, rather than offering the prospect of an imme-diate revivalistic escape from it. The renewal may not yet have found its prophets who can interpret with realism and hope in God's name both the plucking and the planting, the pulling down and the building up. Yet the last chapter is not yet written, and there are signs that the hard process that can turn us from the mirages of escapism to the production of such prophecy is still on track.

All that brings us back to the question that was central for Jerusalem on the threshold of exile, just as it is central for us as we encounter contemporary threats to our Christian future. Who are the true prophets? Are they the ones who offer a dramatic escape from present failures into a scenario of success? Or are they those who tell us that the renewal we seek begins only at the end of a long process of readjustment to God and his purposes in the light of what he is doing with us in our present distressing situation? Both sets of prophets claim to speak in the name of Yahweh and both in different ways offer a way of hope. One holds out a proximate, and even immediate, hope that Yahweh will sweep away the Babylonians from Jerusalem, as just a century earlier he had wonderfully swept away the Assyrians; whereas the other, Jeremiah in fact, points to seventy years of exile in Babylon as the only way to the future that God has for his people.

If you were a prince or a priest in Jerusalem assailed by these contradictory voices, you would have no objective or infallible way of adjudicating between them. You would have lots of reasons to embrace the instant option that would no doubt purify the status quo, because both sides knew the importance of repentance, but that would also reinstate that status quo and guarantee its future and its flourishing. Only by a gift of discernment – always the necessary counterpart of the gift of prophecy, which enables us to distinguish the authentic from the inauthentic word of God – only by that gift could you embrace the hard, demanding, long-term road of Jeremiah and prepare yourself for all that coming exile would impose and require. The prophecy of Jeremiah has canonical status only because in hindsight it was he and not the others who were seen to be pointing to God's way for his people. Jerusalem was not rescued; there was a real ending here for both Temple and crown. It was to be through the exile that threatened to end the covenant that ultimately the covenant would be fulfilled.

It is important to see what the issue between the two schools of prophecy really was; not whether revival was going to come in seven weeks or seventy years, but rather whether Nebuchadnezzar and all that he stood for was an unambiguous evil from which God's people were to be rescued, or an instrument in God's hands whereby his judgements would be executed and his promises fulfilled. Jeremiah is well aware of the evils of Babylonian despotism, he knows that for Nebuchadnezzar also the day of reckoning will come, but for the present in a way quite beyond his own comprehension, he is more than once called God's servant through whom God's will is being accomplished. The nub of Jeremiah's message therefore is to call people away from comforting fantasies that divert them from what ought to be claiming their undivided attention. To reckon with and respond to what God in his providential working is doing now in the collapse of Judah and the coming years of exile in Babylon is the only way forward for them. To face and make an appropriate response to the death of the status quo, rather than dream of its restitution, is the fundamental act of trust in Yahweh that is the only viable route to resurrection and renewal. The question is not about how soon we can get out of our present ills, but how we can discern God's word and will in them and adjust ourselves to them, so that in God's good pleasure and good time we come to the days of refreshment and new life that are beyond them.

The prayer that we finally have to learn to pray is not 'Father, if it be your will let this cup pass from me.' Perhaps there was a moment to pray that prayer, and there is the best of all precedents for starting with it, but if that prayer has consistently not been answered, if the rescuing revivals have failed to appear and the prophecies that have promised them have been consistently proved to be false prophecies, then might not the time have come for us to move on to the revised prayer of Jesus: 'Father, if this cup cannot pass unless I drink it, your will be done'? Gethsemane is a hard place to be, but for Christians Gethsemane is a saving place to be, for it is to be with Christ as he dismisses the twelve legions of angels that might have rescued him and commits himself to the obedience that will bow to and bear the Father's judgement on the sin of the world, and so face the ultimate defeat and come through out of it to the ultimate victory.

I have been leaping back and forward from Jeremiah in Jerusalem on the brink of exile, and Jesus in Gethsemane face to face with the Cross, to ourselves facing the contemporary Christian crisis. I have done so in order to offer the specific discernment that the Jeremiah situation illuminates and exposes the issues at the heart of our situation and that both are specific outworkings of the dynamics of judgement and mercy, demand and grace, death and resurrection that are of the very essence of God's covenant relations with his people. They manifest themselves in the outworking of the old covenant and coming to their ultimate crisis in Jesus' inauguration of the new covenant.

Notice again that I am not making general statements and judgements about something called revivalism. I think the contributions to this volume suggest that in any case the matter is so diverse and complicated that any sweeping statements about it are unlikely to be helpful. I am simply offering a very specific discernment about the concrete Christian situation as I have been encountering it: that the expectations of revival that we have been offered have been unfounded and escapist. They end in inevitable disappointment and disillusion among those who have believed them and a deepened scepticism among those who have not. I am suggesting that on the contrary our way forward is the way of Jeremiah, that our present situation is to be understood as a call to recognise and yield to the judgements of God that are being pronounced and executed through it. Such a discernment is, like that of Jeremiah, vulnerable, disputable and ultimately unprovable. It claims to be faithful to the Christian centralities and to be a credible interpretation of present realities, but in the end it has to be submitted to the discernment of God's people, who alone can decide whether and how far they can hear in it the word of the Lord.

You may well ask who in my scenario plays Nebuchadnezzar. The answer is, of course, that there is no nameable foreign tyrant who has been the agent of the Christian community's internal incredibility to and external alienation from the Western societies in which it is set. For us it is much more subtle and intangible than it was for Jeremiah as he watched the relentless Babylonian war machine roll step by step towards Jerusalem. It is here that we have certainly to listen to all the analyses of modernity and post-modernity that sometimes quite confusingly throng from every side. Just as Jeremiah had to be aware of the political and military realities his prophecy was addressing, so we need to be aware of the philosophical and sociological factors that have shaped our culture. This culture has emasculated and inhibited our own response to the gospel and eroded our communication with and influence upon the surrounding culture.

But with us, as with Jeremiah, sociological analysis has to take second place to theological perception. I do not mean that academic interpretations by theologians have to be rated higher than academic interpretations by sociologists. I mean that we have to understand our situation in terms of our faith in and relation-ship with the God who lives and reigns, who is sovereign over Nebuchadnezzar and all the principalities and powers that have shaped modernity and postmodernity, and who can make the one as much as the other the instruments of his death-dealing judge-ments and his life-giving mercy.

The claim of Jeremiah is, in Brueggemann's words, that 'there is a moral coherence to the political [or in our case read cultural or social] process and that moral coherence is guaranteed by Yahweh, who finally cannot be ignored' (Brueggemann 1998: 192). To put the thing more starkly and memorably: 'Disobedience ends in displacement. A split between historical eventuality and theological claim may separate disobedience from displacement, but the prophets countenance no such illusion' (Brueggemann 1998: 158).

In Old Testament scholarship this connection between disobedience and displacement, between the breaking of covenant and subsequent national disaster, is often referred to as the Deuteronomic schema, because it is in that book that it receives its classical enunciation. In modern times it has not on the whole had a good press. Preference has been given to the insights of the book of Job that displacement can happen to people who have not been disobedient and the insistence of Jesus that suffering can be innocent and indeed the persecution of faithfulness rather than the consequence of sin. To put the matter in terms of formal logic, we are not allowed to convert the Deuteronomic proposition 'All disobedience results in displacement' into its converse whereby 'All displacement is the result of disobedience.' I seem to remember it was called the fallacy of the undistributed middle!

But equally, and by the same logic, we are not allowed to construct the further proposition 'No displacement is the result of disobedience.' The Deuteronomic principle is neither to be dismissed nor universalised; the concept of divine judgement that it implies is applicable in some situations and inapplicable in others. It is again a matter of particular discernment whether and in what way it is applicable to ours.

That contemporary displacement should be the consequence of contemporary disobedience is a possibility that is often either parodied or ignored. It can be parodied in an individualist and atomistic way when particular events are declared to be divine punishments for particular sins, as when the fire in York Minster was prophetically discerned to be God's reaction to the episcopal ordination of the allegedly heretical David Jenkins. But in the perspective of Jeremiah, what is at stake is corporate displacement as a consequence of corporate covenant breaking, and it is about that that we have to ask today.

What has sometimes kept us from asking with any stringency or urgency is our own surrender to the presupposition that the highest conceivable good is a universal and undistinguishing benignity that affirms everything and rejects nothing. This presupposition ignores the contradictions it involves. The universal love of God, which has its biblical context in the death and resurrection of Christ, is misconstrued as a God who in his relationships with us affirms everything and requires nothing, so that the thought that anybody should be excluded from that approval becomes the one remaining heresy that entices to the one remaining sin. That is the kind of thing that many congregations are hearing week in and week out. Of course, it anaesthetises them against what P.T. Forsyth called the holiness of God, the central biblical insight that God is so committed to his own covenant love that he rejects everything in us that defies and contradicts it. Therefore, he hands us over to the displacement and destruction that the prevailing Nebuchadnezzar has in store for us. The only future that we have involves a reintegration into that covenantal obedience.

That message subverted the established ideologies of both Temple and throne when Jeremiah prophesied in Jerusalem, just as it subverts the ideologies of both church and state in our own day. But displacement is a great antidote to complacency and a great dispeller of mythic mists that blind pious eyes. The threat of extinction, even when it is modified into the prospect of exile, gives the prophecy of Jeremiah a compelling credibility that it lacked in quieter and more prosperous days. Displacement, threatened or real, becomes the context in which the community is driven back into a fundamental re-engagement with the covenantal relation with God that is at the basis of its life. It asks again with a depth and urgency that knows that its future depends upon the answer what is involved for its believing and its worshipping but also for its living and its internal and external inter-relating by the promise of Yahweh, which is also the command of Yahweh: 'I will be your God and you will be my people.'

The first commandment of what I have called 'the ethics of exile', the attitude and behaviour of a people that has begun to come to terms with its displacement under the judgement of God, is for a free and unconditional self-exposure to the words and acts of God that called it into being and to the tradition by which it has understood them down the centuries. Does it still believe that the gospel it was given is the source of its salvation in this crisis, as it has been in the crises of the past? What is there in its traditions that obscure that gospel, which its radicals are right to attack? And what is there in its tradition that is faithful to that gospel, which its conservatives are right to defend and retain? Is the morality that it practises an authentic expression of the morality it proclaims – a question that has come home to roost with the Roman Catholic Church in America? If, as Jeremiah urges, it is to relate positively to the Babylonian society into which it has been exiled, is its lifestyle a credible expression of its claim to covenantal relationship with its God that will be relevant enough to the surrounding culture to challenge it, but not to conform to it? Is it able to find answers to the new questions that the alien culture is putting to it that are relevant to the situation and yet faithful to its covenant with God? In that fidelity to the God who has revealed himself in Christ, how are we to relate to a multi-faith world, to an international community in which the exploitation of the poor by the rich that Jeremiah denounced in Jerusalem is still practised on a scale and with a sophistication of which he never dreamed? How are we to relate to the gender questions and the genetic engineering questions and the whole gamut of new concerns that press in upon us?

These are the things with which the Christian community in the West has to deal in the days of its displacement. My point is that it is in dealing with these that we encounter the eschatological issues of life and death, of judgement and mercy, of defiance and repentance, that will determine our future. It is in these terms that it is decided whether we have abandoned the covenant and are in danger of ourselves being abandoned by the God of the covenant. It is not in some fantasy land where all the problems are suddenly solved, but in our walking in uncertainty, doubt and perplexity, bearing the cross of our exile, that we discover the God by whom we have been displaced there in solidarity with us in our experience of Calvary, responding with unexpected generosity when we call upon him even now to remember us when he comes into his kingdom.

Such a prayer did not go unanswered when it was first prayed by one man on a cross to another; it belongs to the heart of Christian hope that it never will. In line with that it is the prophets of the exile who have looked unflinchingly into the abyss of a cancelled covenant and a terminated Israel and who have turned from all offers of instant rescue from God's impending judgements. It is they who, in a glorious paradox, begin to dream dreams and see visions of a resurrection that does not avoid death but that comes after it. It is the same Ezekiel who pictures the departure of the presence from the old Temple, who also envisages the new Temple from whose altar the deepening life-giving streams flow to all the barren and bitter places to refresh the whole land. It is the same Jeremiah who at one dire point proclaims that *hesed*, covenant love, has ended who also prophesies:

> The days are surely coming, says the Lord, when I will make a new covenant with the house of Israel and the house of Judah. [32]It will not be like the covenant that I made with their ancestors ... a covenant that they broke ... But this is the covenant that I will make with the house of Israel after those days, says the Lord: I will put my law within them, and I will write it on their hearts; and I will be their God, and they shall be my people ... for I will forgive their iniquity, and remember their sin no more (31:31–34).

Just as the life of God's people is punctuated by moments of judgement when they look death in the face, so there also keep coming moments of resurrection when they look life in the face, as Mary Magdalene did on Easter morning. The God who has shared the death to which he has sentenced them and who has done the work that can only be done in the darkness of exile now becomes the giver of a life that is not the restoration of the past, but rather its fulfilment. Genuine revivals are never the restoration of the best of yesterday, but always the gift of a tomorrow where what was good yesterday is moved a step nearer to its perfection. True revival is never a sharing of the resuscitation of Lazarus; it is always a participation in the continuities and discontinuities of the resurrection of Jesus.

Such moments of resurrection which surely include but are certainly not confined to the great historic revivals that the Protestant traditions honours are both in their timing and their content sovereign works of God's grace never earned, beyond our control or our contriving, not the results of a previous repentance or the rewards of a previous obedience, but rather the gift of a new heart, a new repentance, a new obedience. 'I will put my law within them, and I will write it on their hearts.'

The call to God's people in our day, as I discern it, is to walk in these dangerous paths of death and life, of the plucking that precedes the planting, of the breaking that goes before the building, to practise the ethics of exile in the company of the crucified Jesus through the undefined seventy years of displacement till the Easter moment arrives when we meet the risen Jesus with his gift of life for the dead. I am encouraged that there are more than a few signs that in our church and our day that call is beginning to be heard.

References

Brueggemann, W. (1998). *A Commentary on Jeremiah: Exile and Home-coming*. Grand Rapids: Eerdmans.

Part 2

Lessons from History

Chapter 5

Revival and Enlightenment in Eighteenth-Century England

David W. Bebbington

The Evangelical Revival of the eighteenth century is the paradigm of all revivals. It was a movement that bound together converts, whether Anglican, Dissenting or Methodist, in a united front for the propagation of the gospel. It was not an isolated local phenomenon, but a national, even international, endeavour that gathered force from the 1730s down to the end of the century. Although this chapter concentrates on England, the salient characteristics of the eighteenth-century revival were to mark Evangelicalism throughout the world deep into the nineteenth century and beyond. So it is important to locate its relationship to the cultural trends of the time. The English revival has often been seen as hostile to the Enlightenment, the movement of thought associated with the *philosophes* of France who cast doubt on the message of the Scriptures, and those in the churches who were tinctured by this way of thinking. Thus the revival has been described as 'a reaction against certain features of the orthodox theology and religious outlook of the early Enlightenment' (Best 1970: 38). According to this analysis, contemporary churchmen appealed only to the head. The attraction of the revival for the heart was a response to the deficiencies of the cerebral approach. Piety challenged reason. The movement was an emotional protest against the intellectual hegemony of the age.

This plausible thesis rests on two premises. Firstly, there is the supposition that the Enlightenment was intrinsically antagonistic to spiritual religion. The grand sweep of eighteenth-century thought is normally depicted as irreligious in tendency (Gay 1967, Hazard 1965). Voltaire, Hume and Gibbon are treated as representative figures. The elimination of religion, at least in its revealed and institutional forms, is presented as the ultimate goal of their endeavours. The Deists of the early eighteenth century were certainly part of such a secularising trend. Its influence was also felt within the churches. The dominant latitudinarianism in the Church of England and the Arians who proliferated among the Dissenters were alike in wishing to make the Christian religion more palatable to educated opinion. Accordingly, it is held, traditional orthodoxy was cast to the winds. 'Reason', wrote an Evangelical critic of Gibbon in 1781, 'has impertinently meddled with the Gospel' (Stromberg 1954: 168). It seems natural to cast the Enlightenment in the role of a liberalising body of thought at odds with the revival's firm grasp of biblical teachings (Young 1998: 1).

The second premise is that the revival was conspicuously unenlightened. The 'emotional transports' of its Methodist dimension have been censured as deluding the common people about their true interests (Thompson 1968: 402). And there is a great deal of evidence suggesting that Evangelicalism was a matter of heat rather than light. 'The dales are flaming,' reported one Methodist to another in 1798 about a spate of conversions. 'The fire hath caught, and runs from one dale to another' (Church 1948: 122). Young converts would open the Bible at random for guidance; an ex-corporal on the fringe of Methodism claimed to be more perfect than the unfallen Adam; and the leading evangelist George Whitefield, who rarely preached without weeping, had his first sermon complained of to the bishop for driving fifteen people mad (Ayling 1979: 211–12, Gillies 1772: 10, Lackington 1795: 62). A catalogue of apparent irrationalism, what the century decried as 'enthusiasm', could be charged against the movement. The ethos of the Evangelical Revival seems at variance with the Age of Reason.

Both premises, however, are open to question. Enlightenment thought may have been as good a medium for vital Christianity as it was for more secularising tendencies; and the Evangelical Revival may have shared the characteristic worldview of progressive eighteenth-century thinkers to a far greater extent than has normally been supposed. The most recent literature has suggested that there were in reality affinities between the revival and the Enlightenment (Bebbington 1993, Ditchfield 1998, Hindmarsh 1996). After all, the metaphor of light was regularly used by Evangelicals to describe the central experience of conversion. Revival in England, as in America, was perceived as the spread of 'New Light'.

It is worth exploring how far revival and Enlightenment were bound up in the same cultural nexus.

The rise of the Evangelical movement in the eighteenth century was associated with a shift in the doctrine of assurance. The Puritans of the previous century had held that certainty of being in a state of grace, though desirable, is normally late in the experience of believers and attained only after struggle. Evangelicals, by contrast, commonly asserted that the norm is for assurance to be given to believers at conversion. Some, including John Wesley and the Anglican William Romaine, believed that certainty of acceptance by God necessarily accompanies saving faith; others, especially John Newton, believed that such certainty is not essential to faith. Yet all insisted that assurance was to be expected early in the Christian life and by all. They were claiming the reliability of knowledge in the field of religion. That was to share the confidence of the age in the validity of experience. The philosopher John Locke, by denying the existence of innate ideas, had cleared the ground for greater trust in the powers of the mind to grasp the world through the five senses. Wesley, like many others in the revival, saw awareness of God as a new sense, analogous to hearing or sight. Faith, he explained, 'is with regard to the spiritual world what sense is to the natural' (Cragg 1975: 46). The rank and file of the revival formulated their experience in the same way. The realisation that the Almighty allows human beings to be certain that they are numbered among the saved was a strengthening of the status of knowledge typical of the thinkers of the century. Here was a fundamental affinity between the revival and the Enlightenment.

There were many other characteristics in common. Both were dedicated to empirical method. The prestige of John Locke in philosophy and, even more, of Isaac Newton in natural science, set a premium on the technique of investigation. It was high praise to call preaching 'experimental', that is, 'explaining every part of the work of God upon the soul' (Telford n.d.: 2: 147[1]). In argumentation, Evangelical leaders such as Henry Venn, Vicar of Huddersfield, habitually appealed for authority not to Scripture alone but to 'observation and scripture' (Venn 1779: 2). The rational evidences of Christianity were valued as much by Evangelicals as by divines of broader schools. Wesley encouraged Methodists to use medical

---

[1] Throughout this chapter any figure prior to the page reference refers to volume number. The abbrevation 'n.d.' will be used throughout the entire book to denote 'no date' and 'n.p.' to denote 'no publisher'.

remedies he had himself investigated and approached spiritual experience in exactly the same scientific spirit. A corollary of respect of empiricism was contempt for more traditional modes of analysis. Disputation was considered an unproductive exercise. Wesley dismissed ancient ecclesiastical debates as 'subtle, metaphysical controversies' (Telford 1931: 7: 21). Likewise, fine Puritan distinctions were criticised by John Newton, since they were 'not scriptural modes of expression, nor do they appear to me to throw light upon the subject' (Newton 1808: 2: 586). Metaphysics, scholasticism, systematisation – these belonged to the darkness of the past. The spirit of enquiry was illuminating religion as much as other fields of knowledge.

The optimism of the Enlightenment was also shared by Evangelicals. Happiness was treated as the proper goal of individuals and of society (Anstey 1975: 163). Wesley went further than the Calvinists in his estimate of the attainability of happiness on earth. According to his *Plain Account of Christian Perfection* (1766), believers may progress to a state where they are free from all voluntary transgressions of known laws. They are then in a state of 'perfect love' (Lindström 1946). All Evangelicals, however, believed that the ultimate welfare of believers, together with that of society at large, is guaranteed by divine providence. 'If we be sincere in intention', avowed John Newton, 'we cannot make a mistake of any great importance' (Pratt 1978: 77). For many, hope of a future millennium of truth, peace and plenty reinforced their optimism. Millennialism was a widespread intellectual concern in the eighteenth century that merged with the beginnings of the idea of progress. Not all Evangelicals embraced millennial expectations: George Whitefield, for example, professed to have no interest in the subject (Gillies 1771: 1: 51). Others, however, especially as the century advanced, were animated by high hopes. The progress of the gospel was certain. 'Slavery and war shall cease!' announced the Baptist John Ryland. '*In fine, the whole earth shall be full of the knowledge of Jehovah, as the waters that cover the depths of the seas!!!*' (Ryland 1791: 21). A sanguine temper undergirded the Evangelical movement as it developed.

Doctrinal moderation, a feature of the Latitudinarianism that prevailed in the eighteenth-century Church of England, was also evident in the theology of the Evangelicals. The Arminianism of John Wesley has been seen as a revolutionary creed because it propagated belief in human free will (Semmel 1974). What has been less widely appreciated is that the Calvinism of non-Methodist

Evangelicals was of a similar stamp. The clergyman Thomas Haweis wrote a biblical commentary as a Calvinist, but hoped that 'there is not a line I have written at which a spiritually minded Arminian need stumble' (Wood 1957: 116). 'That a man is a free agent', wrote the Baptist Robert Hall Snr, 'cannot be denied, consistently with his being accountable for his own actions' (Hall 1781: 236). The statement was possible from a Calvinist, because Hall, like many other Evangelicals in the reformed tradition, embraced the distinction made by the great American theologian Jonathan Edwards between natural and moral inability. Naturally human beings are free, but morally they are unable to obey God. Hence they are culpable and condemn themselves to divine judgement. Since nobody is predestined to reprobation, all have a duty to believe, and the gospel should be preached to all. This theological position, often called 'moderate Calvinism' in the secondary literature, was normal among Evangelical Anglicans. Its wide embrace, its benevolent tone, were symptomatic of the age.

An ethical emphasis was a further feature of the revival that linked it to the Enlightenment. It is true that Evangelicals themselves commonly denounced clergymen for preaching mere morality. They were censuring the idea that salvation can be by works: 'it was *faith* alone that did everything without a grain of morality' (Lackington 1795: 48). Yet their own insistence that salvation is by faith alone did not preclude moral instruction. Haweis's *Evangelical Principles and Practice* (1762) gives far more space to practice than to principles. The idea of sanctification dominates Wesley's theology. Whitefield used to define true religion as 'a universal morality founded upon love of God, and faith in the Lord Jesus Christ' (Gillies 1772: 287). Evangelicals repeatedly repudiated the slander that they denied the duty of the believer to observe the moral law. A few higher Calvinists in both the Church of England and Dissent made remarks that veered towards antinomianism, but only a handful on the fringe of the movement, such as Robert Hawker of Plymouth and the eccentric William Huntington, actually taught it. Faith, according to Henry Venn, 'is not understood, much less possessed, if it produce not more holiness, than could possibly be by any other way attained' (Venn 1779: xi). Evangelicals, like their contemporaries, were eager to enforce the duties of morality.

While they did not apply utilitarian principles to ethics, leaders of the revival adopted the criterion of utility in many areas of policy. That was another bond with theory and practice of the Enlightenment. Field preaching, the grand strategy of the Evangelical movement, was justified on pragmatic grounds: it led to the salvation of souls. To be 'useful' was the highest ambition of a preacher. In a similar spirit, Martin Martin, a London Evangelical clergyman, actually recommended polygamy as a remedy for prostitution, though others hastened to disavow his views (Wood 1957: 159–60). This was not the only question of expediency where there was division of opinion. There were some clergymen, notably Samuel Walker of Truro, whose respect for church order prevented them from endorsing Wesley's employment of laymen as preachers. Even Walker, however, rejoiced that there were 'good men of all persuasions, who are content to leave each other the liberty of private judgment in lesser things, and are heartily disposed to unite their efforts for the maintaining and enlarging Christ's kingdom' (Davies 1951: 71). Wesley was prepared to go much further. 'What is the end of all ecclesiastical order?' he asked. 'Is it not to bring souls from the power of Satan to God, and to build them up in His fear and love? Order, then, is so far valuable as it answers these ends; and if it answers them not, it is nothing worth' (Telford 1931: 2: 77–8). Hence Wesley was prepared to undertake ordinations of clergy for America even though that responsibility was restricted to bishops by the Church of England. Hence, too, he was willing to turn a blind eye to female preaching. The climax of the pragmatic spirit came with the foundation, in 1795, of 'The Missionary Society', later the London Missionary Society, designed to unite Evangelicals of all types in the furtherance of the gospel. '*Expediency*', declared Charles Simeon, the leading Evangelical Anglican by the turn of the century, 'is too much decried' (Brown 1863: 93). It was another attitude of the enlightened world that Evangelicals upheld.

Their taste was similarly adjusted to the spirit of the age. 'The commencement of this century', wrote Haweis in 1800, 'has been called the *Augustan age*, when purity of stile added the most perfect polish to deep erudition, as well as the *belles lettres*. A Newton, and Addison, need only be mentioned, out of a thousand others, whose works will be admired to the latest posterity; and afford the noblest specimens in the English language.' What Haweis most approved about the Augustans was their union of 'conciseness with precision' (Haweis 1800: 3: 221; 1: v). Wesley shared the same ideal in his 'Thoughts on Taste' (1780), and the exemplar was again Joseph Addison (Golden 1961: 252–3). Although Newton was representative of other Evangelicals in moving on in the later eighteenth century to show symptoms of the age of sensibility, he never wholly abandoned Augustan values (Hindmarsh 1996: 284–8). The classical principles of order, balance and harmony appealed to the early Evangelicals as much as to the Augustan *littérateurs*. They formed even Wesley's eye for the natural world, so that he attributed to the Creator an earth before the flood that was 'without high or abrupt mountains, and without sea, being one uniform crust' (Curnock and Telford 1909–16: 5: 351). Dissenters adopted the same criteria. Cornelius Winter, a disciple of Whitefield, quotes with approval William Cowper's identification of elegance with simplicity (Jay 1812: 279). The greatest monument to Evangelical taste, however, is the hymnody of John Wesley's brother, Charles. Disciplined emotion, didactic purpose, clarity and succinctness are qualities for which he is pre-eminent among hymn writers. A single line can exhibit all his traits: 'Impassive he suffers, immortal he dies' (Osborn 1868–72: 4: 371). Charles Wesley turned contemporary literary idiom into a powerful vehicle for revival.

It is evident, therefore, that Evangelical religion was firmly embedded in the progressive cultural milieu of the eighteenth century. It shared assumptions with the mainstream of educated opinion. Its substantial appeal to the elite is often disguised by its numerically larger impact on the common people. Yet the upper classes of England were sometimes attracted. At least three Lincolnshire gentry became staunch supporters of Wesley's Methodism (Church 1948: 164, Church 1949: 44, 117–25). There were 8 'gentlemen' and 21 'gentlewomen' among the 790 Bristol Methodists in 1783 (Kent 1976: 111). Whitefield, perhaps because of his elaborate histrionic skills, drew a significant number of the nobility to hear him and the Countess of Huntingdon became the patroness of a whole denomination. Evangelicals could also find their way into the highest circles of literature and art. Hannah More, an Evangelical bluestocking, moved easily among Sir Joshua Reynolds, Samuel Johnson and Edmund Burke. 'I made such a figure lately', she playfully reported to her family in 1777, 'in explaining Arianism, Socinianism, and all the isms, to Mr. Garrick' (Roberts 1834: 1: 104). Although most of the fashionable world shunned revivalism as a species of enthusiasm, there were points of intersection with those fired by vital Christianity. The Evangelical leaders were not divorced from elite culture.

It was typical of Enlightenment thinkers to wish to bring knowledge from the elite to the masses. The English Enlightenment in particular produced not eminent philosophical systematisers but popularisers in many fields (Porter 1981: 3, 5). The Evangelicals should be numbered in their ranks. Their primary aim was to fit their hearers for heaven, but they also wished to bring the barbarous within the pale of civilisation. Whitefield, dismayed by the absence of cultivation among the colliers of Kingswood, Bristol, gave priority to 'the civilizing of these people' as well as to their evangelisation (Gillies 1772: 37). The darkness of rude ways had to be dispelled. Wesley, like other arbiters of taste, supposed laughter to be a sign of ill breeding. Accordingly, with his usual briskness, he directed that his preachers must avoid laughter (Allen 1937: 1: 94–5). He expressed satisfaction with the effects of his civilising mission at Nottingham:

> although most of our society are of the lower class, chiefly employed in the stocking manufacture, yet there is generally an uncommon gentleness and sweetness in their temper, and something of elegance in their behaviour, which, when added to solid, vital religion, make them an ornament to their profession (Curnock and Telford 1909–16: 6: 156).

Manners had been successfully softened. Similarly, the missionary enterprise that took its rise at the end of the eighteenth century aspired to carry civilisation as well as the gospel to the ends of the earth. Although there was much variety of opinion about the best strategy for confronting barbarism, there was unanimity that missions should aim for its elimination (Stanley 2001). Evangelicals were promoting an Enlightenment programme for the improvement of the people at home and abroad.

Its chief dimension, other than the imparting of vital faith, was education. The revival was often charged with deprecating scholarship, since it flourished among the illiterate and uncritical, and it is true that books were sometimes suspect as sources of error. Whitefield and Wesley concurred that Latin, the foundation of polite culture, was 'of little or no use' to the preacher (Jay 1812: 70). Yet this estimate was part of the Enlightenment preference for the vernacular and is no evidence for a low estimate of learning. On the contrary, Wesley created a publication industry for his followers. He issued grammars of English, French, Latin and Greek, short histories of England and of the Christian church, an outline of Roman history, a compendium of natural philosophy in five volumes and a 'Christian Library' of practical divinity in fifty (Church 1949: 47). The first lay connexional officials were appointed to run the Book Room, and when, in 1778, Wesley launched *The Arminian Magazine* he acquired his own printing presses (Mathews 1949: 171). By 1791, 7,000 monthly copies of the magazine were circulating, in comparison, for example, with 4,550 of *The Gentle-man's Magazine* six years later (Brantley 1984: 118). Wesley prepared a 'Female Course of Study, intended for those who have a good Understanding and much Leisure' entailing five or six hours' work a day for three to five years (Brown 1983: 51), but he concentrated his educational efforts on his travelling preachers, since they were expected to transmit what they learned. At least one claimed to have read every one of Wesley's more than 400 works (Telford n.d.: 6: 148). 'I trust', wrote Wesley of the preachers, 'there is not one of them who is not able to go through such an examination, in substantial, practical, experimental divinity, as few of our candidates for holy orders, even in the university ... are able to do' (Cragg 1975: 296). Every preacher, in turn, was to be a book agent. Wesley was undertaking a campaign of systematic enlightenment.

His efforts were duly rewarded. Methodism produced prodigies of learning. A Lowestoft class leader knew Latin, Greek and Hebrew; a child of Methodist parents read the greater part of the Bible before she was four; and an older girl composed her journal in faultless French. Humbler Methodists would meet on weekday evenings to instruct their unlettered friends in how to sing the Sunday hymns, and by such means literacy spread (Church 1948: 12, 243, Church 1949: 49, 46). Other Evangelicals, though in less dragooned fashion than the Methodists, were equally dedicated to fostering elementary education, since literacy was a condition for reading the Bible. Hence they gave their powerful support to the Sunday school movement as it gathered momentum from the 1780s. The instruction was frequently undenominational, in part a corollary of the policy of pragmatic co-operation in furtherance of the gospel. In the early days, in fact, Unitarians and others often participated alongside the various types of Evangelical, a sign that in educational work the Enlightenment of propagating useful knowledge took precedence over the preservation of gospel purity (Ward 1972: 12–20). It has been estimated that by 1801 there were over 200,000 regular attenders at the Sunday schools, chiefly drawn from the poor (Laqueur 1976: 44). Literary societies and libraries in churches and chapels helped carry education to a higher level. Evangelicalism generated at least its fair proportion of scholars at the turn of the nineteenth century. Isaac Milner, subsequently President of Queen's College, Cambridge, for instance, had his degree results starred 'incomparabilis' (Rosman 1984: 217, 205). The revival did not turn its adherents into ignorant bigots. On the contrary, it proved effective in spreading a thirst for knowledge.

The revival challenged popular culture in the name of reason and religion. The customary ways of the eighteenth century added colour to humdrum lives, but they were shot through with roughness, cruelty and paganism. Traditional holidays gave scope for drunkenness, torturing animals, or indulging in relics of nature worship, like the Abbots Bromley horn dance. Evangelicalism, as is often stressed, opposed such patterns of behaviour. Thus William Grimshaw, the rugged incumbent of Haworth in the West Riding of Yorkshire, attended local feasts to preach the gospel and protested to his parishioners against the annual races. But his normal demeanour was not that of a religious professional, let alone an obsessional fanatic. 'A stranger might be in company with him from morning to night', commented John Newton, 'without observing anything that might lead him to suppose he was a minister; he would only think that he saw and heard a pious, plain intelligent man' (Cragg 1947: 98). Reason dictated Grimshaw's attitudes. William Romaine, a scholarly but angular clergyman, would have claimed the same for his response to the custom of conversing after church. 'He not only spoke against such conversations from the pulpit', according to his biographer, 'but frequently interrupted them, when he came out, by tapping the shoulders of those who were engaged in them; and once, if not oftener, by knocking their heads together, when he found them particularly close' (Cadogan 1796: 7: 101). Those associated with the revival were taking the offensive against the improprieties of popular habits. It is hardly surprising that there was a bitter response, whether (at a higher social level) by means of vituperative satire or (at a lower level) by mob violence. Much of the persecution suffered by gospel preachers must be seen as retaliation against the threat that their civilising mission posed to custom.

Those aroused to serious concern for the welfare of their souls formed a counter-culture shunning worldliness. Wesley formed 'awakened sinners' into classes, admission being regulated by quarterly ticket. The classes were not designed for converts only; indeed, their purpose was to encourage conversions in their ranks. Yet their members were subject to strict discipline, having to avoid evils such as taking God's name in vain, Sabbath-breaking and drunkenness, to do good by charity, visiting the sick and similar means, and to attend the divine ordinances (Lawson 1965: 1: 192–4). Even higher standards were expected of members of bands, which consisted of those professing conversion. Evangelical Anglicans established similar groups, with Grimshaw of Haworth, for instance, holding a parish class. The group was sharply demarcated from the ways of the world. Before conversion, John Iredale, a grocer in a village near Halifax, used to fill the baskets of customers while they attended church on Sunday; after conversion under the ministry of Henry Venn he refused to desecrate the Sabbath and so lost business (Church 1948: 157). Elizabeth Evans, the prototype of the Methodist preacher Dinah Morris in George Eliot's *Adam Bede*, was converted in about 1797. 'I had entirely done with the pleasures of the world', she wrote, 'and with all my old companions. I saw it my duty to leave off all my superfluities in dress; hence I pulled off all my bunches – cut off my curls – left off my lace – and in this I found an unspeakable pleasure. I saw I could make a better use of my time and money, than to follow the fashions of the vain world' (Church 1949: 160). Early Methodists, driven together for mutual support, generated a strong community spirit. Ten soldiers in a regiment, for example, were 'joined in such love for one another that we had in effect all things in common' (Telford, n.d.: 1: 73). The result was a new cultural ambience, the religion of the cottage, where there was particular scope for women to act as counsellors and exhorters (Valenze 1985). If the revival confronted traditional folkways, it created fresh and (it may be suggested) more enlightened patterns of life.

The relationship between revival and Enlightenment was therefore remarkably close. John Fletcher, long Wesley's lieutenant, argued: 'not only that feeling and rational Christianity are not incompatible ... but also that such feelings, so far from deserving to be called madness and enthusiasm, are nothing short of the actings of spiritual life' (Streiff 1984: 241). Emotion, fervour, even irrationality are inseparable from the human condition, but progressive opinion in the eighteenth century kept them bridled. So did Evangelicals, investigating them in a dispassionate spirit of scientific enquiry. Such analysts were following the method of the Enlightenment. It follows that the Age of Reason was by no means necessarily heading in an irreligious direction. England could throw up a Matthew Tindal, the Deist writer, but equally it produced John Wesley, a zealous propagator of scriptural Christianity. The situation elsewhere in Britain was little different. In Wales a literary efflorescence was largely stimulated by a Great Awakening that was intimately allied with the English revival (Morgan 1988). In Scotland alongside the sceptical David Hume there was a group of cultivated ministers of religion who stood at the pinnacle of intellectual achievement, some of whom were latitudinarian in their beliefs, but some of whom, like John Erskine, were promoters of revival (McIntosh 1998). There was a desire throughout Western civilisation during the eighteenth century for religion to be at once purer and more rational (Gilley 1981). Sometimes this aspiration took the form of a suspicion of revelation that tended to strip away the supernatural; but equally it could lead to a confidence in Scripture that rejoiced in God's power to save. There was nothing intrinsically hostile to spiritual religion about the Enlightenment.

Nor was the revival a reaction against the Age of Reason. It is simply wrong to suppose that Wesley intended to debunk the Enlightenment or that the 'burgeoning Evangelical revival anathematized rational religion' (Porter 1981: 16–17). On the contrary, the stronger doctrine of assurance fostered by the revival was associated with the rising confidence of the age in knowledge gained from sense experience. The characteristics of the eighteenth-century Evangelicals – empiricism, optimism, moderation, moralism, utilitarianism and Augustanism – were equally features of the rising cultural mood. And Evangelicals, as much as *philosophes* across the English Channel, wished to propagate their brand of elite culture to the masses, but achieved their aim far more effectively. There was born a popular Christian counter-culture that by the mid-nineteenth century had grown to dominate England. The revival was responsible for spreading enlightened values across the country. Conversely, the Enlightenment provided a vehicle for the gospel to penetrate minds shaped by the assumptions of the times. It has been suggested that to see the Age of Reason as responsible, at least in part, for the success of the eighteenth-century revival is to set up an alternative explanation to the work of God (Haykin 1996). To posit an antithesis, however, between the human agency of a movement of secular thought and the divine agency of a renewal of spiritual vitality would be mistaken. The Enlightenment was not a reason for the rise of Evangelicalism that excludes the Almighty, but rather an instrument in the hands of God for fulfilling his purposes. Just as the early church could see in the Roman Empire, despite its phases of overt hostility to the gospel, a *preparatio evangelica*, so the intellectual climate of the eighteenth century, despite points of incompatibility, made possible the diffusion of revival. The Spirit of God worked through the spirit of the age. The faith John Wesley favoured, he once remarked, was 'a religion founded on reason, and every way agreeable thereto' (Cragg 1975: 55). The Evangelical Revival was closely bonded with the Enlightenment.

Note: I am grateful to the University of Illinois Press for permission for this article to be republished. In an earlier form it appeared in Blumhofer, E.L. and Balmer, R. (eds) (1993). *Modern Christian Revivals*. Urbana, Illinois: 17–41.

References

Allen, B.S. (1937). *Tides in English Taste (1619–1800)*. Cambridge, Massachusetts: Harvard University Press.

Anstey, R. (1975). *The Atlantic Slave Trade and British Abolition, 1760–1810*. London: Macmillan.

Ayling, S. (1979). *John Wesley*. London: Collins.

Bebbington, D.W. (1993). *Evangelicalism in Modern Britain: A History from the 1780s to the 1980s*. London: Routledge.

Best, G. (1970). Evangelicalism and the Victorians. In Symondson, A. (ed.) *The Victorian Crisis of Faith*. London: SPCK.

Brantley, R.E. (1984). *Locke, Wesley and the Method of English Romanticism*. Gainesville: University of Florida Press.

Brown, A.W. (1863). *Recollections of the Conversation Parties of the Rev. Charles Simeon, M.A.* London: Hamilton, Adams.

Brown, E.K. (1983). *Women of Mr. Wesley's Methodism*. New York: Edwin Mellen Press.

Cadogan, W. (1796). The Life of the Rev. William Romaine, M.A. In *Works of the Reverend William Romaine, A.M.* London: for T. Chapman.

Church, L.F. (1948). *The Early Methodist People*. London: Epworth Press.

Church, L.F. (1949). *More about the Early Methodist People*. London: Epworth Press.

Cragg, G.C. (1947). *Grimshaw of Haworth*. London: Canterbury Press.

Cragg, G.R. (ed.) (1975). *Works of John Wesley*, Volume 11. Oxford: Clarendon Press.

Curnock, N. and Telford, J. (1909–16). *The Journal of the Rev. John Wesley, A.M.* London: Robert Culley.

Davies, G.C.B. (1951). *The Early Cornish Evangelicals, 1735–60: A Study of Walker of Truro and Others*. London: SPCK.

Ditchfield, G.M. (1998). *The Evangelical Revival*. London: UCL Press.

Gay, P. (1967). *The Enlightenment: An Interpretation*. London: Weidenfeld & Nicolson.

Gilley, S. (1981). Christianity and Enlightenment: An Historical Survey. *History of European Ideas* 1, 103–21.

Gillies, J. (ed.) (1771). *The Works of the Reverend George Whitefield, M.A.* London: Dilly.

Gillies, J. (1772). *Memoirs of the Life of the Reverend George Whitefield, M.A.* London: Dilly.

Golden, J.L. (1961). John Wesley on Rhetoric and Belles Lettres. *Speech Monographs* 28: 250–64.

Hall, R. (1781). *Help to Zion's Travellers.* Bristol: William Pine.

Haweis, T. (1800). *An Impartial and Succinct History of the Rise, Declension and Revival of the Church of Christ.* London: for J. Mawman.

Hazard, P. (1965). *European Thought in the Eighteenth Century.* Harmondsworth: Penguin.

Haykin, M. (1996). Evangelicalism and the Enlightenment. In Fountain, A.M. (ed.) *Loving the God of Truth: Preparing the Church for the Twenty-first Century.* Toronto: Toronto Baptist Seminary and Bible College.

Hindmarsh, B. (1996). *John Newton and the English Evangelical Tradition: Between the Conversions of Wesley and Whitefield.* Oxford: Clarendon Press.

Jay, W. (1812²). *Memoirs of the Life and Character of the Late Rev. Cornelius Winter.* London: for William Baynes.

Kent, J. (1976). Wesleyan Membership in Bristol, 1783. In *An Ecclesiastical Miscellany.* Bristol: Bristol and Gloucestershire Archaeological Society.

Lackington, J. (1795). *Memoirs of the First Forty-five Years of the Life of James Lackington.* London: for the author.

Laqueur, T.W. (1976). *Religion and Respectability: Sunday Schools and Working Class Culture, 1780–1850.* New Haven: Yale University Press.

Lawson, J. (1965). The people called Methodists – 2. 'Our Discipline'. In Davies, R. and Rupp, G. (eds) *A History of the Methodist Church in Great Britain.* London: Epworth Press.

Lindström, H. (1946). *Wesley and Sanctification.* London: Epworth Press.

Mathews, H.F. (1949). *Methodism and the Education of the People, 1791–1851.* London: Epworth Press.

McIntosh, J.R. (1998). *Church and Theology in Enlightenment Scotland: The Popular Party, 1740–1800.* East Linton: Tuckwell Press.

Morgan, D. Ll. (1988). *The Great Awakening in Wales.* London: Epworth Press.

Newton, J. (1808). *The Works of the Rev. John Newton.* London: for the author's nephew.

Osborn, G. (ed.) (1868–72). *The Poetical Works of John and Charles Wesley.* London: Wesleyan Conference Office.

Porter, R. (1981). The Enlightenment in England. In Porter, R. and Teich, M. (eds) *The Enlightenment in National Context.* Cambridge: Cambridge University Press.

Pratt, J.H. (ed.) (1978). *The Thought of the Evangelical Leaders: Notes of the Discussions of the Eclectic Society, London, During the Years 1798–1814*. Edinburgh: Banner of Truth.

Roberts, W. (1834²). *Memoirs of the Life and Correspondence of Mrs. Hannah More*. London: R.B. Seeley and W. Burnside.

Rosman, D.M. (1984). *Evangelicals and Culture*. London: Croom Helm.

Ryland, J. (1791). *Salvation Finished, as to its Impenetration at the Death of Christ; and with Respect to its Application to the Death of the Christian*. n.p.

Semmel, B. (1974). *The Methodist Revolution*. London: Heinemann Educational.

Stanley, B. (2001). Christianity and Civilization in English Evangelical Mission Thought. In Stanley, B. (ed.) *Christian Missions and the Enlightenment*. Grand Rapids: Eerdmans.

Streiff, P.P. (1984). *Jean Guillaume de la Fléchère, John William Fletcher, 1729–1785: ein Beitrag zur Geschichte des Methodismus*. Frankfurt am Main: Peter Lang.

Stromberg, R.N. (1954). *Religious Liberalism in Eighteenth-century England*. Oxford: Oxford University Press.

Telford, J. (n.d.). *Wesley's Veterans*. London: Robert Culley.

Telford, J. (1931). *The Letters of the Rev. John Wesley, A.M.* London: Epworth Press.

Thompson, E.P. (1968). *The Making of the English Working Class*. Harmondsworth: Penguin.

Valenze, D.M. (1985). *Prophetic Sons and Daughters: Female Preaching and Popular Religion in Industrial England*. Princeton: Princeton University Press.

Venn, H. (1779³). *The Complete Duty of Man*. London: for S. Crowder and G. Robinson.

Ward, W.R. (1972). *Religion and Society in England, 1790–1850*. London: B.T. Batsford.

Wood, A.S. (1957). *Thomas Haweis, 1734–1820*. London: SPCK.

Young, B.W. (1998). *Religion and Enlightenment in Eighteenth-century England*. Oxford: Clarendon Press.

Chapter 6

Creating a Last Days' Revival:
The Premillennial Worldview and
the Albury Circle

Mark Patterson

Introduction

Millennialism (also known as Millenarianism) in its variety of forms[1] can be understood in Norman Cohn's words as 'a convenient label for a particular type of salvationism' (Cohn 1993: 13). It is important to recognise, however, that as a salvific paradigm it also functions as a Weltanschauung. That Millennialism is a worldview is evidenced in how different Millennialists view the world, the church and revival.

Postmillennialism, for example, begins and functions from a profoundly optimistic perspective. The world, while fallen, is not irredeemably lost and the church, while not perfect, is slowly yet certainly prevailing over sin and evil, winning the world for Christ. Revival, like eighteenth-century Methodism, is seen as the ever-increasing movement of sanctification, purification and

---

[1] Millennialism is a non-literalist and spiritual understanding (first popularised in the West by Augustine) of the thousand years of Christ's reign on earth as mentioned in Revelation. Premillennialism believes that Christ will return before a literal reign on earth with the saints for a thousand years (this has a tendency to be presented in a variety of apocalyptic scenarios). Postmillennialism understands the church to triumph before the Second Coming of Christ. This has an altogether more optimistic hue than Premillennialist readings of Scripture.

spiritual empowerment within the church, enabling it to move into ever-greater success and victory. With each year the church becomes a more pure and powerful image of Christ and the world becomes a more holy and godly place fit for his habitation and reign.

Premillennialism, on the other hand, is a profoundly pessimistic perspective looking at the world in nearly the opposite terms. It is not the Kingdom of God that is increasing, but evil, and with each passing year the church is less pure and the world more depraved. The world is not only evil, it is irredeemably lost, and the church, because of its apostasy, is viewed as only marginally better. Revival in this context of depravity is understood as the desperately needed resuscitation of a nearly lifeless church if it (or at least a remnant) is to escape the horrific judgement that Premillennialists expect will soon overtake the world.

Modern Premillennialism[2] is born out of a prophetic reading of Scripture which is based on a literalist hermeneutic that discerns such prophecy as pointing to future events – specifically the final period of history before the end of time. The world as we know it, Premillennialists predict, will be engulfed in an apocalyptic conflagration that will herald the Second Advent of Christ, who on his return will reign on earth with the saints for a thousand years. A corollary of this 'end-time' scenario for students of this school of prophecy is that they always understand themselves as living in the 'end times', which are understood to be but moments away from the fall of the final curtain of history.

This paper looks at one such movement of Premillennialism and its understanding and method of revival, namely the Albury Circle and its journal *The Morning Watch*. This group, I have argued elsewhere (Patterson and Walker 2001: 98–115), is the origin of many of the hallowed beliefs of present-day Premillennialists, from dividing human history into dispensations to believing in a Pre-tribulation Rapture of the saints. To recapitulate the history of Albury is to recognise it as the progenitor of a school of thought that stretches from 1820s England to twenty-first-century America.

---

[2] Primitive Premillennialism, such as the teachings of Irenaeus, is free of the historicism and the language of Dispensationalism, which are the hallmarks of modern versions.

Premillennial Revival:
The Albury Circle and *The Morning Watch*

In 1826 Henry Drummond, MP, invited a coterie of leading prophecy scholars, including Edward Irving, London's most famous preacher, to his Albury Manor to study the biblical prophecies, discern the nonpareil revelation provided through them and correlate this message to the events of their own day. In March 1829, this group, known as the Albury Circle, began publishing a theological journal entitled *The Morning Watch* for the dissemination of prophetic revelation. *The Morning Watch* became the centre of burgeoning interest in eschatological speculation and scholarly exposition upon the prophetic Scriptures, and the primary source of modern Premillennialism.

The Morning Watch was the response of passionate churchmen to an uncertain and rapidly changing age. 'Between 1780 and 1850 (that is, within one man's lifetime) Britain changed more than she had done for many hundreds of years previously' (Harrison 1979: 219). During these brief years the country was transformed from a largely agrarian society of small population to the world's first industrialized nation. Changes in economy and population led to the wholesale restructuring of the political system and traditional social structures. Events on the Continent only exacerbated the fears of those who saw in these changes little more than expanding chaos and anarchy. The horrors of the French Revolution found frequent reincarnation over the first three decades of the nineteenth century, as the rise of Napoleon, wars of coalition and numerous national uprisings redefined Europe. The July 1830 revolution and fall of the restored Bourbon monarchy sent a shudder of alarm through conservative circles everywhere. 'By this new revolution, which seemed to be directed against the Altar as well as against the throne, all established institutions felt themselves to be threatened' (Vidler 1974: 45). Intellectual revolutions too were occurring. Thomas Paine's *The Rights of Man* challenged traditional political theory at its deepest level. Post-Enlightenment rationalism, divested perhaps of its deistic omnipotence, nevertheless posed profound challenges to the concept of revealed religion. These influences, and the belief that the church of their day had become locked in impotence and spiritual lethargy, rallied the men of Albury to pursue revival. But unlike the Methodist Revival a few decades previous, Albury's was a revival shaped wholly by the Premillennial worldview.

From the mid-1820s an unprecedented dynamic transpired as individual strands of prophetic speculation coalesced, allowing, for the first time, the creation of a systematic, universal, Premillennial theology. From 1826 numerous prophetic gatherings took place, uniting the principal scholars. In this year the Society for the Investigation of Prophecy was founded by James Hately Frere, who invited Edward Irving, Thomas White and James Stratton to join him. In 1828 this group published papers contributed to by John Tudor (editor of *The Morning Watch*), Henry Drummond, Dr Thompson, T.W. Chevalier and Thomas White. After 1829 William Marsh – known as 'Millennial Marsh' – held an annual prophecy conference at his parish, with the intention of a broader outreach. Edward Bickersteth, a highly respected Evangelical, became interested in Millennialism during Advent 1832 and entertained Cuninghame of Lainshaw annually at his rectory. 'These yearly visits were made the occasion for local prophetic conferences' (Sandeen 1970: 25). Others, including the Powerscourt conferences in Ireland, the Mildmay conferences in Britain and the Niagara and Northfield conferences in North America would rise to influence and shape Premillennial interests. But among the earliest of these gatherings, and easily the ones of greatest influence, were held at Drummond's Albury Manor. The Albury Circle and its journal *The Morning Watch* became the primary meeting point of multiple prophetic vectors and represents the point at which modern Premillennialism was given its primary shape and characteristics.

The Spirit of Antichrist and the Character of the Age

Albury's criticism of culture and church alike begins with its understanding of Catholicism in prophecy. While resolutely Protestant since the enthronement of William and Mary, Britain had nevertheless grown increasingly tolerant of Catholicism on both the popular and legislative levels. The Gordon Riots effectively marked the end of popular persecution of Catholics in Britain. The Relief Acts of 1778 and 1791 granted Catholics unheard-of liberties, and with the Relief Act of 1829 disabilities had all but disappeared. To Thomas Arnold, Headmaster of Rugby, contemporary of Irving and antagonist of the Albury School, these were hopeful signs of progress; to the Albury Circle these events bore an apocalyptic hue.

The Premillennial worldview and its interpretation of biblical prophecy provided unique illumination on current events and required Rome, the French Revolution and Britain's response to be examined under its iridescence. While the fall of Catholicism in France at the French Revolution was interpreted by Albury as vindication of the Protestant cause, the Circle was nevertheless horrified to find Britain, on the very eve of the 'harlot's destruction', not only reluctant to renounce the sin and apostasy of Catholicism, but to actually receive it as an acceptable alternative deserving legal protections. Britain, they feared, was in danger of rejecting its Protestant heritage for 'another gospel' and of turning from God and the role he had given the nation in the last days to the antichrist and the spirit of the age. The Relief Acts were viewed entirely from an apocalyptic frame of reference: 'As a nation we have even identified ourselves with Babylon, as if to record in the most public manner our disbelief of the threatened vengeance of God' (*The Morning Watch* I: 288 – September 1829).[3] Edward Irving announced the issues at stake with the question 'whether we shall remain an Anti-catholic and Protestant kingdom or whether we shall take the seed of the serpent … again into our councils and administration?' (*The Morning Watch* I: 102 – March 1829).

The nation had fallen into the spirit of the age unleashed by the French Revolution and was destined to face God's purifying wrath. Britain's political acts had revealed her own ungodly stature, affirming the magnitude of depravity and surety of imminent judgement. It remained only to be seen how the church would respond to such unholiness and whether she would turn to faith or fall with the spirit of the time.

Christendom Seeped in the Spirit of Antichrist

'The immediate and proximate cause which brings down the wrath of God is the faithlessness of the professing church,' wrote John Tudor (*The Morning Watch* II: 487 – March 1830). The Albury Circle's perception of the church was a mixture of hope-filled optimism and caustic pessimism: pessimism because they saw the church

---

[3] References to *The Morning Watch* take the form just cited and refer first to the volume number (I–VII) followed by page number. Date of issue will usually, but not always, follow.

as profoundly fallen from its calling, secularised and grievously
unspiritual, and consequently in desperate need of revival; optimism
because they believed such revival was possible and indeed God's
will and work in their day. In these early years of the journal, in spite
of the heat of their rhetoric and the condemnations exchanged
increasingly between the Circle and almost every branch of Christianity in Britain, one perceives that the Circle believed the church –
and thus the nation – could be saved. Even more, they held God had
raised up the study of prophecy, the men of the *Watch* and their journal for just this purpose. Theirs was a special day of mercy, a time of
peerless opportunity, and through their first years they held every
hope that the fruit of their labours would prepare and define the
church for a millennium. With the passion of prophets and energy of
reformers, the Albury Circle set themselves to reverse the spiritual
decline of the nation, check the influence of the French Revolution
and prepare the bride of Christ for the coming of her Lord and bridegroom and the thousand-year reign with him on earth.

James Haldane Stewart, attendee of at least one of the Albury
conferences and the author of *Practical View of the Redeemer's
Advent*, saw the signs of the coming advent in more positive terms
than his colleagues. Like them, he conjectured the decline of the
Turkish Empire and the benevolence toward the Jews were indica-
tions of an imminent advent. But, unlike others, Stewart found the
surest sign of the coming millennial kingdom in the global propagation of the gospel, noting favourably that 41 societies were spending
£400,000 annually to spread the message in 141 languages (Oliver
1978: 71). This reflects a reckoning closer to Evangelical hearts and
is perhaps one reason why the *Christian Observer* would frequently
commend Stewart to its readers for providing a sober and balanced
approach to the prophecies, free of speculative delusions and apocalyptic gloom.

Contrary to Albury's perception, Evangelicals neither denied nor
ignored prophecy. On the contrary, they, like most during the
prophetic revival of the 1820s, saw prophecy as providing an essential part of the church's message. The *Christian Observer* encouraged the study of prophecy during this period, on the premise that
such reflection instilled an awareness of God's sovereignty, not only
over individual lives, but churches and nations. Even more, many of
its reasons for this were in full agreement with those of Albury. Both
saw prophecy as a means of confirming the veracity of the Scriptures through the verification of explicit prophetic fulfilment. Both
saw revelation as occurring in the intertwining of biblical prediction

and later fulfilment. And both saw prophecy as indispensable in bringing renewal and revival to the church and in shaping the morals and behaviour of society. Yet these similarities must not be allowed to hide profound differences in perspective, use and goal of prophecy between the Albury Circle and the Evangelicals.

The Albury Circle, through their journal, castigated almost every aspect and element of the larger Christian world. Through literally hundreds of pages of *The Morning Watch*, through its entire publication from 1829–33, the larger church, particularly its Evangelical wing, was subjected to blistering and unrelenting criticism. The response of the larger church, begun cautiously and with some uncertainty, also took a variety of forms. These initially were little more than casual criticisms of Albury in sermons, theological journals and even the secular press. But by the fourth issue the Circle was responding to full-blown criticism as the church, especially Evangelicals, turned to battle.

In 1830 *The Record*, an Evangelical periodical, accused the contributors to *The Morning Watch* of losing their Christian love in their zeal for prophecy. Albury's response was blunt:

> We tell the editors of the *Record* plainly, and in all love, that unless they are much on their guard, they are on the point of avowing themselves 'no brethren' at all, but rank heretics; in danger of losing their own souls, and destroying the souls of others. The character of their journal has ever been little, petty, and mean (*The Morning Watch* II: 921 – December 1830).

But the full truth of the *Record's* criticism and Albury's maledictions is more complex. To Irving and his Circle, their prophetic zeal and even vitriolic were understood as the fruit of their love, a love for the truth as they understood it and a love for the church to which they were zealously committed. Albury's Premillennial worldview and its hermeneutic had led them to conclude that prophecy was *the* content and message of the Bible, and to turn from its proclamation and dissemination was 'to fall among the students of his false holiness, the Pope; and all those who would shut up the Bible altogether' *(The Morning Watch* I: 400 – September 1829).

The contributors to *The Morning Watch* were well aware of the dangers of prophecy studies and their efforts were a bold attempt to sail between what they perceived were the Scylla and Charybdis of their day. 'The coming of the Lord in glory has acquired a relative interest, maintained and magnified by the discordant opinions and statements which are daily reiterated in all the churches.' This writer goes on to explain how 'diametrically opposed' are these opinions and thus:

> either the one party is deluded by the most visionary enthusiasms, or the other is sunk into a deceitful infidelity; glorying in its own shame under the pleasing title of spirituality ... Either there is Antichristian imagination at work on the one side, perverting the Scriptures; or there is Antichristian scepticism at work on the other side, explaining away the Scriptures (*The Morning Watch* II: 34 – March 1830).

But Irving and the Circle were confident that their system was different. They believed theirs was an objective method of interpretation built upon strict hermeneutical principles and doctrinal unity. Their message bore the weight of ancient truth and fresh revelation conjoined to awaken a distracted and faithless church to the heart and goal of its gospel. And if the promulgation of the Premillennial message was met with consternation and rebuke, this was only to be expected. Irving held the church had always had false prophets leading her astray and these should only be expected to abound in the time of the end (*The Morning Watch* I: 578 – December 1829). Criticism and conflict were a necessary and inevitable element of proclaiming God's truth in a sin-filled world. Their own age was rapidly approaching the nadir of its undying hostility towards God and the only hope for church and world lay in the witness of the prophetic word. The Albury Circle turned to face the storm and courageously raised its voice against the ranks of godlessness.

But criticism was not all they expected. The Albury Prophets, believing their message was one of unprecedented power, authority and urgency, looked with eager anticipation for the fulfilment of all things. The Albury Circle believed themselves destined to succeed and cited evidences that their labour was not in vain:

> Within the last two months men's eyes have become wonderfully opened: the journals which had been foremost in ridiculing the 'novelties' and 'new doctrines' of the prophets, are now themselves recommending a 'judicious study of the prophetic parts of Scripture': and have had the reluctant confession exhorted from them, that all wisdom on these subjects was not hid with themselves (*The Morning Watch* II: 942 – December 1830).

Theirs was a battle to be won, not without cost or strife. And if the world would not turn *en masse* to God, it was fully expected that a significant part might. In this would come vindication, not only of God and his word, but also of those who faithfully and tirelessly endeavoured to voice its proclamation. In prophecy alone lay not only the hope of the world, but their own vindication and reward, given by Christ in his millennial kingdom before the eyes of all who thought them mad.

While the larger church – both Dissenting and established – would see their faults exposed by Albury, it was the Evangelicals, they held, who presented the most dangerously errant ministry. If the established churches were doing nothing to further the millennial kingdom, the Evangelicals were criticised for actually fighting against it. At issue were profoundly differing worldviews. While the men of the *Watch* saw the world through Premillennial apocalypticism, the Evangelical church operated from within a Postmillennial optimism inherited from the previous century. The Kingdom of God was theirs to proclaim, exhibit, and perhaps even usher in as their labours transformed the world. Their ministries and societies in turn reflected this understanding: preaching emphasised a conversion of heart and mission the conversion of the world, while religious societies provided infrastructure for evangelism, missions and social reform. In one sense, both Evangelicals and Albury shared a similar optimism, each viewing the times as divinely nonpareil and ripe with potential. But while Evangelicals perceived their day as one on the very banks of the Jordan, mere steps from the inheritance they had been commanded to take, the *Watch* men saw their times as teetering on the edge of cataclysm, its only hope in Premillennial renovation and a heavenly new Jerusalem.

Edward Irving and the men of the Albury Circle were committed to the church and saw themselves as faithful labourers courageously endeavouring to create a renewal of zeal, direction and depth. It began with the optimism that the church could turn, indeed would turn, if the prophetic truth were clearly set before it, and to this singular aim the men of the *Watch* dedicated themselves. But revival must not be misunderstood. For their focus lay not in the change of the individual heart, but in preparing the larger church and nation for the cataclysm that was all but upon it. The Albury Circle had little interest in revival as commonly understood and held in disdain Evangelicalism's affectional and experiential emphases. Similarly, they were extremely sceptical of the effectiveness of Evangelical preaching and suspected that such experiences of personal crisis, decision and surrender to God, where testified to, were merely evidence of people hearing what they wanted to hear. 'Let their accounts of revivals, be as numerous as they please', remarked one reviewer, 'we may feel assured that the appearances are hollow and false' (*The Morning Watch* I: 712 – December 1829). Indeed, Evangelical preaching, they concluded, was actually a sign and proof 'that religion must be declining' (*The Morning Watch* I: 712 – December 1829) as the majority of preachers, afraid of offending those with wealth or power (*The Morning Watch* I: 711 ff. – December 1829), rendered contemporary preaching anemic, empty and simple. Irving and his circle sought a revival less subjective, emotional and inward, shaped instead by objective historic and biblical realities, and made imminently necessary because of them.

It was not for revival of the heart, but preparation for the end, that Edward Irving and the Albury Circle had set as its course. 'We are now on the eve of a crisis incomparably the most important that the world has yet passed through,' wrote Tudor (*The Morning Watch* I: 185 – June 1829), a fact which gave the journal both its passion and mission. For it was to the church the Lord would first return. It was upon the church that the first and harshest judgements would fall. And thus it was the church, even more than nation or culture, which received the emphasis of Albury's attention, as their every resource and energy was turned to preparing the bride for her coming bridegroom.

The Morning Watch's revivalistic perspective and intentions were immovably centred on the last days and from this perspective alone the larger church was evaluated. The Circle criticised the 'Evangelical sect' for allowing its naïve optimism to blind them to the impotence and arrogance of their labours. Referring to Evangelical Postmillennialists, Irving wrote: 'They speak of the world as winding on its way to a happy Millennium; we preach a world ready to be destroyed by the wrath of God' (*The Morning Watch* II: 553 – September 1830). Likened by Irving to Pharisees who boast in their alms giving, Evangelicals were criticised for their failure to recognise that their best efforts were only doomed to fail. Irving passionately lamented:

> Oh, it is a cruel system, a most cruel, hateful system of pharisaical pretense, which is working over this land. We talk of our charities and alms-deeds: they are as a drop of that bucket which is filled with the sweat and tears of an over-wrought and miserable people ... Woe unto

such a system! Woe unto the men of this land who have been brought under its operation (*The Morning Watch* I: 666 – December 1829).

For the *Watch* men, no greater example of Evangelicalism's folly could be found than their efforts to convert Jews and Catholics. Seen by Evangelicals as an integral part of the gospel mandate, such efforts were interpreted by Albury through the Premillennial worldview and hermeneutic, and judged antithetical to the will of God. Albury's Premillennial chronology had determined that the Jews had not yet come to the time when they would hear the gospel, repent of their previous rejection of Christ as Saviour and turn in mass conversion to become, again, the people of God on earth (see *The Morning Watch* I: 38, 72–5, 157, 247, II: 311, III: 102, 105, 311 et al.). In addition, Catholicism, the antichrist prophesied of old, had been destined for destruction, not salvation. 'But all churches, that have put forth any form of doctrine, have agreed in this, that to destroy Antichrist is Christ to come. The conversion of the Papacy is a dream of Evangelical Liberality; and so is spiritual advent, that precious absurdity of the same learned school' (*The Morning Watch* I: 607 – December 1829). It was this perceived liberalism that stirred the ire of those contributing to *The Morning Watch*. 'The Evangelical Clergymen, who have been for many years the principal writers in *The Christian Observer*, have become so deeply imbued with Liberalism, which is but a modified Infidelity, that they have leaned much more to the infidel than to the High-Church party in the country' (*The Morning Watch* IV: 235). Thomas Arnold was criticised for what *The Morning Watch* felt was a rejection of ultimate truth by his support of the Catholic Relief Act. This led Albury to identify Arnold with the 'Evangelical Prelates who patronize and circulate his opinions'. While the principles of 'equal rights' are argued 'very successfully' by Arnold, they 'have nothing to do with Christianity; that they are the very same which are discussed by Plato, Tully, and Plutarch; and that therefore they are not *higher principles* upon the same level, and no higher, than those which are to be found in every radical club in the kingdom, in Jerry Bentham and in the *Westminster Review*' (*The Morning Watch* I: 498). To the men of the *Watch*, Arnold and the 'liberal' Evangelicalism conjoined to him embodied the very anti-Christian principles unleashed in the French Revolution. The principles of the age were drawing Protestant Britain ever closer to the full acceptance of Catholicism, capitalism and democratic principles, and were thus a sign and part of the problem, not its

solution. Evangelical attempts to seek the conversion of either Jew
or Catholic was indicative of their liberal *naïveté*, arrogant confidence, parochial interests and striving against, rather than for, the
Kingdom of God.

To these indictments were added numerous other sins and
failings, yet all bound to the Premillennial worldview. Spiritual
qualities of the church had been lost, being replaced by religious
activity that built chapels, printed Bibles, collected funds for char-
ities (*The Morning Watch* I: 650 ff.) and sent missionaries across
the globe. Thoroughly ignoring deeper spiritual realities rendered
such activities powerless. Evangelicals were characterized by
greed and covetousness (*The Morning Watch* I: 648), were in
competition with the rest of the church (*The Morning Watch* I:
126), and sectarian (*The Morning Watch* I: 259, 702, IV: 210).
They, like the established churches, were spiritual hypocrites, obliv-
ious to the real nature of God's kingdom, and propagating, instead,
the very spirit of the age the church had been called to tear down.

The established and Dissenting churches were also rebuked by
the men of Albury. If the Evangelicals were viewed as 'Pharisees'
intent on building their own party, the larger church was deemed
'Sadducees', who had bought wholesale into the culture and associated themselves with free thinkers and scientists. The 'High-Church
party' was guilty of enjoying a life of wealth and privilege while
oppressing the poor and even their own curates, with all but a few
forgetting 'that civil government and ecclesiastical establishments
are institutions of God for the well being of man' (*The Morning
Watch* III: 200). Calvinists had together fallen with 'Wesleyan
Methodists', the latter being chastised for allowing feelings to
become 'too powerful for their judgment', while the emphasis on
knowledge in the former had 'puffed them up, so that they think
they know all of God that is revealed. Besides this, they mistake a
knowledge of doctrines for a knowledge of God; and place the seat
of religion in the intellect, and not in the affections' (*The Morning
Watch* III: 369 – June 1831).

The Albury Circle concluded 'that Christendom was full of
infidelity' (*The Morning Watch* I: 247). From the perspective of the
prophetic Scriptures, this had several practical implications. Firstly,
'Infidelity' is easily disguised and 'may be found in the temple of
God' (*The Morning Watch* I: 619 ff. – December 1829). Regardless
of apparent sincerity, fruitful labours and alleged piety, the
dominant character of the church had come to be identified with
apostasy. Furthermore, this apostasy, once identified strictly with

Rome, had now expanded to include fallen Protestantism, the two being evermore closely linked. 'It would scarcely be credited, by those who have not made the comparison, how close a resemblance there is between the statements of doctrine in the published sermons of the Evangelical clergy, and those of the Church of Rome' (*The Morning Watch* I: 720 – December 1829). Secondly, hidden within this larger apostate body was a faithful remnant of true believers, marked primarily by their understanding of the last days and faith in the prophetic word. Thirdly, the witness and labour of this faithful remnant would illicit persecution not primarily from those outside the church but those who were false within it (*The Morning Watch* I: 115). And finally, judgement upon this apostate body was inevitable and imminent:

> I stand in awe of God's judgment; and the more because I perceive that the very thought of a sin-visiting God is departed from the governors of our nation, and the memory of it is not recalled by those who stand in the room of the prophets, – the ministers of the Word and pastors of the people, who, if they do not teach lies, give place and encouragement to lies by not teaching the truth (*The Morning Watch* I: 325.5 – September 1829).

As the fiery polemic between *The Morning Watch* and the Evangelical world intensified, it is not surprising that the Circle found figural references to their struggles predicted in Scripture. 'The spiritual antitype of Moab has never been fully made out till of late, when it has been shewn to belong to the Evangelical church of the present time' (*The Morning Watch* VI: 290). Albury proclaimed the Evangelical church was prefigured in the plagues inflicted upon Egypt, which were, in their day, finding antitypical manifestation. The Egyptians who dug holes in the sand at the Nile's bank are likened to 'Evangelicals in these days, who would strive after some influence of the Spirit while they reject the Spirit himself ... the Tomlines, Mants, Gills, Wesleys, Clarkes, Henrys, Scotts, &c., the whole army of Libri Critici – all alike want the life of the living, all alike shew water turned to blood' (*The Morning Watch* VII: 34 – March 1833). Conveniently, another enemy of Albury, 'the half-brethren of the Evangelical church, the Presbyterians of the North', was found to be typically prefigured in Ammon (*The Morning Watch* VI: 291). The malleable character of prophecy and typology allowed the literal to take a diversity of forms, all founded upon the expectations of the Premillennial worldview, all proclaimed as the literal and explicit fulfilment of the prophetic Scriptures, and all a creation of Albury's imagination.

The Failure of Millennialist Revival

In the end, Albury failed to win the church to its Premillennial worldview.[4]

Albury's strident attempts to interpret prophecy were little more than a reflection of their own presuppositions, hopes and doctrine, read into the message they so confidently interpreted. Original context, historical setting and authorial intent were altogether ignored and replaced by Albury's imagination, eisegetically read into the texts without any knowledge, awareness or concern of their having done so.

Albury's labours reflect the weakness of the Premillennial worldview, its hermeneutic and the entire theological system created from it. Never slowed by lack of knowledge, ever confident of their abilities, and certain they had grasped with near perfection what all others had missed, the Circle approached the prophetic Scriptures, collocating each detail into a single philosophy of history and grand doctrinal system almost wholly derived from their own imagination. Carefully reasoned and expressed with precision, clarity and passion, it remained a neologism built upon the speculations of men anxiously contemplating a changing world. The men of the *Watch* stood convinced that in a world of bumbling, incompetent interpreters, they alone had grasped the proper meaning of the texts and the truth of God's revelation. Thus, more often than not, they utterly rejected the opinions of the larger church and mocked the labours of all who saw things differently. Their interpretations of prophecy blossomed always into the grandest of schemes, as words were made to refer beyond their simple meaning to a universal structure, motion and message. At Albury, a system was created which gave meaning to the motion of stars and empires, nations and individuals alike. The words of Scripture, twisted beyond all authorial intent, were shaped into the massive Premillennial system raised to calm the corporate angst of a small but influential group contemplating a changing world. Yet in their study of prophecy, the men of Albury were inter-

---

[4]   And hence failed to precipitate revival; though in time, especially in the United States, premillennialism became a regular feature of revivalism.

preting a language they neither knew nor understood, and in their ignorance and zeal they merely arranged the characters according to their own presuppositions, hopes and polemic, creating a message utterly unconnected from the text. The resulting 'translation' has profoundly shaped the eschatology of the church into the twenty-first century. Today, 170 years later, their theological heirs continue to scan the newspapers, confidently correlating events of the day to specific biblical prophecies and claiming their creative (and repeatedly wrong) interpretations are only the simple and literal word of God. Albury's attempts to bring revival to the church through the interpretation and proclamation of prophecy find their reflection in today's *Left Behind* series, the *Omega Code*, and claims that Saddam Hussein is the antichrist. These are but the heirs and progenitors of Albury's Premillennial angst, presuppositions and methodology.

The Premillennial system created by Albury is perhaps best described as a proto-foundationalist myth. Here, traditional and even ancient elements, replete with heroic individuals under a divine hand, combine to give a narrative that provides an essential order to their worldview, by explaining elements of the natural world and human society – with its history, psychology, customs or ideals – and uniting them to a course of ultimate meaning. In the midst of a world undergoing rapid and profound change, the men of *The Morning Watch* turned to prophecy to provide order and hope. Upon the premise of the imminent return of Christ, they designed a last-days revival, building a magnificent theological structure before which their chaotic world received order, design and meaning. Here, the uncertainty of their times, with its revolutions, both violent and cultural, could be given ultimate meaning. From its first gathering, Albury had concluded that most of the Continent had already foundered, swept from its biblical foundation into the tide of secularism, modernity, democracy and rationalism. Through the pages of their journal they warned that this swell was rising against Britain. In their first year, John Tudor explained the crisis in terms of teleological realities: 'at the close of the Christian dispensation the simple word of God would be less regarded than the traditions and interpretations of men ... Among the Germans the authority of the Apocalypse has been questioned by many, and among ourselves symptoms of a doubting spirit have appeared' (*The Morning Watch* I: 275 – September 1829). The irony in this – and perhaps their costliest mistake – was the failure of the Albury Circle to see how their own Premillennial worldview and hermeneutic was but one more of these 'traditions and interpretations of men'. While reflecting biblical concepts, their Premillennial belief system was built entirely from their presuppositions and shaped by a cultural worldview and their own polemical interests. This combination, imposed upon the Bible, was then proclaimed and defended as the Bible's inherent character and message. Unknowingly shaped by the modernity they decried, Albury's interpretive and doctrinal system was turned from a Christological to historicist centre. Thus their message was limited to one of their time, but incapable of bringing to it any real revival.

References

Primary Sources

The Morning Watch; or Quarterly Journal on Prophecy, and Theological Review, Volume I, 1829. London: James Nisbet, 1830.

The Morning Watch; or Quarterly Journal on Prophecy, and Theological Review, Volume II, 1830. London: James Nisbet, 1831.

The Morning Watch; or Quarterly Journal on Prophecy, and Theological Review, Volume III, March–June 1831. London: James Nisbet, 1831.

The Morning Watch; or Quarterly Journal on Prophecy, and Theological Review, Volume IV, September–December 1831. London: James Nisbet, 1832.

The Morning Watch; or Quarterly Journal on Prophecy, and Theological Review, Volume V, March–June 1832. London: James Fraser, 1832.

The Morning Watch; or Quarterly Journal on Prophecy, and Theological Review, Volume VI, September–December 1832. London: Regent Street, 1833.

The Morning Watch; or Quarterly Journal on Prophecy, and Theological Review, Volume VII, 1833. London: James Fraser, 1833.

Secondary Sources

Abanes, R. (1998). *End-Time Visions: The Road to Armageddon?* New York: Four Walls Eight Windows.

Barkun, M. (1974). *Disaster and the Millennium.* New Haven: Yale University Press.

Baumgartner, F.J. (1999). *Longing for the End: A History of Millennialism in Western Civilization.* New York: St Martin's Press.

Bebbington, D. (1995). *Evangelicalism in Modern Britain: A History from the 1730s to the 1980s.* London: Routledge.

Boyer, P. (1992). *When Time Shall Be No More: Prophecy Belief in Modern American Culture.* Cambridge, Massachusetts: Belknap Press.

Cohn, N. (1993). *Pursuit of the Millennium.* London: Pimlico.

Harrison, J.F.C. (1979). *The Second Coming: Popular Millenarianism, 1780–1850.* London: Routledge & Kegan Paul.

Hennell, M. (1979). *Sons of the Prophets: Evangelical Leaders in the Victorian Church.* London: SPCK.

Hofstader, R. (1979). *The Paranoid Style of American Politics and Other Essays.* Chicago: University of Chicago Press.

Knight, F. (1995). *The Nineteenth-Century Church and English Society.* Cambridge: Cambridge University Press.

Oliver, W.H. (1978). *Prophets and Millennialists: The Uses of Biblical Prophecy in England from the 1790s to the 1840s*. Auckland: Auckland University Press.

Patterson, M. and Walker, A. (2001). 'Our Unspeakable Comfort': Irving, Albury, and the Origins of the Pre-tribulation Rapture. In Hunt, S. (ed.) *Christian Millenarianism*. London: Hurst.

Sandeen, E. (1970). *The Roots of Fundamentalism: British and American Millenarianism 1800–1930*. Chicago: University of Chicago Press.

Stewart, J. Haldane (1825). *Practical View of the Redeemer's Advent*. London.

Vidler, A.R. (1974). *The Church in an Age of Revolution*. London: Penguin.

Chapter 7

Making Sense of the 1859 Revival in the North-East of Scotland

Kenneth S. Jeffrey

'The Lord', wrote Henry Williamson, 'is walking through the land' (Anon. 1860: 6). Williamson, an Ulster-born Free Church minister at Huntly, was describing the revival of 1859 as it spread across the north-east of Scotland. This chapter intends to examine the manner in which the Lord walked the land as the religious movement spread across Aberdeenshire and appeared in a variety of different situations. Previously, the 1859 awakening has been presented as a uniform experience. James Edwin Orr's account of the revival assumes that it was an unvarying movement that began in the south-west of Scotland before being diffused in an unbroken manner across the rest of Britain (Orr 1949: 58–77). Similarly, John Kent judged the 1859 Revival to have been a traditional awakening that was consistent across the whole of the land (Kent 1978: 71). These broad, national interpretations of the revival assumed it was a homogeneous event. More recently, however, scholars of religious movements elsewhere have begun to uncover the particular details of an awakening in a given situation. This has revealed the diversity of manner and expression that has lain within a single movement (Long 1998: 136). It has been demonstrated that revivals are often not uniform. Rather, they have appeared in a variety of forms that depend upon the different features of the indigenous circumstances within which they are felt.

This study examines further the influence that local contexts exercise over the appearance of revivals by exploring the 1859 religious movement as it arose in the north-east of Scotland. This region has been chosen because it affords the opportunity of studying the awakening as it appeared in at least three separate situations. In the first instance, the city of Aberdeen provides a typical mid-Victorian urban setting within which to study this religious movement. Meanwhile, the rural hinterland of Aberdeenshire presents a very different set of circumstances for a study of the awakening. Finally, the fishing communities dotted along the Moray Firth produce a third distinct situation for an examination of this revival. An attempt will be made to uncover the various textures of this simultaneous movement as it occurred in a range of separate places within the same vicinity. As a result, it will be shown how local factors affected the manner in which the Lord walked the land.

Part 1: The Revival in the City of Aberdeen

The revival began in Aberdeen towards the end of November 1858 during a course of religious meetings for children, conducted by the itinerant evangelist Reginald Radcliffe (Anon. 1859a: 10). After the initial burst of excitement that lasted three months, the momentum of the revival slowed considerably. It quickened again during the autumn of 1859 before entering another period of suspension the following winter. The final period of the revival came towards the end of the summer of 1860. It is noteworthy that the ebb and flow of the religious movement was affected by the patterns of work and rest that governed the lives of those who lived in Aberdeen. The industrial developments at the beginning of the nineteenth century had created a new urban environment where men and women worked long, regulated shifts in factories and other places of employment (Evans 1983: 228–32). This shift from task-orientated work to timed labour was accompanied by a change in people's appreciation of the value of time. It became currency that was no longer passed, but spent (Thompson 1967: 56). During this period a plethora of recreational and sporting activities emerged in the city, which competed against each other to fill the free time of the townsfolk (Skene 1905: 16). Consequently, the city's work patterns and leisure opportunities impinged upon the time that people could devote to attending religious meetings. This required the leaders of the city's revival to target vigorously the free time its workers enjoyed.

As a result, the Aberdeen awakening was highly organised. One of its chief features was the summer evening open-air meeting. These gatherings often attracted large crowds, numbered in their hundreds

(*Aberdeen Free Press* 29 July 1859: 6). Their popularity lay not only in the novelty of such occasions, but also in their success in targeting the free time the townsfolk enjoyed during the long summer evenings. Similarly, the Music Hall rallies that marked the second period of the revival demonstrate further the attempts of its leaders to attract the city dwellers during their spare time. These meetings were held on Sunday evenings, during the only period of the week when everyone was not at work (*Banffshire Journal* 18 October 1859: 5). In addition, the final heightened period of the revival was marked by a number of carefully planned meetings that were arranged to coincide with local public holidays (*Stonehaven Journal* 28 July 1860: 3). Perhaps the defining characteristics of the Aberdeen Revival were its two daily prayer assemblies. These reveal further how the movement's leaders planned events to fit around the labour and leisure patterns of the city. The first meeting, held between two and three o'clock, 'gathered together [people] from the drawing room, lowly hearth side, shop and office' (Omicron 1859: 4). This assembly was organised to appeal to those who lived and worked in businesses in Aberdeen. In order to attract those who laboured longer shifts in factories outwith the town's centre, a second meeting was arranged specially 'for the convenience of the working people' (*Aberdeen Journal* 2 February 1859: 3). In this way the city revival was planned in order to fit around the disciplined working routines of the townsfolk, and to target their free time.

The organised nature of Aberdeen's revival reflected the character of its leaders. The movement was conducted principally by a group of young business laymen, many of whom were members of the Young Men's Christian Association (YMCA 1859). Their professional influence was displayed in the orderly manner in which revival meetings were conducted. The daily prayer assemblies were restricted to an hour in length and followed a regimented pattern that left little room for spontaneity (Omicron 1859: 6). Similarly, the evangelistic rallies followed a standard format, with two ordinary meetings followed by a special gathering for anxious enquirers. Even the open-air events were carefully stage-managed to begin and end at certain times in order to allow those who wanted to be converted to attend a second special meeting (*The Revival* 30 July 1859: 6). These were never protracted beyond ten o'clock. This reveals further the disciplined fashion of the Aberdeen Revival.

The strict control exercised by the city's revivalists is illustrated by the manner in which they counselled those who wanted to be converted. They decided not to use the 'anxious seat', a special pew set aside at the front of a hall where those who were spiritually concerned were invited to come and sit at the end of a service. During a previous religious movement in Aberdeen in 1840 the use of the 'anxious seat' had served to create uncontrolled emotional scenes (Aberdeen Presbytery 1841). Instead, enquirers were invited to remain after the public gathering for a second brief meeting (*The Revival* 15 October 1863: 241). This more respectable method of dealing with those who wanted to become Christians guarded against displays of physical prostration. Indeed, the absence of such spectacles was a distinguishing feature of the Aberdeen Revival. Anxious to preserve the movement from any accusation of religious excitement, the leaders of the revival controlled its meetings diligently. Thus the *British Messenger* reported: 'there has been a total absence of exciting preaching, of noise or confusion' (*British Messenger* 5 1859: 230). The restrained expression of the city awakening suggests further that it was an organised revival.

The key players in the Aberdeen Revival were a number of itinerant evangelists. They included Peter Drummond, Grattan Guinness, Brownlow North and Reginald Radcliffe (Anon. 1859b: 12). These gentlemen preachers created considerable excitement when they appeared in their morning suits preaching in churches. They commanded a particular influence over congregations during this period (Omicron 1859: 11). However, many of Aberdeen's ministers distanced themselves from this work because they had grave misgivings over the manner in which the lay preachers dealt with anxious enquirers (Matthews 1910: 108). The evangelists taught that conversion was an instantaneous event, which depended upon an immediate act of will (Radcliffe n.d.: 40). Consequently, ministers became suspicious that conversion was becoming too effortless. They believed, in accordance with the traditional Calvinist view, that regeneration was preceded by a protracted work of the law and that the leaders of the revival were 'too ready to accept a demonstrative sentiment for a vital conviction' (*Aberdeen Journal* 22 August 1860: 8). They were concerned when they overheard 'youths talking of going to be converted, as if conversion were but an evening's entertainment' (Omicron 1859: 39). Nevertheless, the evangelists continued to invite men, women and children to be 'born again' immediately, in an instant. This particular understanding of conversion was another distinguishing feature of the Aberdeen awakening.

Perhaps the most significant feature of the 1859 Revival as it appeared in the city of Aberdeen was the gender composition of its converts. During previous awakenings, most notably at Cambus-lang in 1742 and in Aberdeen in 1840, women outnumbered men among those affected by at least three to two (Aberdeen Presbytery 1841, Smout 1982: 116). However, in an attempt to redress the gender imbalance within their churches, American revivalists around the middle of the nineteenth century began to organise special services designed to attract men. Indeed, this was a feature of the 1857 New York Revival that led to a noteworthy rise of male piety (Long 1998: 69-71, 90). In Aberdeen particular meetings were organised whose purpose was to draw certain groups of men into the church. The following advert appeared in the *Aberdeen Herald*:

> Open-air Meeting for WORKING MEN. A meeting will (D.V.) be held on the Links of Aberdeen, on Saturday the 10th inst. (Today), at five o'clock. It is hoped that a SPECIAL MEETING, for men exclusively will be held on Thursday evening, at eight o'clock, in St Nicholas Lane U.P. Church. A MEETING for SAILORS, and those connected with the Shipping and Trade about the Harbour, will be held on Wednesday evening, at seven o'clock, at Weigh-House Square, or, in case of rain, in Free Union Church (*Aberdeen Herald* 10 August 1861: 4).

It appears that the leaders of the Aberdeen Revival made a concerted effort to target men. Upon an examination of the gender of those converted during the city's religious movement, it was found that 45 per cent were male and 55 per cent were female (Jeffrey 2002: 105). The Aberdeen Revival of 1859 attracted a disproportionate number of men, which represented a significant shift in the gender balance of the city's churches. Accordingly, this manifestation of the awakening was broadly similar to modern religious movements that had begun to appear in America during the 1850s.

Part 2: The Revival in the Rural Hinterland of Aberdeenshire

Around the springtime of 1859, after the initial burst of religious enthusiasm in Aberdeen had begun to wane, the revival began to appear in the villages of the rural hinterland (Matthews 1910: 54). It was diffused into these communities both through students who travelled into the countryside to lead meetings, and also by farming people who were converted in Aberdeen (Anon. 1860: 36). Notwithstanding the important role played by itinerant evangelists as the catalyst of the revival in many villages, it was ordinary men, women and children who were the principal agents of this movement. Robert Reid, the Free Church minister at Banchory, acknowledged how 'God had made those who were awakened and changed the means of awakening others, and turning them to the Lord' (Anon. 1860: 8). Indeed, the strength of the farmfolk's revival lay in the large number of cottage prayer meetings held across the countryside. William Smith, Free Church minister at Keig and Tough, described how these were conducted 'either wholly or in part, by the people themselves' (Anon. 1860: 38). Henry Williamson reported 'a farmer addressing ... about a hundred people gathered in a mill loft ... [and] a quarrier's prayer meeting assembled in the smithy belonging to the work ... [that] was originated entirely by the workmen, and is usually conducted by them' (Anon. 1859a: 40). A particular feature of the rural awakening was the role played by local ordinary converts in conducting small cottage meetings. The popular strength of this revival lay within these unplanned gatherings.

Besides the support of ordinary people, local Free Church ministers undertook the role of leading the revival (Anon 1860: 28). These men exercised great influence upon the course of the rural awakening. Their authority was reflected in the traditional manner of the revival. An indication of the nature of their guidance may be speculatively inferred from the contents of Robert Reid's library, which were auctioned in 1894. Among his books for sale were some written by George Whitefield, Andrew Bonar, Richard Baxter, William Couper and Matthew Henry (Anon. 1894). Conspicuous by their absence from Reid's library were works by Finney and Colton, who were widely regarded by many as authorities on religious movements around the middle of the nineteenth century, but who also advocated modern revival techniques. Thus the contents of Reid's library suggest that his sympathies lay with traditional Presbyterian revivalists.

The control exercised by local ministers over the rural awakening is demonstrated by the manner in which conversion was understood and experienced. These men were staunch Calvinists who believed that regeneration was most often a gradual awakening, preceded by what they described as 'a work of the law'. During this unspecified time men and women became distressed in their conscience by the weight of their own sinfulness, and only after this were they able to receive God's gift of faith. Then they would be enabled to repent and be converted. This model of religious experience appears to have been the standard among the farmfolk. They were said to have had a 'growing feeling of earnestness and solemnity towards religious matters' before they were converted (Inverurie Free Church Kirk Session Minutes, 12 January 1860, Oyne Free Church Kirk Session Minutes, 7 February 1860). Meanwhile, George Bain, Free Church minister at Chapel of Garioch, remarked: 'of these persons [converted] the great majority obtained peace in waiting on the Lord Jesus in the course from one to four weeks' (Anon. 1860: 29). The farming people were not exhorted to be 'born again' in an instantaneous way like their fellow anxious enquirers in Aberdeen. On the contrary, the new birth was for them a protracted ordeal that could last for weeks or even months. Conversion in the rural revival, then, was experienced in a traditional manner.

In addition, incidents of physical prostration accompanying conversion were rare in the rural hinterland. In this area there were only a few reports of isolated cases. One concerned an elderly woman who cried loudly during a church service. Another involved a young woman who became so affected that she required the help of several friends to leave a meeting (*Aberdeen Free Press* 13 January 1860: 6). More often, it appears that physical manifestations affected the farmfolk in their dwelling places. William Leslie, Free Church minister at Macduff, reported two accounts of prostration from his parish, both of which occurred at home (Anon. 1860: 38). William Ker described another incident when a man 'tried to sleep, but a trembling seized him so that the bed shook under him, and he was forced to his knees to cry for mercy, so loud that all in the house heard him' (Anon. 1860: 17). However, such cases were not common. Physical manifestations were not a prominent feature of the rural revival. Public services were usually orderly, and prostrations, when they did appear, were often in people's homes. There is no doubt that the undemonstrative nature of this awakening reflected further the guiding influence of the ministers.

The pattern of the rural religious movement was also quite distinct, as it followed the unregimented rhythm of the farmers' working life. David Kerr Cameron, a local author, described how 'the turn of the seasons imposed their own order on the lives of the folk of the farmtouns ... the grieve might order the farmtoun day but God and the soil itself set the rhythm of the year' (Cameron 1984: 75). According to this natural pattern the busiest period for the farmfolk was between August and October, while the winter afforded more time for leisure (*Aberdeen Almanac* 1860: 13). This annual cycle of work and rest had an important influence upon the religious practices of the farming communities and the timing of the revival (Ardclach Free Church Kirk Session Minutes 7 November 1860). Although the awakening began during the spring of 1859, newspaper reports suggest that its momentum slowed considerably towards the end of the summer, and that its most effective period lasted from November 1859 until February 1860 (*The Revival* 26 November 1859: 139, *Wynd Journal* 21 January 1860: 123). The correlation between the farmfolk's awakening and their periods of rest is perhaps best illustrated by its appearance during the principal holidays in the agricultural calendar, the biannual feeing market. Held in the terms of Whitsunday and Martinmas, these farming community carnivals became the opportunities of the revival's greatest influence (Anon. 1860: 21). Hence the rural revival flourished during those periods when the farmfolk were not consumed with work and had free time to devote their attention to religious concerns.

This is clearly shown by the most significant feature of the farm village awakening – its association with the traditional communion season. These long-established five-day religious festivals, held twice each year, acted frequently as the principal occasion of the rural movement. Robert Reid described how 'in regard to the commencement of the work, he might state that it seemed to begin the week after their spring communion, on the first Sabbath of May, which not a few had felt to be a very solemn season to their souls' (Anon. 1860: 7). Moreover, he planned additional communion seasons, believing they would 'have a beneficial effect and serve to advance the Lord's work in our midst' (Banchory Ternan Free Church Kirk Session Minutes 1 June 1859). Meanwhile, George Bain also recognised the tremendous potential of the traditional communion season to serve the purposes of the revival. Like Reid, he organised a special celebration of the sacrament in January 1860. Afterwards, his kirk session minutes recorded: 'there has been a truly wonderful awakening ... on the occasion of a special communion ... there were more communicants added to the roll than there was during the whole past nine years of the minister's incumbency' (Chapel of Garioch Free Church Kirk Session Minutes 30 January 1860). Clearly the traditional communion season, which was knitted into the annual rhythm of the farming calendar, had a profound influence upon the timing of the rural revival. The high points of the movement regularly coincided with these great religious festivals.

Planned to correspond with the communion seasons were large open-air field services. These became the most important characteristic of the farmfolk's awakening (*Aberdeen Free Press* 9 August 1861: 5). Such 'camp meetings' became popular during eighteenth-century revivals in America, where they were used as an instrument of evangelism in rural areas (Carwardine 1978: 106). Their popularity waned during the first half of the nineteenth century. However, they reappeared and were used with enormous effect in agricultural villages during the Ulster Revival (Carwardine 1978: 172). Upon their return from visiting scenes of the Irish awakening, Aberdeenshire's ministers began to organise such meetings in their own parishes. Associated most frequently with the spring and early summer communion seasons, these open-air meetings, held in fields adjoining the local church, became very popular (*Aberdeen Free Press* 17 August 1860: 5). Approximately 9,000 attended a gathering at Huntly in the grounds of the estate belonging to the Duchess of Gordon, while 3,000 met at Banchory Lodge, the home of Colonel Ramsay (*Aberdeen Free Press* 7 September 1860: 8). It is noteworthy that the farmfolk's awakening flourished at open-air religious meetings held in fields. This indicates further how the distinct manner of the rural revival was influenced fundamentally by the setting within which it appeared. Furthermore, it reveals how this manifestation of the awakening bore a close resemblance to traditional seventeenth-century Presbyterian revivals.

Part 3: The Revival in the Fishing Villages along the Moray Firth

'A more unlikely place for a revival of religion did not exist' (McGibbon n.d.: 89). John McGibbon, a local author, made no attempt to hide the astonishment felt by local people after the Moray Firth fishing villages were overcome by the 1860 awakening. This coastline was more renowned for its smuggling and drunkenness than for its spirituality. The villages of Portknockie, Findochty and Portessie, wherein the movement began, were said to have a 'deplorable moral and spiritual condition', which had been 'notorious for generations' (*British Messenger* 4 1860: 318). Meanwhile, Thomas Baxter, the United Presbyterian minister at Banff, described how 'the moral and spiritual condition of our town has been long a matter of reproach' (*Missionary Record of the United Presbyterian Church* 9 1860: 165). Thus it came as an enormous surprise to many when the Moray Firth was overwhelmed by this remarkable tide of revival in 1860.

This length of coastline was affected by the awakening in an unprecedented manner. At the time, it was recognised that these villages had had a more profound encounter with the revival than any other area in Scotland. It was reported how 'the excitement which has been prevalent in the coastline villages of the western district of Banffshire, for the last three weeks, has been … quite unequalled, it is believed, by anything which has yet taken place in Scotland in connection with the present revival movement' (*Aberdeen Herald* 3 March 1860: 6). It was matchless because its influence extended across whole communities. The *News of the Churches and Journal of Mission* described how 'a general awe has been diffused over the whole population, as in the days of the apostles, when "fear came upon every soul" ' (*News of Churches and Journal of Mission* 5 1860: 119). This religious movement affected entire communities. In this way the Moray Firth enjoyed an unrivalled experience of the 1859 Revival.

Two features of these communities serve to explain why they were affected by the revival in such a remarkable manner. Firstly, they were remote and secluded. This comparative isolation had a note-worthy influence upon how the revival affected these communities. One minister described how:

> the remarkable awakening which seems to be extending along our coastline has a special significance from the character of the fishers. Their isolation in locality, but more in sympathy and interests from the agricultural and trading populations naturally tends to keep them untouched by those waves of religious excitement which are passing over the inland districts (*Aberdeen Free Press* 3 February 1860: 8).

Furthermore, these were tightly knit villages. This is illustrated by parish reports contained in the New Statistical Account of 1843, which invariably commented upon how the fisherfolk were 'a distinct class of society, with sentiments, sympathies and habits peculiar to themselves' (Smith 1991: 55). Even in the larger towns of Fraserburgh and Peterhead, the fisherfolk lived apart in well-defined areas that became known as the 'Seatowns', with the result that they were often regarded as an alien people (Gray 1978: 10). There is no doubt that the geographical isolation and the homogeneous character of the fishing villages serve to explain why they experienced the revival in such a singular manner.

It was indeed the indigenous environment of these mid-nineteenth-century fishing villages that helped to fashion a distinct experience of the awakening. In particular, the annual patterns of work and leisure that governed their lives had a strong influence upon the nature of this religious movement. The people were engaged in three main fishing industries during this period. The inshore summer haddock season lasted from March to May. Carried on in small lighter boats, teams of four men and a boy rarely sailed more than an hour's journey from their village and returned home each night (Smith and Stevenson 1989: 38). The more lucrative herring season began in June and lasted until the end of October. Throughout this season, fishermen slept at home on Saturday and Sunday evenings, but for the rest of the week they worked day and night and slept for around two hours each afternoon (McGibbon n.d.: 141). Once they returned from the herring season in November, the fisherfolk spent the winter at home collecting bait, and only occasionally did they go to sea (Anon. 1843: 378). During this period it was anticipated that:

> there will be no regular work for weeks. The boats and gear will be overhauled, and the nets spread out to air and dry in the fields ... It will be a month of weddings. The lights will go out late, in some cases not till morning ... they do not get up early in these days of semi-holiday (Leatham 1930: 7).

Hence a clear seasonal pattern of work and rest governed the lives of these fishing villages.

The timing of the fishing village revival demonstrates clearly how it was determined by this model of labour and leisure. The first signs of awakening began to appear at St Combs on 6 December, but it was at Portknockie, from 28 January 1860, that the movement began in earnest (Robbie 1863: 49–51). During a second wave of revival among the fisherfolk in 1863 it was remarked how 'in God's kind providence, the time for their special visitation was arranged when they were constantly at home, and thus able to unite together in a joyful reception of his blessing' (*The Revival* 1863: 53). In addition, this movement barely lasted for more than a month. It was an intense affair that overwhelmed these communities to such an extent that normal patterns of life were temporarily suspended. At Findochty it was reported how there were 'fishermen who have for nearly three days and nights been praying and singing and exhorting their neighbours. Labour is totally suspended and has been during these five days. Even the cooking of victuals is much neglected' (*The Revival* 1860: 61). Services were not planned and targeted for particular times. On the contrary, they began spontaneously and were continued throughout days and nights for several weeks at a time. The fervent nature of this movement was only possible within a fishing community where, during this time of year, people could afford to suspend their labours indefinitely and devote their entire attention to spiritual matters.

The distinct character of the fishing communities also affected the particular expression of its revival. The movement in these villages was accompanied by physical prostrations that were not experienced elsewhere. There are a number of reasons why the conversions of the village fisherfolk were accompanied by these manifestations. Undoubtedly, a vital factor was their emotional character, which was often described as unrestrained and excitable. Women from these communities were also afflicted more than men. According to one reporter, 'instances were numerous of females fainting and falling quite helpless into the arms of those near them' (*Elgin and Morayshire Courier* 2 March 1860: 6). Moreover, prostrations also regularly attended meetings conducted by young people. Indeed, a great furore arose in Elgin one weekend when some young converts from Lossiemouth held a particularly excited religious meeting in the town. Afterwards, a member of the town's union revival prayer meeting disavowed any connection with the service (*Morayshire Advertiser* 28 March 1860: 4). It appears that physical manifestations were experienced almost exclusively by the village fisherfolk. Excitable women and young people, who were generally unaccustomed to regulating their behaviour before others in public, were the principal casualties of this emotional and religious distress.

There were also two specific situations that gave rise to a large number of prostrations. Firstly, they appeared at revival meetings led by laymen. Manifestations that affected men and women at Gardenstown occurred at gatherings conducted by four fishermen who had arrived from Portknockie. However, once they left, the prostrations ceased and there were no reports of manifestations at subsequent services led by John Munro, the local United Presbyterian minister (*Banffshire Journal* 10 April 1860: 5). Indeed, local ministers appear to have been anxious to stem the tide of religious enthusiasm as quickly as possible. At Garmouth, for instance, John Allan, the Free Church minister, 'at once came forward and took the direction of the meeting, so as to prevent any undue excitement or extravagance' (*Elgin and Morayshire Courier* 13 April 1860: 5).

Physical manifestations did not occur at every revival meeting that was conducted in the fishing villages and towns along the north-east coast. They were actively discouraged by ministers of religion and as a consequence appeared only at gatherings that were presided over by local lay evangelists.

Secondly, physical prostrations occurred most frequently at what became perhaps the defining feature of the fisherfolk's revival, the crowded, protracted meeting that usually began in the early evening and was often carried on until between four and six o' clock in the morning. In March 1860, the *Aberdeen Herald* reported in detail the proceedings of one of these meetings held in Portgordon, which illustrates how physical manifestations were generated. It described how 'the school got heated almost to suffocation by the people's breath, and in this state of atmosphere the meeting was kept up for nine and a half hours, many of the people remaining there the whole time without meat or drink'. Hymns and spiritual songs were repeated until 'the audience was quite in an excited state, boys and girls holding one another by the hands and rocking and rolling with their bodies, and even beating with their feet on the floor to the time of the music'. Then a series of prayers was offered, and as people's names were mentioned they shrieked, 'especially females, and commenced crying aloud, and throwing themselves into the arms of some of their neighbours'. Following this, James Turner, a Methodist lay preacher, addressed the congregation, telling them: 'every unconverted man and woman had a devil or devils in their breast, which must be plucked out before they could be saved'. According to the report, this animated address was followed by several cases of physical prostration. However, the greatest commotion did not occur until around midnight, when during a period of prayer a number of women fell into an unconscious state. The meeting began to draw to a close around one thirty a.m., only because the lights were nearly all burnt out and the meeting place was beginning to get dark (*Aberdeen Herald* 3 March 1860: 6).

This account reveals clearly the peculiar circumstances wherein prostrations most commonly occurred along the north-east coast. There is no doubt that the excitable character of the village fisherfolk and the nature of their gospel meetings were largely responsible for the physical phenomena that accompanied their experience of this movement. This particular feature of the Moray Firth revival, alongside other distinct aspects, demonstrates how the fisherfolk experienced the 1859 awakening in a dissimilar manner. Their religious movement was markedly different from that which affected Aberdeen and its surrounding rural hinterland. Moreover, this manifestation of the revival was remarkably like the excitable Methodist religious movements that were common towards the end of the eighteenth century.

Conclusion

Undoubtedly one of the most fascinating features of the 1859 Revival, as it swept across the north-east of Scotland, was the rich diversity of forms in which it appeared. Within this one movement there were a number of separate campaigns. Each manifestation, set in a particular social context, displayed a different ethos and belonged to a separate tradition of revival. The farmers' movement, built around the traditional communion season, emerged in a settled community and reflected the Presbyterian model of seventeenth-century revivals. The awakening that took place among the fisherfolk was altogether very different. Located along a 'neglected' coastline, it bore the characteristics of a more emotional late eighteenth-century Methodist Revival. Finally, the movement as it appeared in Aberdeen took the form of a modern evangelistic campaign. It belonged to a new common Evangelical school of revival that had emerged in the mid-nineteenth century and was set to continue through Moody and Sankey, Billy Sunday and Billy Graham into the later twentieth century. The 1859 Revival in the north-east of Scotland was not a single, uniform religious movement, as has usually been supposed. Simultaneous in its appearance and yet heterogeneous in its manifestation, this 'season of grace' demonstrates the definitive influence that local circumstances exercise when 'the Lord is walking through the land' (Anon. 1860: 6).

References

Aberdeen Presbytery (1841). *Evidence on the Subject of Revivals taken before a Committee of the Presbytery of Aberdeen.* Aberdeen: Gray and Davidson.

Anon. (1843). *The New Statistical Account of Aberdeenshire.* Edinburgh: Blackwood.

Anon. (1859a). *The Appearance of God's Work in the Chief Towns of Scotland: With Special Reference to Aberdeen and Dundee.* Aberdeen: King.

Anon. (1859b). *Times of Refreshing: Being Notices of some of the Religious Awakenings which have Taken Place in the United Kingdom, with Special Reference to the Revival in Aberdeen.* Aberdeen: King.

Anon. (1860). *A Report of a Conference on the State of Religion and Public Meeting held in the Free Church, Huntly, January 5, 1860.* Huntly, n.p.

Anon. (1894). *Catalogue of a Collection of Books being Portions of the Libraries of the Late Rev Robert Reid, Banchory, and Others, to be Sold by Auction, by the Aberdeen Auction Company Limited within their Rooms, 120 Union Street, Aberdeen, on Successive Evenings, Commencing 28 February 1894. Sale at 6.30 pm Each Evening.* John F. Smyth, Auctioneer. Aberdeen: Smyth.

Cameron, D.K. (1978). *The Ballad and the Plough.* London: Futura.

Cameron, D.K. (1984). *The Cornkister Days: Portrait of a Land and its Rituals.* London: Gollancz.

Carwardine, R. (1978). *Transatlantic Revivalism: Popular Evangelicalism in Britain and America, 1790–1865.* Connecticut: Greenwood.

Evans, E.J. (1983). *The Forging of the Modern State: Early Industrial Britain 1783–1870.* London: Longman.

Gray, M. (1978). *The Fishing Industries of Scotland, 1790–1914.* Oxford: Oxford University Press.

Jeffrey, K.S. (2002). *When the Lord Walked the Land: The 1858–62 Revival in the North East of Scotland.* Carlisle: Paternoster.

Kent, J. (1978). *Holding the Fort: Studies in Victorian Revivalism.* London: Epworth Press.

Leatham, J. (1930). *Fisherfolk of the North East.* Turiff: Deveron.

Long, K.T. (1998). *The Revival of 1857–8: Interpreting an American Religious Awakening.* New York: Oxford University Press.

Matthews, T.T. (ed.) (1910). *Reminiscences of the Revival of Fifty-Nine and the Sixties.* Aberdeen: Aberdeen University Press.

McGibbon, J. (n.d.). *Fisherfolk of Buchan.* London: Marshall.

Omicron. (1859). *Five Letters on the Religious Movement in Aberdeen: With an Appendix on the Nature, Probability and Necessity of a Religious Revival.* Aberdeen: Milne.

Orr, J.E. (1949). *The Second Evangelical Awakening*. London: Marshall, Morgan & Scott.

Radcliffe, J. (n.d.). *Recollections of Reginald Radcliffe*. London: Marshall, Morgan & Scott.

Robbie, W. (1863). *The Life and Labours of the Late James Turner of Peterhead*. Aberdeen: Wagrell.

Skene, W. (1905). *East Neuk Chronicles*. Aberdeen: Aberdeen Journals.

Smith, J.S and Stevenson, D. (eds) (1989). *Fermfolk and Fisherfolk: Rural Life in Northern Scotland in the Eighteenth and Nineteenth Centuries*. Aberdeen: Aberdeen University Press.

Smith, R. (1991). *One Foot in the Sea*. Edinburgh: Donald.

Smout, T.C. (1982). *Born Again at Cambuslang: New Evidence on Popular Religion and Literacy in Eighteenth-Century Scotland*. Oxford: Oxford University Press.

Thompson, E.P. (1967). *Time, Work Discipline and Industrial Capitalism*. Oxford: Oxford University Press.

YMCA (1859). *Fourth Annual Report of the Aberdeen Young Men's Christian Association*. Aberdeen: Milne and Stephen.

Chapter 8

Does Revival Quicken or Deaden the Church?
A Comparison of the 1904 Welsh Revival and John Wimber in the 1980s and 1990s

Nigel Wright

I am grateful for the opportunity given me in this chapter to revisit areas of thought and concern that I have previously touched on but not fully expressed or developed. For this reason, the basic thesis I am testing is a tentative one, and can be contested at a number of points. Although the title may give promise of a more historical analysis, my concern is primarily with issues of religious experience and spiritual discernment. Whereas it is readily assumed that the purpose of revival is to quicken the church and that as a consequence revival must be altogether desirable, I advance the thought that in fact revival, precisely because it is a human experience, is a more ambiguous affair and that in some aspects and at some times it may serve to do the opposite, to compound the church's spiritual ineffectiveness.

The presenting issues that draw me to examine this theme are twofold. In the case of the Welsh Revival, there is the historical observation that the century following on from the revival has seen a relentless decline in the life of Welsh Christianity, to the point that Wales can now be regarded as one of the least Christian countries of Europe. Is there here a suggestion that the revival, despite the reputed 100,000 added to the church, was in the longer term unhelpful to the cause of Christianity? In the case of John Wimber, there is the more personal observation derived from direct participation that, dramatic and exciting though the events surrounding what came to be called the Third Wave may have been, they left in their wake a degree of deflation, despondency and disillusionment. This may have hindered the church, serving in the longer term to compound its decline rather than enliven its mission. In Angus Kinnear's biography of the Chinese Christian leader Watchman Nee, he records a period in the 1930s during which there was an outpouring of the Spirit of God associated with Nee's ministry and an emphasis over a year or two on spiritual excitement and subjective experience. This was expressed by means of 'jumping, clapping, laughter, unknown tongues that conveyed no message to hearers or even speaker, and a flood of dramatic healings, some undoubtedly real but not a few mistaken' (Kinnear 1973: 134). Kinnear adds Nee's judgement in about 1935 that 'some revival methods ... worked like spiritual opium. Addiction to them compelled an ever-increased dosage.' The loss of restraint led to Nee's assessment after three years that 'We find on looking back over this period that the gain has been rather trivial, the loss rather large' (Kinnear 1973: 135).

It may immediately be objected that the Third Wave cannot be considered a revival on a par with the Welsh Revival – it may count as revivalism, but not as revival. The distinctions between renewals, revivals and awakenings is a debate I am keen to avoid. The connecting link between these two movements as I consider them in this paper concerns the experience of striking and unusual phenomena, of profound spiritual intensity, that is common to both and the catalytic involvement in those events of personalities of a certain kind. The subtext of the paper therefore is to do with the evaluation of the longer-term value of external phenomena. The spirit with which I approach this particular topic is not one of hostility or disdain for such phenomena. I am not a stranger to them and have from time to time shared in, and indeed enjoyed, the religious intensity. But in the midst of them I have also been prompted to ask how and to what degree they are helpful or unhelpful to the church and its mission and whether approached in a certain way they hinder rather than help spiritual growth. To enable this analysis we need first of all to establish a positive framework within which phenomena such as those associated with the Welsh Revival, the Third Wave and indeed prior and subsequent movements might be understood and then evaluated.

The Elemental, the 'Natural' and the Primal

The Elemental

A television programme and a sermon come to mind. Some years ago, the journalist Michael Frayn presented a television programme about Jerusalem. We saw him exploring its highways and byways and musing on its place as a holy city of three world religions: Judaism, Christianity and Islam. The dominant metaphor in the programme was of radioactivity. Jerusalem the Golden was presented to us as being alive with an immensely powerful and potentially highly dangerous energy, which seeped through the very stones of which it was built. The radioactive core, the nuclear reactor at the heart of the city, was, of course, the Temple Mount, on which at one time the Temple itself had stood, whose inner sanctum was the Holy of Holies, where the Lord was enthroned above the cherubim. The site now is home to two of the most imposing mosques of Islam. Because holiness is like radioactivity, God could, in Old Testament religion, only be approached with the greatest of care, lest those who infringed upon him be contaminated and die in his presence. Once a year, after taking elaborate sacrificial precautions and following a minutely prescribed procedure, much as scientists deal with dangerous nuclear substances, the High Priest was allowed to enter this Most Holy Place to make atonement for the uncleanness of the people.

In this sustained metaphor it is not difficult to recognise the elements of biblical truth – the ways in which God is portrayed, specifically in the Hebrew Scriptures, as an elemental force, a danger to those who approach in uncleanness. We are reminded of Mount Sinai and the warnings given by Yahweh. Around the mountain a cordon sanitaire is to be thrown. Moses says to the Lord:

> 'The people are not permitted to come up to Mount Sinai; for you yourself warned us, saying, "Set limits around the mountain and keep it holy." ' The Lord said to him, 'Go down, and come up bringing Aaron with you; but do not let either the priests or the people break through to come up to the Lord; otherwise he will break out against them' (Ex. 19:23–24).

There is here a strong note of the divine or the holy, which is presented almost as something impersonal, an uncontrollable power, an awesome power, a *mysterium tremendum*. The holy is portrayed as something contagious (radioactivity is not a bad metaphor) which can adhere not only to people but also to places and objects which must be carefully preserved from becoming contaminated and unclean and which in their turn can become contagious with holiness. It cannot be doubted that at the heart of the religious quest is some kind of sense of the elemental, the power and grandeur of the divine. Neither would it be incorrect to describe this as primitive, as belonging to the beginnings and foundations of religious experience.

Here, we turn to the sermon, preached during Lent in 1990 by Dr Colin Morris on BBC1 (Morris 1990). It is a sermon on the Holiness of God and traces the idea of holiness in the Scriptures, a notion that begins once more with the idea of energy. In the unfolding story of Scripture we are introduced to holiness as raw and sometimes savage energy, with minimal ethical content. To get in the way of this energy is fatal, as Uzzah discovered when, however well intentioned, he put out his hand to steady the Ark of the Covenant (2 Sam. 6:6–11). 'The anger of the Lord was kindled against [Uzzah]' and he was struck dead. He was not entitled to touch the Ark and suffered the consequences of disobedience, all personal considerations swept aside in the presence of elemental and seemingly impersonal power. Other instances could be given.

Colin Morris comments:

> The Hebrew words that describe the inner fire of God's being mean foaming, snorting, boiling under pressure and energy. When the Old Testament writers looked for suitable images of God's nature, they lighted upon the roaring lion, the hissing serpent, the angry bear. Untamed power! The American poet, Walt Whitman, said 'that in all true religion there's a touch of animal heat' … We say that the days have long gone when people lived in terror of God; we say that our religion is now much more sophisticated, and so it is. The God we project is very often a milk and water deity, so sloppily benevolent as to attract polite disregard rather than awe – and it's a mistake (Morris 1990: 8).

Morris goes on to describe the progress of the human apprehension of God's holiness first through the prophets to 'ethical holiness' or 'moral energy' and then through Christ to the holy as 'redemptive' or 'saving' energy. God is a Holy God and therefore a saviour (Morris 1990: 11). But his point is a vital one: we cannot eliminate from our understanding of God the notion of the elemental power of God that overwhelms and sometimes threatens us, or at least threatens the sin that clings so closely to us. Those who are educated in the ethical and redemptive dimensions of the Holy One nonetheless need to be reminded from time to time of the elemental, of the primitive, of the threatening, without which we risk not magnifying God but taming God and therefore despising God.

The 'Natural'

This leads me to talk about the 'natural'. Elsewhere (Wright 1995: 73–5) I have argued that this is an essential category for our understanding of religious experience in general and of the phenomena associated with revivals and revivalism in particular. For all human experience of God is experience of God with and through the natures that we have been given and for which we remain responsible. For human beings at least there can be no non-human experience of God. Divine agency is mediated agency. When God acts, God acts in and through the natural that has been created and given. The supreme paradigm for this remains the incarnation. The sacraments of water and bread and wine reinforce it. The effects of an understanding of the natural along these lines are immediate. Religious experience is de-sacralised and it becomes both appropriate and reverent to examine it without fear that in doing so we are doing so in defiance of God. It becomes human experience, not supernatural experience, and so it becomes questionable, ambiguous, fallible, since not only are humans finite, they are also fallen, and the potential for distortion and failure is always to hand. It becomes as varied and diverse as are the human beings who participate in it. Therefore strait-jackets and legalisms go out of the window.

None of this is intended to be reductionist or dismissive, but rather elucidatory. Nor is it to deny God's activity, but rather to understand the shapes that human experience may take under the inspiration of God's Spirit. When human beings respond to God those responses may be described at different levels, psychologically, physiologically, sociologically, theologically. Each of these perspectives complements the others. An appropriate model may be that when God's presence draws near that presence awakens within us a variety of responses which are particular to ourselves even as, because we share a common humanity, there are patterns of response that recur from generation to generation. Or the notion of inspiration may serve as a model: our humanity is breathed upon and so made attentive and alert to a Reality that transcends us even as it engages us.

In the Steven Spielberg film *Close Encounters of the Third Kind* there is a scene in which a spacecraft approaches a house. The force of its energy causes the house to shake and its electrical equipment to go haywire. If God is also to be understood as elemental, as holy energy, then it should not surprise us if when the human encounters the divine all manner of responses become possible and even likely. This, I suggest, is one way of thinking about the place of unusual phenomena in religious experience. It is unhelpful in my view to seek to legitimate the details of this kind of response by reference to specific biblical texts. It would seem to be enough to draw a broad analogy between the undoubted fact that in Scripture there are varieties of unusual response to the divine from time to time, with the fact that the same order of response happens from time to time in the history of the church.

In exploring the concept of the natural I have also suggested in other places (e.g. Wright 1989: 118–21) that the category of the 'psychic', by which essentially I mean the unconscious, may also assist us in exploring the nature of religious experience. To suggest, as is often done, that we are temperamentally different and that therefore experience of God will be shaped by our particular temperament is no doubt true, but it also appears to me as a state-ment to be somewhat bland. Human beings are a mystery, most of all to themselves. If it is the case that the conscious mind is a minor-ity part of our total mental and emotional existence, then we should not be premature in defining what our temperament consists of. Beneath the surface we are all capable of kinds of response, or reaction, to the divine presence, which we cannot predict or quan-tify. It is in this realm, which I and others call the psychic, that we are to look for those unusual responses that we find in times of revival, all the time remembering that these are human experiences. It is not therefore that God makes certain things happen to some and not to others, but that in the presence of God varying responses are evoked, sometimes dramatically and sometimes not, which are appropriate to the particular configuration of body, soul and spirit that constitutes each person. And lest this begin to sound too indi-vidualistic, the picture we paint here should recognise that who and what we are is in part constructed by the group(s) in which we participate. What happens to that group is therefore apt to shape what happens to ourselves, and as groups change this will change our experience from place to place and time to time. To develop the category of the natural is to broaden out our analysis of the nature of religious experience.

The Primal

This in turn brings me to the 'primal'. What we have come to be is the accumulation of those things that have gone before and which have been instrumental in forming and shaping our conscious and unconscious selves. We are in part products of the past, with events and relationships leaving their deposit within us. Most especially is this true of the earliest relationships and experiences, which lie at the root of our personality formation. Such experiences are negative and positive. At this point the evoking from us of unusual phenomena in times of revival or dramatic renewal can be the rising to the surface of otherwise repressed and contained feelings. There are clear parallels here with what may happen to people under the conditions of hypnosis or therapy, and the parallels do not invalidate. A positive outcome of these experiences would be the acknowledgement of hidden emotions in order to put them, finally, in their place. Catharsis is involved as the unconscious is cleansed of the unwanted. I suggest that it is because this experience is potentially releasing and because it awakens new depths of emotional energy into people's lives that it is more often than not – against the odds – an enjoyable experience, one which people are apt to want to be repeated.

This account of the elemental, the natural and the primal enables us within a constructive framework and seen in the best light to describe what may be happening in revival phenomena. Seen in these terms, revival may be said to quicken the church in the sense that it intensifies human experience of God and leads to greater personal wholeness. In turn, this may make an impression on the non-church community by awakening awe and the fear of the Lord and lead to conversion. It is conceivable and demonstrable therefore that revival accompanied by such phenomena quickens the church. To do justice to the title with which we are working, however, we also need to give an account of how the analysis I have offered may succeed in doing the opposite.

Revival and Revivalism – the Inducement of Phenomena

It is not uncommon to draw a distinction between revival and revivalism, and such a distinction will be in evidence in this book. The former is where there is a free work of God among human beings that comes as divine gift, although it may be prepared for in prayer and the search for God. I would suggest that where this is the case there is a new sense of the holy God, which may not be contained within ordinary patterns of behaviour. If this is accompanied by unusual phenomena this is not something that should be considered intrinsically problematic from either spiritual or biblical perspectives. The sense of the divine would normally come where there is an openness to God in prayer and where the word of God is accurately and effectively proclaimed. There is a difference between this and revivalism. Revivalism is the attempt to reproduce through human methodology what is essentially a response to divine gift. My contention is that revival quickens, revivalism deadens. The crucial, and apparently difficult, distinction between the two concerns is that between serving a free work of God and manipulating phenomena by force of human personality and suggestibility. Since it is difficult to discern where this line happens to fall, it is easily crossed, leading to the ambiguity concerning revival to which I have referred.

The analysis of religious experience I have offered above stresses the human side of such experience. The corollary to this is to say that those human, psychic energies that are awakened by the sense of divine presence are potentially to be manipulated by other agents with similar external, though not spiritual, consequences. Two other factors come into play here. The first is that because the release of primal energies can be pleasurable and indeed addictive, there is a tendency on the part of those who experience them to collude with their inducement. The second is that in states of mind in which the psychic is being tapped there is a high degree of suggestibility; those who minister in these circumstances can find themselves possessed of a degree of power to make things happen that is exciting and deceptive in equal measure. It belongs to the self-restraint of the responsible believer not to transgress these boundaries. People who are psychically open are both receptive and vulnerable, as, I believe, we see profoundly and movingly illustrated by King Saul. Saul is, arguably, the most dramatically responsive character in the Old Testament if such is to be gauged by external phenomena. And it was Saul who suffered from manic depression. When genuine renewal or revival overlaps into its humanly induced alternative my contention is that this deadens the spirit by pushing people into themselves in an unhealthy subjectivism that in time produces disillusionment or self-distrust. The consequences of this could be reaction against the whole experience, cynicism, or, in the extreme, loss of faith.

The Latent Power of the Soul

Let me go back for a moment to the reference to the life of Watchman Nee. He came to the conclusion after a period of renewal and phenomena that, although there had been gains, they were offset by losses. Nee went on to develop his thinking in a book entitled *The Latent Power of the Soul* (Nee 1972). In it he identifies the power of 'psychic force'. In Nee's thinking, the spirit belongs to God, but the soul belongs to man, and they are distinct, indeed even opposed. Where the soul is confused for the spirit, disaster and deception ensue. Adam, the first man, possessed as a living soul 'unthinkable supernatural power' (Nee 1972: 19), which in its original form was lost at the Fall. But this is not to say that this ability was fully forfeited. Rather, it was subjugated to the flesh, and it becomes buried in Adam as a latent power that Satan seeks to break open and gain access to. Various religions gain access to this latent potential and release its miraculous power (Nee 1972: 21–2). This explains their spiritual, but counterfeit, content, as it does that of mind movements, such as Christian Scientism. The analysis, argues Nee, is confirmed through sciences such as psychology and parapsychology (note the appearance of the word 'psyche') and explains phenomena such as telepathy (Nee 1972: 24 ff.), which are to be given credence. The capacity to gain access to the latent power of the soul, or 'psychic force' as Nee also calls it, is increasing with the passage of time, but there remains an absolute distinction between soul-force and spirit-force, the operation of one being of Satan and the other of God (Nee 1972: 43).

We can see in this description where Nee is taking us. He highlights the danger of the mingling of soul and spirit that it leads to. In many areas of putative spiritual experience the danger needs to be recognised, and even (perhaps especially?) in revival meetings the danger of soul-force as opposed to spirit-force is identified (Nee 1972: 67–8). Discernment and refusing to rely upon the energies of the soul are paramount if we wish not to fall prey to the counterfeit, which in Nee's terms means to Satan.

Despite reservations concerning Nee's assumptions and theology, I do believe there are significant human and spiritual insights here. Let me display first of all my reservations. Watchman Nee works with a tripartite view of the human constitution, according to which human nature is comprised of body, soul and spirit, each of which is distinct from the other almost to the point of separation. I regard this as theologically and biblically suspect and prefer to understand human nature as a radical unity, although one that can be looked at from different perspectives. Nee accompanies his tripartite view of the human constitution with a dualism that works at two levels: the spirit and the soul are to be radically contrasted, one being of God, the other of man. Similarly, the soul in fallen humanity is prey to Satan, so that soul-force is closely identified with Satanic counterfeit. When soul-force and spirit-force operate alongside each other this is tantamount to God and the Devil vying for dominance, not least in the manifestation of revival phenomena.

The foundations I have previously laid concerning the 'natural' enable us to give a less fraught account of religious experience. The Spirit of God works by inspiration upon and within the humanity that has been bestowed upon us. Such inspiration embraces the conscious and unconscious realms of the human person and produces effects. In the unconscious or psychic realm these effects may take unusual and dramatic forms as energies are unlocked. Because these are essentially human experiences, they are always potentially to be induced or evoked by other forms of inspiration, supremely by other human beings or groups. There is no particular need to resort to the category of the demonic at this point (although I would not want absolutely to exclude it) and it is usually unhelpful and high-blown to do so, just as it is to assess all unusual phenomena as being necessarily inspired by God. There is something much more human going on. However, humanly to induce such phenomena, intentionally or otherwise, is spiritually unhelpful, since it pushes people into their own subjectivity rather than into God and ultimately leads to spiritual emptiness.

Evan Roberts and Lonnie Frisbee

This brings me to what is probably the most tentative, if perhaps also the most tantalising, aspect of this essay. It is also the part that properly justifies the reference in the title to a comparison between the Welsh Revival in 1904–5 and the movement associated with John Wimber in the 1980s and 1990s. The comparison is specifically concerned with two central characters in those movements: Evan Roberts and Lonnie Frisbee.

Evan Roberts

I have referred to Watchman Nee, who, it should also be pointed out, was indebted for much of his thinking to the writings of Mrs Jessie Penn-Lewis, a figure of some significance in the Keswick movement and in the Welsh Revival itself. In *The Latent Power of the Soul* he quotes frequently from her work. Jessie Penn-Lewis was herself a close associate of Evan Roberts and co-wrote her most famous and most controversial work, *War on the Saints*, with him (Penn-Lewis with Roberts 1973). It is a major theme of that book that 'Full "abandonment to God", unless guarded by the knowledge of the methods by which the Spirit of God reveals himself, may open the life to the invasion of spirits of darkness' (Penn-Lewis with Roberts 1973). The book is fundamentally concerned with the pervasiveness of spiritual deception. It is clear that this derives in large measure not only from the general experiences of the Welsh Revival, but specifically from the personal experiences of Evan Roberts.

Roberts, as a young man candidating for the Calvinistic Methodist ministry, was a central figure in the revival at its brief heights at the end of 1904 and the beginning of 1905. He was a catalytic figure mediating intense spiritual fervour accompanied by the typical phenomena and manifestations of revival. He understood himself to be a prophet and became a figure attracting both intense devotion and critical opposition, which took its toll of his sensitive and vulnerable personality. His methods were chaotic and unconventional. He avoided expository preaching and relied instead upon insights (words of knowledge), inner voices, erratic behaviour and confrontational behaviour seemingly out of character for an otherwise gentle and retiring person. Pierce Jones, in his highly sympathetic biography, ventures, 'It cannot be denied that in the heat of the moment, Evan Roberts was claiming powers for himself that no individual can ever have' (Jones 1995: 101). The same historian records at length how, 'The great victories of the revival period gave place to an era of spiritual slump and depression' (Jones 1968: 79). When the excitement died down many of the promoters of the revival 'denied the original inspiration of their work', thousands of converts lapsed and some observers came to regard the revival as a 'flash in the pan'. More importantly, a major shift took place away from the search for spiritual wisdom towards the desire for political solutions (Jones 1968: 79–80), and the Welsh drift from Christianity got underway. We are left to speculate whether the revival attenuated or encouraged this shift.

Roberts himself proved highly vulnerable and suffered a series of nervous breakdowns, becoming effectively a semi-invalid until his death in 1951. In reflecting upon his part in the revival, Roberts was to question himself about whether it was the Holy Spirit who commanded some of the things he did and whether he used power aright (Jones 1995: 120). Under the tutelage of Jessie Penn-Lewis, who believed that because he was transparently spiritual he was all the more vulnerable to evil spirits, he appears to have concluded that he had been open to deception. He came to be distrustful of mystical experiences such as tongues, prophesying and visions (Jones 1995: 173). However, this essay points in a more humane and matter-of-fact direction: Roberts was a sensitive and psychically gifted man. He was undoubtedly used by the Spirit but could not easily distinguish between what was of God and what arose from his own unconscious. He was a patently good man, but dangerously exposed by virtue of his own sensitivity. Intense spirituality and the consequent exposure to public gaze was more than he could bear. However, a primary catalyst in the revival in the form of Evan Roberts was also an inherently unstable one, and it is this dimension that renders the revival experiences ambiguous and potentially unhelpful for the onward progress of the church in the wake of the revival.

This is not to say that the revival was without many positive fruits. Leadership of the revival was not in the hands of Roberts alone, but rested also with figures such as R.B. Jones and Geraint Nantlais Williams, who brought wise, expository ministries to bear and conserved much that was good. If the sociologist Margaret Poloma is to be followed in believing that the continuing value of revivals is to be found in the institutions to which they give rise and in which their impact is extended (Poloma 2001: 99–127), then a major impact of the revival was in the Pentecostal movements to which it was the mother and evangelists such as George and Stephen Jeffreys who were at their heart. The intense blessing of the revival was thus transmuted into enduring and productive spiritual enterprise, the effects of which are still to be felt.

Lonnie Frisbee

Similarities are to be found between Roberts and Lonnie Frisbee, the catalytic figure of the Wimber movement. Lonnie is a figure of mystery. I have indicated elsewhere that a fuller understanding of the Vineyard movement associated with John Wimber awaits an honest and informed assessment of Frisbee (Wright 1998: 254). Who was he and what happened to him? It was through Frisbee, who had previously been influential in the Jesus Movement of the 1960s, and was associated with Chuck Smith, that the dramatic spiritual movement associated with Wimber came into being. As far as I am aware, Frisbee was later to leave the Vineyard and his fate is unknown to me except by way of rumour. However, it is clear enough to me that Frisbee was himself an unstable element in the Wimber cocktail. His methods were, like those of Roberts, unconventional and at times chaotic. He struck the pose of a prophet and wonder-worker (Wimber called him a 'fun-maker'). He worked by means of words of knowledge, individual and group confrontations and impartations of the Spirit. When first converted he would strike people with his coat in order to impart the Spirit to them – having learned this directly from Elijah in the Scriptures! At the root of this essay lies a remark I heard him pass during a visit in 1982 to the effect that even before he was converted he could 'do this' – that is, make strange phenomena come to pass. This suggests to me that he had already prior to his conversion to Christ learned to tap into the 'latent power of the soul' in individuals and groups, and that many of the phenomena that accompanied him wherever he went were essentially psychic in origin. Once more there is no need to interpret this in anything other than a merely human framework.

In so far as Frisbee's impact was defined and channelled by the influence of essentially sound people such as John Wimber the strange signs following could be contained and interpreted constructively. Cut loose from it, they were likely to become destructive – religious experience without a secure context to give it shape and meaning. Once more it is my contention that this ultimately deadens rather than quickens the church, since it creates a subjectivism that absorbs energy and attention away from that which matters more and leaves people with a few gains but probably more losses. But this is not to say that this is all the Wimber movements amounted to. The enduring value of those early days is also to be found in what was left behind. On the one hand, there is the Vineyard denomination with its thrust towards growth and church planting. On the other, there is the Alpha movement, which owes something at least (and in my view probably a great deal) to John Wimber's impact upon its originating church, Holy Trinity Brompton, and particularly upon its dominant and gifted advocate, Nicky Gumbel.

Conclusions and Evaluations

I have tried in this paper to offer a positive way of interpreting revival phenomena as well as pointing to their perennial downsides. It is appropriate to draw together some conclusions on the basis of what has been said.

In using the distinction between revival and revivalism I have
sought to point up the difference between an act of God that comes
freely and sovereignly, sometimes with strange wonders attached,
and the human propensity to help it on its way by the use of suggestion and the power of psychic energy. It is hard but necessary to
resist this temptation and to do so requires both high levels of
discernment and self-knowledge. There is nothing quite as intoxi-
cating as 'spiritual' anointing. If I have a criticism of the Wimber
movement and the subsequent derivative known as the Toronto
Blessing it is precisely here. Whether or not a biblical mandate can
be offered for such experiences, it is surely beyond question that
their propagation by a kind of consumption-driven promotionalism can find no such basis. The longer such a promotional drive
lasts, the more likely it is to become debased and corrupted with the
merely psychic: by 'soul-force', as Watchman Nee would have it.
The temptation to begin with the Spirit and end in the flesh is as old
as Christianity itself (Gal. 3:3). The Spirit of God is not a commodity to be promoted. The Welsh Revival, the Wimber or Vineyard
movement and the Toronto Blessing were all marked by a rush to
'get a slice of the action', and this instinct causes me unease, even as
I can understand the desire to catch the contagion.

Yet the waves of spiritual frenzy that we see attaching to these
events was also in each case marked by an equal and opposite frenzy,
the frenzy to denounce and oppose the phenomena as demonic or
occultic. Both tendencies are unhelpful. McCarthyism is a paranoid
frenzy of its own, which panders to feelings of spiritual elitism and
pride in its own way. To downplay the demonic, as I have sought to
do in this paper, and stress the sheer humanity of religious experience
of the divine ought surely to help us behave more mercifully towards
our fellow humans and offer fruitful possibilities for the future.

As a participant in the Wimber movements, when the Toronto
Blessing came I was surprised at how little reference back there was
to the Wimber visits. It was as though something completely new
was happening and that no wisdom from the previous decade was
available. It is a feature of the charismatic movement that emphases
come and go and are swiftly consumed. Since further movements of
spiritual intensity are sure to break upon us sooner or later, this
seems a pity. Wisdom gained now might help to maximise the
positive sides of future movements and minimise the negative. One
piece of wisdom concerns how important it is not to be overly
impressed or distressed by the external phenomena of spiritual
experience, but to take them in our stride. In this way we might

avoid divinising them or demonising them, and see them instead as part of the simple but fascinating variety of human religious experience.

References

Jones, B. Pierce (1968). *The King's Champions (1905 – 1935)*. Cwmbran: Christian Literature Press.

Jones, B. Pierce (1995). *An Instrument of Revival: The Complete Life of Evan Roberts 1978 – 1951*. Monmouth and South Plains: Bridge.

Kinnear, A. (1973). *Watchman Nee: Against the Tide*. Eastbourne: Kingsway.

Morris, C. (1990). 'The Holiness of God' in sermon series *Let God be God*. London: Broadcasting Support Services.

Nee, W. (1972). *The Latent Power of the Soul*. New York: Christian Fellowship.

Penn-Lewis, J. with Roberts, E. (1973[9]). *War on the Saints*. New York: Thomas E. Lowe.

Poloma, M. (2001). A Reconfiguration of Pentecostalism. In Hilborn, D. (ed.) *'Toronto' in Perspective: Papers on the New Charismatic Wave of the Mid 1990s*. Carlisle: Paternoster Press.

Wright, N. (1989). *The Fair Face of Evil: Putting the Power of Darkness in its Place*. London: Marshall Pickering.

Wright, N. (1995[2]). The Theology and Methodology of 'Signs and Wonders'. In Smail, T., Walker, A. and Wright, N. *Charismatic Renewal: The Search for a Theology*. London: SPCK.

Wright, N. (1998). A Baptist Evaluation. In Pytches, D. (ed.) *John Wimber: His Influence and Legacy*. Guildford: Eagle.

Chapter 9

George Jeffreys, Revivalist and Reformer: A Revaluation

Andrew Walker and Neil Hudson

Introduction

In the history of Evangelical revivals, distinction can be made between those who can be said to have left a lasting legacy, and those who did not. In the Great Awakening of Europe and North America in the eighteenth century, for example, George Whitefield was arguably the most dynamic speaker and crowd pleaser of the day, and yet, with the exception of some influential printed sermons, he left behind him nothing in the form of a body of knowledge, a religious movement or an organised church (Stout 1991). John Wesley, however, who had neither Whitefield's panache nor his gift for publicity, left a major denominational legacy in Methodism, an innovative approach to Christian discipleship, and a perfectionist doctrine, which was itself to spawn a host of holiness traditions and churches in the nineteenth century.

Pentecostal revivalists can be similarly divided into those who left a lasting legacy and those who did not. Arguably the two most talked-about preachers and healers of that tradition in Great Britain were Smith Wigglesworth and Stephen Jeffreys, yet they left nothing behind except blessed memories and fitful legends. Stephen Jeffreys' brother George, however, who had none of the hwyl and raw power of Stephen, nor the spectacular healing methods of Wigglesworth,[1]

---

[1] Wigglesworth would run at those in the prayer line waiting for healing, and would punch the source of the illness. See Gee (1980: 90–91).

left behind him a Bible College and a denomination that has lasted for over three generations.

Jeffreys himself died in obscurity in Clapham in 1962. The *Daily Mail*, which had once trumpeted his exploits in rousing headlines, carried a *sotto voce* news item of his death, whispering his demise under the rubric the 'Mystic of Maesteg'.[2] The newspaper reminded its readers that once long ago Jeffreys had been a man who mesmerised crowds and was reputed to possess great spiritual power.

Even the denomination Jeffreys had founded, the Elim Church, did not make much of a fuss over his passing. Nor did they celebrate his life with fulsome praise (though the *Elim Evangel* paid tribute to his earlier glory, when he had held the denomination in the palm of his hand, and was the focus of attention by the British press).[3] Elim's muted mourning was due to the fact that in a very real sense the church was still in denial over Jeffreys' foundational role in its life; this denial followed Jeffreys' resignation as leader in 1940 only to form a new denomination in opposition to the one he left behind.[4] This denomination, the Bible Pattern Church Fellowship, effectively died with Jeffreys in 1962, and even during his lifetime it never escaped from the shadow of Elim.

Indeed, from 1940–62 we could also reasonably say that Jeffreys was little more than a shadow of his former self. He could still command platform privileges at international Pentecostal conferences in Europe. There he traded on his revivalist reputation, and as late as 1946 he could still draw a crowd in the United Kingdom, but he was unable to raise any great enthusiasm for his message, which by now had increasingly become centred upon ecclesiastical policy rather than an evangelistic appeal.[5] Even *The*

---

[2] 'The man who once seemed to work miracles', *Daily Mail*, 27 January 1962. The *Daily Express* (27 January 1962) ran the story of his death under the headline 'Man who worked "miracles" dies forgotten'.

[3] The *Elim Evangel* made mention of his death in the edition dated 17 February 1962. However, there was only a six-line reference to his death in the editorial (98), the rest of the editorial being taken up by the threat of communism, and two and a half pages containing the reflections of three of the senior leaders in Elim (104–7). Only one veiled reference referred to his departure from the movement.

[4] A move unique in the annals of Pentecostalism. For the full story of the break, see Hudson 1999.

[5] See A. Lloyd, 'George Jeffreys', *Picture Post* 11 May 1946: 10–13 for evidence of the crowds that still came to hear him.

Pattern's effusive hagiographic account of Jeffreys' life had to reach back to the inter-war years to provide any evidence that once Jeffreys was the pre-eminent revivalist in Britain.[6]

In this paper we offer a re-evaluation of Jeffreys' ministry and legacy by contrasting his role as a revivalist with his role as organisational reformer. Having given due weight to the evidence that Jeffreys was the most successful revivalist in Britain since the Great War (not least because many of the converts at his meetings were unchurched), we will argue that as a reformer his effect on Elim was catastrophic. We shall also contend that his undoubted success as a revivalist was a mixed blessing for the denomination, an ambiguous beneficence that has lasted to the present day. Despite this ambiguity, however, we wish to attest to the positive substantiation of Jeffreys' legacy, and note in conclusion that in Elim, sixty years after Jeffreys' resignation, he is finally being rediscovered.

George Jeffreys: his Background, Development and Evangelistic Success

The *Sunday Chronicle* (28 April 1931), under the banner headline 'Religion is Reviving', reported: 'The greatest religious revival for many years is sweeping Britain and preparations are now being made to tend the thousands of converts who are expected to fill the Church during the autumn and winter.' Such headlines as these were common in Jeffreys' heyday: the press would congregate in their dozens to witness a thousand converts baptised in a makeshift canvas baptistery at the Crystal Palace. Or they would tell of the hundreds of souls converted at Bingley Hall in Birmingham. And again they would report many scores of people healed of diseases at the Royal Albert Hall, surrounded by the 'wall of sound' erected by the great Elim Youth Choirs as they sang and swayed, almost imperceptibly, in swinging waltz time, 'Saved, Saved, Saved, I'm Saved by His wonderful grace.'[7]

---

[6] *The Pattern* April 1962. In 1928, for example, 10,000 people turned up to hear Jeffreys preach in the Royal Albert Hall.

[7] G.O. Webster, 'Saved by His Wonderful Grace', *Redemption Hymnal* no. 624. The *Redemption Hymnal* was a collection of all the hymns that had circulated amongst Pentecostals over the previous forty years.

His Background

George Jeffreys, the man orchestrating these extraordinary events, was born into a lower-middle-class family in Maesteg, South Wales, in 1889. He was converted at the age of fifteen, in November 1904, the year that the Welsh Revival began: his whole life and ministry would reflect the fact that he was a child of the Welsh Revival.

From his youngest days, George seemed to be possessed of a high sense of personal self-esteem and divine destiny, which in part was nurtured by his mother's protective attitude towards him. In his book *Healing Rays* (Jeffreys 1932: 56–7) he writes of his awareness of having been 'called to preach the gospel' from the 'earliest days of childhood'.

In September 1912, Jeffreys, with no higher education and having worked for a while in the Co-operative Stores, applied for a place at the Pentecostal Missionary Union Bible School with a view to entering the ministry.[8] The finances for his studies were paid for by Cecil Polhill (1860–1938), President of the Pentecostal Missionary Union, after Jeffreys had met him whilst ministering at the Tro'r Glien Mission (Llewellyn 1997: 37).[9] To Jeffreys, an unknown young man from South Wales, Polhill's support was interpreted as evidence of the divine seal of approval on his call to the ministry.

In winter 1913 he abandoned his studies to support his brother, Stephen, in evangelistic campaigns in Swansea, where he attracted the attention of the Sunderland-based Anglican vicar Alexander Boddy. Boddy had been at the centre of British Pentecostalism since 1908 and was the editor in chief of the Pentecostal publication *Confidence*. In 1913, Boddy went to Wales to visit the two brothers. Whilst there, he invited George to speak at the Sunderland Convention. It was Jeffreys' task to preach each evening, after the other main speakers had delivered their addresses. Jeffreys, in effect, then, was snatched from obscurity and catapulted into the midst of leaders who were older than him and vastly more experienced in

---

[8] Cartwright (1986: 30–31) gives the School's address as 134 St Thomas' Road, Preston. Jeffreys was accepted by the Council in September and began his studies in November 1912. He was only at the school until January 1913, when Stephen asked for his help with the campaign at Cwmtwrch.

[9] Polhill had attained national fame as one of the 'Cambridge Seven' (Pollock 1959: 100–105).

ministry. The opportunity to play a major role in the Conventions, which was a focal point for European Pentecostalism in those early days, set him on the road to success.[10]

Jeffreys believed his sudden elevation to the status of 'platform speaker' to be further confirmation of God's commendation on his life and ministry.[11] His rhetoric had certainly commended itself to Irish Pentecostal William Gillespie. After hearing Jeffreys preach at Sunderland, Gillespie invited him to evangelise in Ireland. In 1915, soon after arriving in Belfast, Jeffreys formed the Elim Evangelistic Band. The aim of this group was to conduct evangelistic meetings and open new churches. It was from the work of this 'band of brothers' that the Elim movement began.

The Golden Years

The years of 1915–34 were the golden years of Jeffreys' remarkable success, when almost without exception every town and city he visited saw him conducting huge meetings. The crowds who attended did not merely listen to the Welshman, but responded in large numbers to his message and the call to conversion. The sheer scale of these Pentecostal gatherings, beginning in Northern Ireland and then spreading to the British mainland, attracted the national press, whose stories were syndicated in many of the provincial papers. In 1928, for example, the *Daily News*, *Daily Express*, *Daily Telegraph* and *Daily Herald* all contained reports of the thousand people baptised at the Royal Albert Hall on Easter Monday (Phillips 1936). These reports subsequently appeared in

---

[10] *Elim Evangel* 25 September 1976: 8–9 carried a picture of the male delegates at the 1913 Sunderland Convention. There are seventy-eight pictured. With the addition of women and any possible men who were not included in the picture, the number present could be estimated at around 150–175. Gee (1967: 37) comments that although the numbers were never large, attracting 'a few hundreds at the most', the significance of the Conventions was 'in their formative influence in attracting and helping to mould not only the immediate leaders of the multitudinous little Pentecostal meetings ... but (also) the younger men who were destined to become leaders of the Movement'.

[11] Jeffreys wrote: 'From the moment I uncompromisingly entered the open door of the Christian ministry right up to the present day, God has been faithful and His abundant grace has been lavished upon myself and the work entrusted to my charge' (Jeffreys 1929: 529–30).

fifty-three local papers, not to mention the *Indian National Herald* (16 April 1928).

The following statistics gleaned from 1929–35 give some sense of the measure of Jeffrey's achievement as revivalist. In 1929, 600 people professed conversion in the evangelistic campaign held in Brixton; of these, nearly 300 were baptised at the Elim Bible College, with 3,000 in attendance (Phillips 1936). The highlight of the following year, which was the pinnacle of Jeffreys' popularity, was the mission in Birmingham. This evangelistic campaign had begun in the 1,200-seater Ebenezer Chapel, but out of necessity had to move to the town hall, which could seat 3,000. The services then moved again to the skating rink, seating 8,000, until on Whit Monday the 15,000 capacity Bingley Hall was booked and filled (Coates 1930: 321).

The number of reported converts from the 90 meetings held in Birmingham was in excess of 10,000, many of whom professed no church affiliation (Cartwright 1986: 105). Brooks (n.d.: 28–32) reported that in 1934–5 1,400 people responded to the altar call in York, 1,500 in Brighton, 1,500 in Dundee, 1,200 in Nottingham, 2,000 in Leeds, 3,000 in Cardiff and 12,000 in a series of meetings held in Switzerland.[12] The quantitative success of these campaigns is further exemplified by the fact that the number of Elim churches increased from 15 in 1920 to 233 by 1937.

Behind the raw statistics of Jeffreys' success lay a grass-roots charismatic movement founded not only on ecstatic religious experience but also on songs of eschatological hope – 'I shall see the king, where the angels sing, I shall see the king someday'[13] – and personal encounters with Christ in the here and now – 'Standing somewhere in the shadows you'll find Jesus, He's the only one who cares and understands.'[14]

But it is misleading to think of Jeffreys' role in these Pentecostal revivals as no more than the mouthpiece of an essentially spontaneous

---

[12] cf. Edsor 1964: 29–43. Wilson's comment that people may have made multiple conversion decisions (Wilson 1961: 111) is valid. The 'decisions' made may well have been for many different reasons, other than as a first-time commitment to Christianity. However, that so many people attended the services and made public responses needs to be noted.

[13] *Redemption Hymnal* no. 789.

[14] *Elim Choruses* no. 558. A note was included with this chorus that stated it was 'specially arranged as sung in Elim revival campaigns'.

movement. On the contrary, like D.L. Moody before him, Jeffreys was the author of carefully orchestrated and organised evangelistic events.[15]

The Easter Pentecostal Conventions, for example, were not unrestrained outbursts of religious fervour, but were carefully staged theatrical occasions – more sacred dramaturgy than camp meeting revival. At the 1928 Easter Convention at the Royal Albert Hall, a reporter from the *Manchester Despatch* noted the great care that had been taken in decorating the front stage: 'The platform was a striking patch of colour – a veritable arboretum. There were roses, lilies of the valley, palms, firs, ferns, and rhododendrons peeping out from a bower of green.' And while the music on Easter Mondays sounded easy on the ear, it did not rise up unbidden from the congregation in a voluntary of extempore praise. On the contrary, it was carefully regulated from the platform, with chosen hymns and choruses, and sacred songs rendered mainly by soloists, but sometimes performed as duets or close harmony quartets. Dominating the musical scene during the 1930s were the set choral pieces conducted by a professional musician, Douglas Gray, who commanded a choir of a thousand voices. Jeffreys' sermons, the centrepieces of these divine dramas, were not wild or ranting in the American style of the Deep South, or brimming over with demotic bathos, but were exceptionally well crafted and emotionally restrained.

Accounting for Jeffreys' Success

Jeffreys' fellow pastors thought the reasons for his success were clear. Above all else, it was believed that Jeffreys had been 'anointed with the Holy Spirit', and that this divine unction accounted for the harvest of souls (Brooks n.d.: 28). In 1936 an illuminated manuscript in the style of Victorian Gothic revival script was presented to Jeffreys on behalf of all the Elim Church members in gratitude and

---

[15] See McGuire 1987: 115. Bryan Wilson's sober assessment, made as long ago as the 1950s, was that the whole scale and *modus operandi* of revival in Elim significantly changed from the glory days of the 1930s. It had become, he said, 'the planned proselytising of a denomination' rather than the 'spontaneous, unorganised and naïve desire to convert the nation' (Wilson 1961: 58). In reality, the late 1920s and early 1930s were the years that displayed the 'planned proselytising' in contrast to the early pioneering days in Ireland.

praise for his ministry over the previous twenty years. The manu-script (see Edsor 1964: 69–72) was addressed: 'To Principal George Jeffreys' (Elim's favourite title for the revivalist). It read:

> As an Apostle, you have pioneered the Full Gospel message and estab-lished churches in the largest cities and towns of the British Isles.
>
> As an Evangelist, your ministry has been signally owned and blessed of God.
>
> Through your faithful proclamation of the old-fashioned gospel you have led countless thousands to Christ.
>
> As a preacher and teacher, you have stood uncompromisingly for the Word of God, your expositions of the Sacred Scriptures have enriched our minds and hearts.
>
> As a leader, you have stood like a bulwark in the midst of backsliding and departure from the faith.

But not all Pentecostals accounted for Jeffreys' success exclusively in terms of apostolic anointing and preaching the old-fashioned gospel. Assemblies of God pastor Donald Gee (1941: 157) believed that Jeffreys' success was partly down to media attention. The Pentecostal revivals, he wrote, caught the attention of the press because of the healings that accompanied Jeffreys' ministry and the size of crowds he attracted. The press reports in turn advertised the revivals and in so doing magnified them by boosting the crowds still further.

Media reports were legion. While the size of the crowds always merited comment, it was descriptions of Jeffreys as healer that occupied the most column space. In 1927 *The Evening News*, for example, reported a sixty-year-old woman who had been healed of blindness, and a wife of a Harley Street socialite who had been healed of asthma. The news report finished with the words, 'women of all ages who had suffered, they said, from cancers and tumors openly avowed that their illnesses had disappeared'.

Other contemporary accounts of Jeffreys' success stressed the natural rather than the charismatic gifts that he possessed. The consensual picture of Jeffreys as a platform speaker was of a man with a magnetic personality and a beautifully modulated speaking voice. Well-known journalist Rom Landau, who had introduced the British public to such men as Krishnamurti and Frank Buchman of Moral Rearmament (Landau 1942: 122), described Jeffreys in his book *God is my Adventure* as a man with 'a strong face with rather a soft mouth, dark curly hair and a fine presence'. But it was to the cadence and timbre of Jeffreys' voice that Landau attributed his popularity: 'I did not doubt that the strong and sincere tone of the voice of Jeffreys was responsible for much of the veneration in which his followers held him' (Landau 1942: 113).

The reporter for the *Belfast Weekly News* (1928) was in concert with the majority journalistic approach to Jeffreys, stressing his revivalistic fervour. He also praised his balanced presentation and eirenic approach to other Christian confessions. 'Pastor Jeffreys', he wrote:

> is a Welshman, possessed of all the fire and enthusiasm which charac-terises his race, with the gift for graphic word painting and an earnest-ness of purpose which seem to cast a spell over his hearers. He eschews everything in the nature of sensationalism and avoids theatricals and vulgarity in speech or action; neither does he attack others engaged in the many spheres of Christian activity.

There are other more structural reasons why Jeffreys came to a position of prominence and popularity during this time. His golden years spanned the aftermath of the Great War with its Depression, unemployment, the rise of Communism and Fascism. Jeffreys' message of the 'old-time gospel' rang out with a confidence and certainty that enabled the predominantly working-class members of the Pentecostal movement to retain some security and control over their own lives.

The revivals also, let it be said, provided them with some enter-tainment and glamour in an age of austerity. The Pentecostal message may have been the old-fashioned gospel of holiness fire and Evangelical piety, but it came dressed in exotic clothes. The possi-bility of healing, speaking in tongues and swooning under the power of the Spirit all gave a frisson of excitement to the Pentecostal convert. While the music may not have been risqué – it was not syncopated rhythm – it did fulfil the function of light entertainment, for it came packaged in waltz, marching time, and sacred simulacra of music hall songs – 'Everybody's loved by someone.'[16]

Speaking of entertainment and glamour is to remind us that Jeffreys' own popularity with the press and general public was boosted by the British tour of the controversial revivalist from California, Aimee Semple McPherson. In 1926, she became an

---

[16] A popular duet sung by R.E. Darragh and A.W. Edsor at evangelistic meetings.

overnight sensation with the British press who, used as they were to covering 'flappers', had no experience of women evangelists! As it turned out, Aimee was ultimately too theatrical and outrageous for British tastes. Her relationship with British Pentecostals was also ambivalent: on the one hand, she was the most famous Pentecostal in the public view and thus positively attracted attention to the 'Four Square Gospel'; on the other hand, some of her off-stage antics caused many Pentecostals to cringe. However, her celebrity status undoubtedly rubbed off on George Jeffreys and bolstered his public profile as well as his confidence. He soon found that he could fill the Royal Albert Hall without her.

Jeffreys as Reformer

But whatever reasons we may muster in accounting for his success, the sad truth is that from the mid-1930s onwards, Jeffreys slowly ceased to be the successful revivalist he had been for the last twenty years as he became increasingly embroiled in attempts to reform the Elim Church. In 1934, Jeffreys took the surprising step of ceasing to hold revival services with the intention of opening new churches around the country, preferring instead to revisit the churches he had previously established. This decision had a number of consequences. One was that he became more focused on the organisational side of church life and less on evangelism. He believed that the movement he had created had been reshaped by his lieutenant, E.J. Phillips, into a system in which the Spirit had been muzzled by clerical control. With the containing of the Spirit, he claimed, had come a loss of freedom.

Jeffreys' concerns were consistent with his Welsh revivalist experience, for as a child of the revival he had cherished the liturgical openness and organisational fluency of those days, so much so that his experience of 'living in revival' before the Great War had become the template for what he believed normal church life should be. His plan for Elim after 1934, in effect, was to decentralise the movement with its Presbyterian structure and autocratic executive control, and move the church towards a more Congregational system, where the laity would have greater democratic rights in the local churches and more say in the annual national conference.

This seemingly legitimate concern for a loss of freedom, however, coincided in 1934 with an increasingly public row with the Elim executive over his ardent support for British Israelism.

What had previously been a debate conducted in private between Jeffreys and Phillips developed into a public rift between the charismatic leader and his administrative officer. It was Phillips' abiding belief that Jeffreys used the issue of organisational change in favour of more local autonomy as a smoke screen for his real intention – which was to use his outstanding rhetorical gifts to persuade the rank and file church members to adopt British Israelism as a normative belief.[17]

The struggle for control of the denomination between Phillips the executive leader and Jeffreys the charismatic apostle can be tracked in their correspondence. In a letter written to Phillips in 1935, before a vote on his organisational plans, Jeffreys assured him: 'I will still be their [the pastors'] leader whichever way the voting goes.' However, fifteen months later, Phillips questioned Jeffreys' grip on reality. 'You must appreciate', he said, 'the fact that we are more than you in touch with our Ministers and Churches' (Phillips 1937). This was not an altogether unfair comment, because Jeffreys, a lifelong bachelor, lived in an almost hermetically sealed world of private male company, away from the prying eyes of media and church alike. He hid within the sanctuary of the exclusively male society of the Revival Party,[18] moving from venue to venue with them, and having little daily contact with or knowledge of local church life.

Phillips believed that his chief goal in this conflict was to protect the churches from the force of Jeffreys' personality when he came out on show. Jeffreys, on the other hand, was certain that God had spoken directly to him in 1937 and told him 'put your house in order'. Therefore he was convinced that he had been given a divine mandate to shake Elim to its foundations and build again if necessary from the bottom up.

As this public row escalated so did the voluminous correspondence between Phillips and Jeffreys, many of the letters consisting of holding tactics, protestations and legal manoeuvres. By 1939,

---

[17] Phillips, like many Elim and Assemblies of God pastors, considered British Israelism not only to be historically unproven but also an unhelpful if not heretical doctrine as it privileged Anglo Saxons by virtue of their alleged Israelite status over the rest of humankind. The fact that E.J. Phillips was also Jewish by birth may have played a part in his distaste for the pseudo-Israelites.

[18] The Revival Party was the group of men that worked with Jeffreys in the planning and execution of his revival meetings. All within this group were unmarried, and totally devoted to ensuring that Jeffreys' meetings ran as smoothly as possible.

the Ministerial Conference (the primary decision-making body of Elim) was to witness undignified scenes of their leaders attempting publicly to demolish each other's ministries and characters. By the following year estrangement between Jeffreys and the majority of Elim leaders was complete: they voted to curtail and redefine Jeffreys' authority, which in turn led him to resign and form a new denomination against the very church he had brought into existence.

Jeffreys, as we have seen, believed that he had been given a divine mandate for the reformation of the movement in 1937, when he received the command to 'set your house in order'. In his own mind, therefore, Jeffreys believed that he had to be obedient to all that God had told him, whatever the cost. Since he believed that Elim headquarters was embroiled in 'Babylonish control' of churches, he was not able to rest from his fight for the freedom of the people within them.

By the same token, Elim believed Jeffreys was under the devil's thrall. In 1945, Pastor Canty stated bluntly that he believed Jeffreys to be 'doing the devil's own work of scattering'. This view had been expressed more guardedly at the 1941 Representative Conference[19] (Minutes, 1941) in a formal motion that stated:

> We are of the unanimous opinion that the strife and contention that has lately arisen among us has not been engendered by the Spirit of God, but rather by the Adversary, an endeavour to divert and distract our attention from the main purpose for which God Himself brought this work into being [i.e. the Foursquare Gospel].

For some Elim pastors, Satan had managed to turn Jeffreys through appealing to his own pride. Phillips (1939) believed that the central problem lay in Jeffreys' unwillingness to yield to an accountable body and step down from power. Other contemporaries of Jeffreys, including some of those who had been the closest to him, couched their disenchantment with him somewhat differently: they thought that he was simply deluded in his belief that God had spoken to him about reforming the church. McWhirter, an original member of Jeffreys' Revival Party, believed that his major success had been as an evangelist, and that this was the area in which God had particularly gifted him. It was when he directed his efforts to work as a

---

[19] The Representative Conference was a gathering of ministers and appointed laymen from all the Elim churches.

reformer that problems arose. He wrote years later: 'When the Revivalist became a reformer of church order he lost his extraordinary power' (McWhirter 1983: 85). In an earlier reflection, McWhirter pointed to the results of Jeffreys' reformation (he meant both the split and the failure of the Bible Pattern Church) as evidence of the fact that he had been mistaken in his vision (1975). He wrote: 'The bad fruit of his reformism is the evidence that he was not motivated by the Holy Spirit. What he called a vision was only an illusion' (McWhirter 1975).

This inside view from one of the members of the Revival Party was echoed in 1993 by senior Elim Pastor J.T. Bradley. Reflecting on the split, he wrote: 'I have seen a Movement brought to the brink of destruction and only saved therefrom by men who adhered to the Word of God. Alas, when men and women get what they feel is a word from the Lord it seems impossible to convince them that they are mistaken' (Bradley 1993).

Another theory that sought to understand why Jeffreys had fallen from grace was the suggestion that God, not Satan, had removed him from his position. In a letter written in 1941, Pastor Joseph Smith wrote that he believed there to be a biblical parallel to Jeffreys' removal in the story of Solomon, who was replaced by God when he caused division. Solomon had built the Temple, but was removed from his position when the dissension he provoked led to worship being divided between Jehovah and other gods. A variant, though more specific, version of the theory that God removed Jeffreys from office was held by Assemblies of God evangelist Nelson J. Parr. He believed that God withheld his anointing from Jeffreys because he had diverted his gaze from the Jesus of the foursquare gospel to British Israelism (though we would add that the love affair Jeffreys had with British Israelism was linked to the flattering attention he received from members of the upper classes and minor aristocracy that were the dominant force in British Israelism between the two World Wars).

Because both sides in the Elim dispute took such opposing views, it was virtually impossible for there to be a reconciliation, let alone a *modus vivendi*. The moment that Jeffreys framed his desire to change the movement in terms of obedience to a divine command, the stakes were raised from organisational disagreement to out-and-out spiritual warfare. Phillips and many of the ministers in Elim believed that Jeffreys had become a distraction from the work they were engaged in, and because of his retracted dissension from collegial authority they lost the heart for attempts at mediation.

Conversely, Jeffreys could not step down and thereby end the dispute, for to do so would be to lose face and deny the authenticity of his divine mandate.

Conclusion

Wading through the prolific correspondence between Jeffreys and Phillips and the minutes of the Elim executive is to realise that Phillips may have been unbending and implacable, but Jeffreys from the mid-1930s was a man no longer in control of himself. While there is no reason to doubt that his desire to reform Elim and make it democratically accountable was genuine, this has to be balanced against the evidence that he became increasingly volatile and authoritarian. Many Elim leaders, not only Phillips, became alarmed at his oscillations and protestations. Pastor Kennedy, one of Elim's pastors at that time,[20] suggested in later years (Interview, 1993) that Jeffreys was an insecure man who panicked when he realised that he did not have sufficient influence to sway the movement to his way of thinking.

It would seem, then, that nothing good came from Jeffreys' reformation period. Yet the irony of his reforming zeal is that although it, more than anything else, led to the split in the Elim movement, eventually by the 1990s Elim did adopt a denominational structure very similar to Jeffreys' vision of a greater lay participation with more power devolved from the centre to the local congregation. An unintended consequence of the Elim schism in 1940, therefore, is that in the long term it facilitated Jeffreys' wishes and has to be counted as part of his legacy.[21]

We might be tempted to say in contrast to his reforming zeal that only good came from Jeffreys' revivalism. However, taken as a whole, while Jeffreys' revivalistic legacy is substantial it is not without ambiguity. On the positive side, one could cite the fact that his ministry during the golden years proved to be the catalyst for large numbers of conversions and the growth of many new churches. Furthermore, to state it bluntly, Elim owes its very existence to Jeffreys, and the denomination, along with its Bible College, now a degree-awarding seminary, are the lasting fruits of Jeffreys' labours.

---

[20] During his time as an Elim minister he served, alongside J.T. Bradley, as a member of the Executive Council.

[21] Though in fact changes began as soon as Jeffreys left.

Yet when the split took place in 1940 Jeffreys' very success as a revivalist was initially a problem for Elim. It had come to believe that Jeffreys achieved the establishment and growth of Elim single-handedly – a view that Jeffreys constantly liked to reiterate himself. The feeling of evangelistic inferiority in Elim became so acute when Jeffreys left that there was an attempt to reassess Elim's successes in this area and downgrade Jeffreys' contribution to it. The executive leaders' reasoning seemed to be that if Jeffreys could not be taken down a peg or two they would be consigned to live in the shadow of his abiding memory, and would never be able to strike out on their own.

In 1942, senior statesman W.G. Hathaway began to question the claims that Jeffreys had made for himself and, in effect, began dismantling the mystique that had been cloaked around him. He wrote to Phillips enclosing a list of churches that Jeffreys had not opened (Hathaway 1942).[22] These were ones that others had pioneered or which had already been in existence before his campaigns. Phillips, from this information, estimated that only one in three churches had actually been founded by Jeffreys and suggested that Hathaway include this information in the next Ministerial Circular (Phillips 1943). Hathaway expressed his excitement to Phillips when he wrote to him after doing some more mental arithmetic: 'Pastor Brewster and I had quite a thrill when from memory I named well over 100 that I could think were not founded by George Jeffreys' (Hathaway 1943). This revisionist account of Elim's history, and the attempt to push Jeffreys somewhat into the background, may seem petty and rather vindictive now, but at the time it was probably a necessary exercise if Elim was to survive without him.

But Jeffreys' influence, in a more subtle and ambivalent way, remained with Elim long after he had resigned and had been successfully marginalised by Elim's executive. This was because Elim headquarters could not imagine church life without a major revivalist as its figurehead. Their initial solution to the absence of Jeffreys as their premier revivalist was to find a replacement for him in the person of Percy Brewster, who was a friend and a disciple of the Principal.

Brewster's first great success came at Wigan in 1946 when after seven weeks campaigning Hathaway was able to report that over

---

[22] It has to be said, there was a certain 'creative accounting' going on here. This was re-visioning of history, and as such was never completely accurate.

600 people had responded to the call for conversion and that a new church was to be established. On hearing this news, and thinking ahead to the future of Elim without Jeffreys, Canty was able to say, 'I knew it would be alright' (Canty 1965).

Canty was right. Brewster was never to be as popular and as successful as Jeffreys, but then Pentecostal confidence itself was to evaporate in the post-war period as revival dried up and Britain entered the long descent into a post-Christian nation. In this context Brewster, from the end of the war to the late 1960s, was a remarkable success, opening forty new churches during this period.

Elim, however, like so many other evangelistic churches, did not come to terms with the rapid changes of modernity after World War II: they assumed that the revivalistic methods so successful in Jeffreys' day were the tried and tested methods for the future. This blinkered, and frankly mistaken, approach explains why Brewster, who was, as it were, a little Jeffreys, was the man under whose tutelage Alex Tee and Wynne Lewis were groomed as the next generation of revivalists (the 'little Brewsters'). Tee was to be the man for the 1960s and 1970s, Lewis for the 1980s and early 1990s.[23]

The quest for the new Jeffreys in the post-war years suggests that Elim were torn between the nostalgic need to recapitulate revival and rally behind a new dynamic leader, and the ongoing pastoral need to nurture and maintain an established community of Christians. This cognitive dissonance meant that on the one hand there was the pull of an orderly, principled, but essentially rational approach to ecclesiastical affairs, while on the other hand there was the push to sacrifice all on the altar of revival. In Weberian terms this 'push-me-pull-you' scenario left open the possibility that Elim may have reverted to charismatic authority after having settled down under the legal authority of bureaucratic control – the so-called 'routinisation of charisma' so typical of second-generation revivalistic movements.

In the event, the return to a revivalist figurehead did not materialise. Post-war evangelists were decent men, but due to changes in British culture – and certainly through no fault of their own – they had little of the success of Brewster, let alone Jeffreys. While in command and at the height of his popularity in the late 1980s,

---

[23] And it could be said that under Lewis' patronage, Elim's present day revivalist figurehead is Colin Dye of Kensington Temple in London (though Dye seems to have altogether a more realistic grasp of the evangelistic problems ahead than many of his predecessors).

Wynne Lewis was an altogether more flamboyant and powerful personality than most post-war Pentecostals. But although Lewis has probably been the most popular and charismatic figure in Elim since Jeffreys, he was not to see results to match those of his illustrious predecessors.

But Pentecostals can take heart that sixty years after Jeffreys' departure there are signs within Elim that they are awakening, as if from a long and forgetful sleep, only to discover, with the immediacy of a new revelation, their revivalistic founder. The way was opened for this new interest in Jeffreys by the re-release in the 1980s of a selection of early recordings of his sermonettes, surrounded by the songs of the revival, and presented as a memorial to Jeffreys under the title 'Precious Heritage'.[24] This was followed in the late 1990s by a reworked and reprinted publication of Pastor Boulton's biography of the Principal (Boulton 1999). Wynne Lewis played his part in this fresh look at the once-honoured apostle by rekindling Elim's revivalistic spirit.

This rediscovery of Elim's founding father has accelerated under the watchful eye of John Glass, the recently appointed General Suprintendent of Elim.[25] Glass, a third-generation Pentecostal, is by no means a romantic man: he will not condemn Elim to repeat the mistakes of the past by once again capitulating 'to the man of the hour', however anointed he may appear to be. He favours collegial authority over the charismatic overlord, and backs the team against the prima donna every time. Nevertheless, in his early fifties, he bridges the old world of the disenchanted pastors who survived the loss of the Principal through a subliminal process of induced collective amnesia, and the new generation of younger pastors untouched either by the shame or the sorrow of the past. Glass knows that while the survivors of Elim's discerption have lived in the shadow of an absent founder, this new generation of Pentecostals have never really known the father of their movement, and hence have never been able to name and claim him as progenitor or hail him as hero.

What Glass seems to be doing is putting back in his rightful place the forgotten father of an orphaned movement. Jeffreys is beginning to reappear in image and text for open distribution throughout the churches; and the Principal's face is now proudly stamped on Elim's web site. Even the prosaic walls of Elim headquarters are newly lit

---

[24]   The collection is undated, but Kingsway gave permission for the copying, and ICC studios in Eastbourne were responsible for the production.

[25]   Since 2000.

with iconic reminders of the Principal from his golden days and anointed hours. In this season of anamnesia, it would seem that the time has come when Elim can forgive its fallen idol and move on in the realisation that George Jeffreys, revivalist, has finally gone, but will never again be forgotten.

References

Boulton, E.C.W. (1999). *George Jeffreys, Ministry of the Miraculous.* Cartwright, C. (ed.). Tonbridge: Sovereign.

Bradley, J.T. (1993). Letter to D.N. Hudson, 12 May.

Brooks, N. (n.d.). *Fight for the Faith and Freedom.* London: Pattern Bookroom.

Canty, G. (1945). Letter to E.J. Phillips, 14 November.

Canty, G. (1965). The Past? What Past? *Elim Evangel,* 6 November.

Cartwright, D. (1986). *The Great Evangelists.* Basingstoke: Marshall Pickering.

Coates, E. (1930). The Nineteenth Century of Pentecost. *Elim Evangel,* 23 May.

Edsor, A. (1964). *George Jeffreys.* London: Ludgate Hill.

Gee, D. (1941). *The Pentecostal Movement.* London: Elim.

Gee, D. (1967). *Wind and Flame.* Croydon: Heath Press.

Gee, D. (1980). *These Men I Knew.* Nottingham: Assemblies of God.

Hathaway, W.G. (1942). Letter to E.J. Phillips, 30 December. (Mattersey Hall, Donald Gee Archive.)

Hathaway, W.G. (1943). Letter to E.J. Phillips, 5 January. (Mattersey Hall, Donald Gee Archive.)

Hudson, D.N. (1999). *A Schism and its Aftermath: An Historical Analysis of Denominational Discerption in the Elim Pentecostal Church 1939–1940.* Unpublished PhD thesis, University of London.

Jeffreys, G. (1929). Christmas and New Year Greetings. *Elim Evangel,* 25 December.

Jeffreys, G. (1932). *Healing Rays.* London: Elim.

Jeffreys, G. (1935). Letter to E.J. Phillips, 18 November. (Mattersey Hall, Donald Gee Archive.)

Landau, R. (1942). *God is my Adventure.* London: Faber & Faber.

Kennedy, J. (1983). Interview with D.N. Hudson, 22 April.

Llewellyn, B. (1997). *A Study in the History of the Apostolic Church in Wales in the Context of Pentecostalism.* Unpublished MPhil thesis, University of Bangor.

Lloyd, A. (1946). George Jeffreys. *Picture Post,* 11 May.

McGuire, M. (1987). *Religion: The Social Context.* New York: Wadsworth.

McWhirter, J. (1975). Letter to J. Du Plessis, 9 December. (Mattersey Hall, Donald Gee Archive.)

McWhirter, J. (1983). *Every Barrier Swept Away.* Cardiff: Megiddo Press.

Phillips, E.J. (1936). Handwritten notes for the Coming of Age Celebration. (Mattersey Hall, Donald Gee Archive).

Phillips, E.J. (1937). Letter to G. Jeffreys, 23 February. (Mattersey Hall, Donald Gee Archive.)

Phillips, E. J. (1939). Letter to G. Jeffreys, 18 January. (Mattersey Hall, Donald Gee Archive.)

Phillips, E. J. (1943). Letter to W. G. Hathaway. (Mattersey Hall, Donald Gee Archive.)

Stout, H.S. (1991). *The Divine Dramatist: George Whitefield and the Rise of Modern Evangelicalism*. Grand Rapids: Eerdmans.

Wilson, B. (1961). *Sects and Society*. London: Heinemann.

Chapter 10

Revivals as Historically Situated Events: Lessons for the Future

Meic Pearse

What is Revival?

It is worth asking what we mean by the term 'revival'. Since biblical scholars are mostly honest enough to admit that we cannot – except by some hermeneutical sleight of hand – derive much information from their principal academic subject matter, the task devolves to church historians to plunder the 2,000 years since and to weigh up what phenomena might, or might not, answer to that description. I shall argue that most of those 2,000 years are scarcely more useful to us than the biblical records in this search, but more of that hypothesis anon.

Which events in church history might count as 'revivals'? If we can agree on that, we might advance towards a definition. Alas, the lists of some people make a motley assortment. One frequently hears the rise of Lollardy and Hussitism and the Reformation referred to as revivals. An American writer recently insisted that the high-church Oxford Movement of the 1830s was 'a revival movement' (Bercot 1989: 149). Such usages, prone to describe any and every new movement as 'a revival', make it evident that the resultant definition of the term must inevitably be 'all those bits of church history of which I approve'. I was present recently at a conference on 'The Religious Radical Tradition'. This took a somewhat laudatory approach to its subject matter and, whilst it mostly concerned itself with the usual suspects (groups teetering on the brink of orthodoxy and occasionally slipping over the edge), various participants insisted on roping in Erasmus, Celtic Christianity and

William Booth's Salvation Army – groups with nothing in common with one another, and even less with the Diggers, Ranters and Quakers who formed the centrepiece of discussion – as equally parts of 'the radical tradition', on no firmer foundation than their own approval of them. There are certain views of which it has been well said that 'to describe them is to refute them', and this, I think, is such a case. We need not detain ourselves with it.

But what else? It has been more sensibly urged that revival starts with the church. Judgement, after all, begins with the household of faith. Before conversions can begin on a large scale, the church must be revived in itself. Revival, on this view, is not simply the inrush of converts, but the spiritual blood-rush-to-the-head that may (God willing and allowing) precede and facilitate it. There are advantages to such a view. It would certainly let us off the hook in a hard-to-evangelise society such as contemporary Britain, and made it possible to argue that the Toronto Blessing of 1994 was 'a revival' even in the absence of a flood of new converts – though wiser heads soon amended such talk, and spoke instead of 'times of refreshing'.

But can we really speak of a 'revival' that might, if we were to stick to the last, result in no converts whatsoever? On this criterion, the 'Toronto' phenomena might (at least arguably) count as revival, despite their minimal evangelistic impact, whilst the Great Awakening in England and Wales, led by John Wesley and George Whitefield, Hywel Harris and Daniel Rowland – which (even allowing for the later exaggerations of Methodist historians) occurred against the back-cloth of a miserable state of the church – would not! Where is the sense in such a definition?

Nor is this the end of our problems. If a rush of new spiritual experience and fervour is the main criterion of a revival, who is to say what it is and should be like? Were those staid Christians – or just more sober-minded charismatics – who were unhappy about 'Toronto' really the enemies of revival? They would hardly agree! Is a 'revival' a deepening of the kind of spirituality and doctrine that you like, or of the kind that I like? The question is not absurd: one fairly recent publication (I forbear to mention names, but *cognoscenti* will know the book to which I refer) denied that the revivals in early nineteenth-century America – and especially those associated with Charles Grandison Finney – were revivals at all, for no more persuasive reason than their failure to be conducted on the basis of Calvinistic principles.

To describe is to refute? Probably so, but perhaps a more charitable judgement of this striking instance of myopia is in order, for

I think that the term 'revival' does indeed imply a certain kind of theological content, albeit nowhere near so narrow as the stalwarts of a particular 'banner' might insist.

Consoling though the theory that revival is principally a refreshing of the church might be to us in Britain in the early twenty-first century, I think we have to face the fact that 'revival' unavoidably entails large numbers of people becoming Christians within a short (short, that is, relative to the numbers involved) compass of time.

But we do not include an influx of numbers simply by any means. No one, for example, counts as 'a revival' the Christianisation of Kievan Rus under the orders of Prince Vladimir in the years after 986 – a process concerning which, even 200 years later, the chroniclers were unable to put any finer gloss than to claim that his subjects 'wept with joy and exclaimed in their happiness: "If this were not good, the prince and his boyars would not have accepted it" ' (*Povest' vremennych let* ['The Narrative of Bygone Years'] in van den Bercken 1999: 31). Neither do we include the Baltic Crusades of the thirteenth century, in which the original Prussians and other Baltic tribes were massacred and then their remnants subjected to cultural, linguistic and religious assimilation into Christendom. The Spanish conquests of the Aztecs and Incas are similarly not counted as revivals, and with good reason.

And here we come to the theological element. For when we speak of many people becoming Christians, we have a fairly clear idea, I think, of the general nature of that conversion: we mean that it is personal, that the individuals concerned have some notion that they are dealing with – or being dealt with by – God, rather than simply changing their religious affiliation at the point of a sword, or even under more modest social pressure.

To that extent, 'revival' is a category that belongs to the thought forms and behaviour patterns of Evangelicals, rather than to Roman Catholics, Eastern Orthodox or even to Protestantism broadly understood. By 'revival' we do, after all, mean a closer affinity (if only in aspiration) between present events and those described in Acts 2 or even Acts 13:14–39 than is generally apparent in the celebration of matins or evensong. This observation is, I hope, no bigotry or special pleading; the other groups are more or less happy to let the Evangelicals have the term to themselves. Perhaps Catholics have come a little closer to this model of activist propagation in more recent years, especially in the Third World, though the Eastern Orthodox have not. Liberal Protestants famously scorn conversions – and revivals along with them.

De-conversions are more in their line, to judge by the direction in which all their polemical artillery is deployed, and where these have numbered millions, as in Britain, their achievement (if that is what it is) might perhaps qualify as a 'remortal'.

In sum, we find that the most rational meaning of our term, and the one least prone to individual quirkiness or to being hijacked as a piece of unanswerable, super-spiritual rhetoric, is that it refers to the conversion to Christ, as a result of divine encounter, of large numbers of people within a relatively short period. These converts may come into a relatively healthy church, as with the Welsh revivals of 1859 and 1904–5, or to an unhealthy, unspiritual one, as those of the 1730s. Indeed, the revival may be the instrument of bringing a church into existence in the first place, as among the Dani people in the Bariem Valley of Irian Jaya. (Some people may wish to question whether 'revival' is an appropriate term for events among a population previously unChristianised, even nominally. I do not insist upon the point, but I think it more useful to include it within the category, for reasons that will become apparent.)

When is Revival?

Having observed that 'revival' is a term generally used by and about Evangelicals presents us with another problem. Evangelicals insist that their version of the faith most faithfully reflects the New Testament vision and experience. But, allowing that claim for the moment, surely Evangelicals must themselves acknowledge that Evangelicalism as we now understand it is a product of modernity; its combination of key ingredients (conversionism, biblicism, activism and crucicentrism, as David Bebbington has mapped out so well) are visible from the 1730s onwards, but the lacuna from the first three centuries of the church is considerable. Are revivals a phenomenon of modernity also?

It seems that the answer is, mostly, yes. Professor M.E. Dieter has asserted with good reason that: 'Modern revival movements have their historical roots in Puritan–Pietistic reactions to the rationalism of the Enlightenment' (Dieter 1984). The isolated word 'Puritan' in that definition does not justify dragging our origins back to the Elizabethan period, let alone to the beginnings of the English Reformation, for Professor Dieter was clearly referring to the interaction of the later (especially American) Puritan tradition with Pietism and the Enlightenment – i.e. to the early eighteenth (and at the very earliest to the late seventeenth) century.

Most revivals before the twentieth century occurred in the various countries of Britain and North America: the Great Awakening in all of them; the Second Great Awakening in America; many localised revivals in nineteenth-century Wales; and the revival of 1859 in all of these countries. Professor W.R. Ward has helpfully drawn our attention to revivals elsewhere in Europe – and even as far afield as Siberia – under the influence of Germanic Pietism during the eighteenth century (Ward 1992, *passim*). The early nineteenth century also witnessed a revival in parts of Protestant Switzerland (Stunt 2000: chs 2–4).

Coming into the twentieth century, we note the Welsh Revival of 1904–5 (an event which, incidentally, still awaits a scholarly history), the Scandinavian awakenings in the following years (Orr 1973: ch. 7), and the Pentecostal revivals of the opening decades of the twentieth century. But the twentieth century is much more notable for the rapid advances of Christianity in sub-Saharan Africa, and for the huge progress of Pentecostalism in South America and parts of Asia. At least some of these took place against a background of little or no previous church attendance amongst the target populations, and so would not count as 'revivals' by some definitions, though I would wish to include them. Perhaps understandably, Edwin Orr judiciously referred to such events, especially in his exhaustive multi-volume coverage of them in the non-West, as 'Awakenings' rather than as revivals (Orr 1975–8).

Yet even Orr's coverage concerns itself almost exclusively with the nineteenth and twentieth centuries – that is, with the modern period. He thereby bears out our contention that as revivals (or awakenings) are associated almost exclusively, in practice, with Evangelicalism, so they are by the same token modern phenomena.

It will at once be objected that all of our criteria of 'revival' (except that which insists upon the background of a generally Christian population) are answered by the events of the Book of Acts. And that is hardly modern! Let Evangelicals be mollified, however, by the assurance that this is yet further evidence that their version of the faith is the one which most closely approximates to the biblical norms. The temporal lacuna between the early centuries and the eighteenth is so great precisely because the interim saw so few instances where promoters of a form of Christianity that was a reasonable approximation to the faith once delivered to the saints propagated that faith in a way that addressed the minds, wills and consciences of audiences who were free, if they wished, to reject their blandishments. Only in such circumstances, I would submit, can a revival ever happen.

These two conditions – orthodoxy and freedom – are a constant of all revivals. Distorted versions of Christianity might, theoretically, produce similar responses under certain conditions, but in general they have not. Efforts to spread the faith by force, such as the Crusades or other 'Christian' conquests, are unlikely to evoke an answering chord in the consciences of the target population: sullen acquiescence is the optimal response – and conviction, if it happens at all, will occur only after several generations. In the first generation, resentment is a more likely response than conviction of sin. And if the missionary movement's spread under the aegis of the British Empire is brought as an example against this contention, the answer must be the politically incorrect but factually accurate one that the increase in trade, the benefits (in Africa, at least) of literacy and the advantages of the Pax Britannica outweighed, in the minds of many if not of all, the vexations of alien rule. (In any case, most missionaries distanced themselves easily from the colonial authorities who, as often as not, resented their presence.) To reproduce the Book of Acts in the present, one needs broadly the same combination of elements in the message, and an audience that is free to say 'No'. Late antiquity aside, those conditions have only generally been met with in combination during the modern period.

Two Kinds of Revival

Until now, we have overlooked another crucial distinction in examining revivals, and one which is of the foremost importance in understanding our own situation. Most of the really turbulent historical events that answer to the description of 'revival' have been what we might call 'meeting-driven': conversions have been the response of listeners to preachers, or of participants in prayer and worship meetings. Our dominant image of the Great Awakening, or of the 1859 and 1904 Welsh revivals, or of the massive responses even today to Reinhard Bonnke's crusades, is of the towering figure of the preacher, declaiming about the horrid nature of sin, the judgement to come, a Saviour who loves sinners and died and rose again for them, and of the forgiveness and new life available at the foot of the Cross.

That dominant image is well justified. Not all who were – and are – converted in revivals experience a personal crisis in meetings, but most do so. The question arises as to how and why this should occur. For thousands upon thousands of ordinary people to see any purpose in attending Christian meetings they must, at an absolute minimum, inhabit a society in which Christian meetings are a commonplace. In such a society great swathes of the population – very likely including the putative converts themselves – profess Christianity in the first place, or are at least well acquainted with most of its central tenets. Christianity is unavoidably a meta-narrative (one of the reasons why it is so hard to promote in a postmodern society), and entire metanarratives are not gleaned and adhered to within the space of a forty-five-minute sermon, no matter how persuasive. The overwhelming majority of converts from meeting-driven revivals did – and do – inhabit societies which are already superficially Christianised or in which central Christian tenets are already widely accepted.

This is true of the day of Pentecost. Luke tells us that the hearers were all 'devout Jews' (Acts 2:5) and, as such, they would already have been aware of who God was, what the moral law was, and that they had transgressed it. They would have known who Jesus was, for he had been amongst them until only a short time before. As preacher, Peter's task was to remind them of what they already knew, and then give those facts a keen, evangelistically Christian gloss – and press the point home very hard indeed! The result? Bingo! Three thousand 'decisions'.

Reinhard Bonnke could hardly have asked for more. His own hearers are ready for him now. At the start of the twentieth century they would not have been, for Christian ideas would have seemed very strange to most of the population, and would have required extended explanation just to make sense, never mind to make a deep mental and moral impression. But Christianity (and here we include even superficial forms of it) is now widely dispersed south of the Sahara: when the evangelist speaks of God and Jesus, almost everyone knows – and very many already believe – what is meant.

In the 1960s the philosopher Ola Winslow edited a popular abridgement of the most important works of Jonathan Edwards. She included her own sagacious commentary on much of the material. Her remarks upon Edwards' famous sermon 'Sinners in the Hands of an Angry God' are extremely telling and worth quoting at length:

Two centuries and more later, it is still a grim sermon on the printed page, and delivered to a packed auditory under the strain of 1741, it was almost unbearable. What made it so was not only the earnestness of absolute belief for the speaker, as he painted the wrath of God, the pains of fire everlasting, the unending hopelessness of doom, but the fact that the congregation also believed it, ancestrally, as it were. The 'unsaved' among them had always intended to accept the terms of eternal safety, but as yet they had postponed the day. What Jonathan Edwards was doing as he turned page after page in the little booklet was to make this July Sunday, 1741, seem their last chance ...

Overwhelmed by this sense of immediacy of doom, no wonder strong men clung to the pillars of the meetinghouse and cried aloud for mercy. It was a scene that could not be reenacted in a later generation to whom these preachments would not spell unqualified certainty. Had the preacher confronted his congregation with a new doctrine, such terror could not have been induced. It was the familiar certainty that had won (Winslow 1966: xix–xx).

As I am in the habit of emphasising to my students, every class of whom includes one or two would-be revivalists who fantasise about driving strong men to clutch pillars, these teachings do not occupy the same status in their minds (that is, of the would-be preachers) as they did even to the listeners in 1741. Are we ungodlier than they? Very possibly, but the difference is mostly sociological: we hold these beliefs, if we do so at all, conscious that we are a cognitive minority. We think them true in spite of the fact that all of the organs of our society – schools, media, peers and governing authorities – scream at us day in and day out that it is all nonsense. For even the most ardent and godly among us, hellfire is a nagging worry: it can never be a 'familiar certainty'.

Jonathan Edwards' New Englanders are an extreme case, perhaps: a good proportion of them – or of their ancestors – had gone to live there precisely on account of their religious zeal. Even so, eighteenth-century London cutpurses, nineteenth-century Ceredigion farmhands and superficially Catholic Nicaraguans today all have a greater predisposal to think the words of the evangelist a likely approximation to the truth than do we who have been brought up to think of sexual restraint as practically immoral and dogmatic belief as tantamount to Fascism.

Consequently, Evangelicalism is easier to spread in (even superficially) Christian social milieux. Furthermore, when it does so, it may well be meeting-driven. Like the Jews on the day of Pentecost, many people require no more than a rhetorical nudge over the edge into 'decision'.

Inhabitants of societies like ours, however, where Christianity is marginal and its thought forms alien to that of the majority, require more. They require a longer acquaintance with the central Christian verities than they are likely to gain from an evangelistic sermon, no matter how well constructed or delivered. Emotional sensationalism – such as 'Toronto blessings' – may have a marginal effect, but in the absence of cognitive backup (that is, of familiarity with the principal Christian ideas) any 'conversions' elicited are likely to be very superficial and probably fleeting. Amongst the cutpurses' descendants, the unreflective awareness of Christian realities has been eroded almost to nothing, and replaced by its contraries. Greater time and exposure than that afforded by meeting-driven attempts at revival are required to counteract these disadvantages.

We now come to the central question raised by these considerations. Does this mean that societies where Christianity has become – or always has been – marginal, and where its chief ideas contradict common perceptions of 'common sense', cannot experience revival? I wish to argue 'No'.

Contemporary Britain and other woefully under-evangelised societies can indeed experience revival (or, *pace* certain tight definitions of that term, at least Orr's 'awakening'). But it will not look like the day of Pentecost, or like Jonathan Edwards' meeting room.

We mislead ourselves, as so often, by treating Scripture as a flat book, as if it has only one model to offer us. It has, of course, more than that. Peter's listeners on the day of Pentecost were all devout Jews, but Paul's audience at the Areopagus were nothing of the sort. The Hellenic intellectuals heard him out with ironic smiles until he spoke of the resurrection of the dead. At that point, their culturally conditioned 'common sense' was affronted, and many began to sneer. The best response Paul elicited that day was: 'We will hear you again about this' (Acts 17:32). Nevertheless, he succeeded in establishing a church there, as he did among other 'mere' pagans.

Well before the late first century, and on into the second and third, such evangelism accounted for the large majority, and eventually almost all, of the church's growth. Neither the day of Pentecost nor the later, smaller-scale versions in the synagogues of the Diaspora could be repeated among peoples who knew nothing of the Old Testament God. Growth was fast – certainly fast enough to qualify as a 'revival', or at least as an 'awakening' – but individual conversions were slow, drawn-out affairs, the result of hard graft, much explanation and much prayer by evangelists and other existing Christians.

The reason? New converts (or rather those in the process of becoming Christians) knew almost nothing of Christian faith and were suspicious of what they did know. (Does that sound familiar?) In consequence, many churches instituted 'catechising', a foundation of teaching and training in Christian behaviour (which latterly Alan Kreider has called 'rehabituating') that often lasted up to three years (Kreider 1994: 7–38).

Is it so startling that Alpha groups work better in our situation than do tent campaigns, or that 'Foundation' courses, or membership classes, have become again a frequent recourse of congregations seeking to protect themselves against uninformed mavericks demanding treatment and privileges on the same basis as known and trusted disciples? Alpha and Foundation courses do not amount to revival, of course, or to anything like it. They may or may not be useful as models in a revival situation. But they do confirm that we are, at least, on familiar ground. It makes sense to expect that conversions, in our circumstance, will happen over a long period of time. In 1967, 70 per cent of British Evangelicals could put a date on their crisis experience; now the large majority cannot. That is fine – as long as we are making sure that something (as opposed to nothing much) really has happened to the people coming into our churches!

China may be a very different country from contemporary Britain, but it has this much in common with it: its unconverted populace has little idea of what the gospel is all about, and so conversions will, mostly, be gradual. The difference is this: China is experiencing a revival ('awakening'), whilst Britain is not. Large numbers of people are becoming Christians in the most populous nation on earth, whilst the erstwhile home of revivals and the mother of the missionary movement is still stuck on the ground.

There may be many reasons for this situation, of course, and the last thing I wish to do is to propose yet one more simplistic 'solution' to our problem in a field where simplistic 'solutions' abound. But I would suggest this: our fixation with the meeting-driven model of revival, so entrenched in our Evangelical tradition by the experience of the eighteenth and nineteenth centuries, is causing us to put our energies, faith and expectations into something that cannot 'deliver'. By predicting 'revival this year' from some platform, or by urging us to yet more hysterical meetings in the expectation of revival somehow emerging from them, the faith of existing Christians is actually undermined, for the promised goal does not – cannot – arrive. It also misdirects, and so wastes, the spiritual and emotional energies of many good people. On both counts, it pushes revival further away, when we could be drawing it closer.

The super-spiritual put-down to this conclusion is precisely that: rhetoric. It may sound very superior to say that the arguments I have put forward here are somehow questioning the power of God, or the sovereignty of the Holy Spirit – and, of course, God can indeed do whatever he wants. If he wants a meeting-driven revival in a society where most unbelievers don't know their rear ends from their elbows, then undoubtedly he can do it. I observe merely that he does not, and historically has not. Rather, revivals in minimal-Christian-presence societies such as ours tend to come from the hard work, prayer and witnessing of the many, rather than from the high-profile pulpit declamations of the few.

The conclusion is as unwelcome to the slothful 'ordinary Christian' as it is to the would-be pulpit superstar and driver-to-pillar-clutching. But until we confront it I see no way ahead. Beyond that, however, if we do confront it and take steps accordingly, who knows what God might do?

References

Bercot, D.W. (1989). *Will the Real Heretics Please Stand Up?* Tyler: Scroll.

Dieter, M.E. (1984). Revivalism. In Elwell, W.A. (ed.) *Evangelical Dictionary of Theology*. Grand Rapids: Baker.

Elwell, W.A. (ed.) (1984). *Evangelical Dictionary of Theology*. Grand Rapids: Baker.

Kreider, A. (1994). Worship and Evangelism in Pre-Christendom. *Vox Evangelica* 24.

Orr, J.E. (1973). *The Flaming Tongue*. Chicago: Moody.

Orr, J.E. (1975–8). *Evangelical Awakenings* 5 Vols. Minneapolis: Bethany.

Stunt, T.C.F. (2000). *From Awakening to Secession*. Edinburgh: T&T Clark.

van den Bercken, W. (1999). *Holy Russia and Christian Europe*. London: SCM.

Ward, W.R. (1992). *The Protestant Evangelical Awakening*. Cambridge: Cambridge University Press.

Winslow, O. (ed.) (1966). *Jonathan Edwards: Basic Writings*. New York: Signet.

Part 3

The Contemporary Scene and Multidisciplinary Approaches

Chapter 11

'God came from Teman':
Revival and Contemporary Revivalism

Steve Latham

When I was an undergraduate in the 1970s my research project involved reading every issue of the *Church of England Newspaper* published in the 1950s. They contained many calls for revival – words I heard repeated some two decades later in my own church. In both periods the longing was never rewarded with realisation. There was more heat than light, more revivalism than revival.

Definitions

We need to distinguish between revival and revivalism: revivalism is the deliberate cultivation of and preparation for revival. I aim to clarify the meaning of the term 'revival' as used by revivalists and examine the social context of contemporary revivalism.

History has seen many revivals in Christianity: Anglo-Catholicism and the social gospel, for example. These are not revival in our sense. 'Revivalism' is specifically an Evangelical phenomenon, a resurgence of that form of conservative Protestantism associated with personal faith in Christ (Edwards 1990: 27). Evangelicals recognise that revival is not a biblical term, but claim the phenomenon is described in Scripture (Ortlund 2000: 7).

Evangelicals see revival as God's activity (Edwards 1990: 29): a visitation or manifestation of his presence (Wallis 1979: 14). The term, however, is used in different senses. I identify six levels in the understanding of revival, each gradually expanding in scope, and acknowledge my debt to Andrew Walker for the form they take.

R1:   a spiritual quickening of the individual believer.

R2:   a deliberate meeting or campaign especially among Pentecostals to deepen the faith of believers and bring non-believers to faith.

R3:   an unplanned period of spiritual enlivening in a local church, quickening believers and bringing unbelievers to faith.

R4:   a regional experience of spiritual quickening and widespread conversions, e.g. the Welsh, Hebridean, East African and Indonesian revivals, and possibly Pensacola in the 1990s.

R5:   Societal or cultural 'awakenings', e.g. the transatlantic First and Second Awakenings.

R6:   the possible reversal of secularisation and 'revival' of Christianity as such.

Distinctions

I am not original in describing different understandings of revival. Revivalists themselves distinguish true from false definitions. Brian Mills, former Secretary for Prayer and Revival at the Evangelical Alliance, wrote that revival did not mean charismatic renewal, evangelism, meetings or an organisation, but the Holy Spirit's outpouring, primarily to revive Christians and secondarily to convert non-Christians (Mills 1990: 24–6). Similarly, supporters of the Toronto Blessing debated whether it was revival, renewal or a refreshing. Prophetic minister Rick Joyner said that the Toronto Blessing was only a 'bridge to revival' because it lacked mass conversions (Joyner 1998: 1–4).

My analysis, however, is a phenomenological typology that lays alternative senses alongside each other. Revival is a tensive symbol embodying desirable outcomes for different sectors of Evangelicalism. In practice the meaning is slippery. Revivalists slide easily from one level to another in a confusion of semiotic codes in which the gap between speaker and hearers can result in a message about R2 being understood as implying R5. For example, while a preacher may say that revival [R2] is happening 'tonight', listeners may think he or she means a reversal of Christian decline [R6]. Hopes are perhaps unintentionally inflated. Evangelicals eagerly desiring worldwide revival may discern it within the smallest spiritual infusion. This we can see in responses to the Toronto Blessing during the 1990s, and in the way the Great Awakening itself was 'invented' by revivalists who saw Jonathan Edwards' *particular revival* [R3] in Northampton as the harbinger of *general revival* [R5] (Lambert 2000).

Time Waves

Another aspect of revivals is their short-lived nature. Mills maintains that, as God's means of rescuing a moribund church, revival cannot last into the next generation because it depends on direct spiritual experience. A lessening of the initial impulse is bound to institutionalise it or reduce its vitality (Mills 1990: 38 ff.). Waves of revivalism therefore are not merely faddism but revivalism's essence. Especially within Pentecostalism, the weakening of the anointing requires periodic outpourings to re-energise the movement, a Weberian transmission of charisma which counters routinisation (M. Hill 1973: 175).

We need a Kondratieff theory of 'long waves' to explain the general topology of revivalism (R1–6) and the lesser fractals of local revivals (R1–4). Today's dilemma, however, arises from the absence of any fresh Californian-induced transatlantic wave. As Christian decline in Europe continues, the strength of succeeding waves gets lesser, not greater. If there are movements, they are 'waves' of programmatic teaching (Alpha or Cell Church, for example), not of spiritual renewal.

Catholic experience of revivalist spiritual movements is different. Here, the chief distinction is between those remaining in the church (for example Focalare and charismatic renewal), and those that are not containable (Gérest 1973). Peter Hocken suggests that Catholics prefer the term *renewal* to *revival*, because while Protestantism stresses discontinuity in the Spirit's work, Catholicism emphasises its continuity with hierarchy and tradition (Hocken 1995).

Variables

Sometimes it seems people simply have lower standards. I remember hearing Dale Gentry at Marsham Street and Roberts Liardon in Bromley saying that revival was happening 'tonight'. At a service conducted by my worship leaders and myself, many people came forward for prayer. My leaders exclaimed that it was 'nearly revival'! Rather than lower standards, however, they unconsciously adopted the R3 model, whereas I cautiously reserved the term for

R5. Higher levels are distinguished by 'atmospheric revival' where a whole community is transformed (Dunn 1992: 222).

Another variable is the time scale. R5 takes longer: 100 years for the Evangelical Awakening and 300 years for the conversion of the Anglo-Saxons (Mayr-Harting 1990). Instead of short evangelistic campaigns, this requires long-term *Kulturkampf* to ascend the commanding heights of the cultural and intellectual economy and control the hegemonic ideology.

Further variation arises from the importation of revivalists' pet interests. We make revival in our own image. Hence I.D.E. Thomas's study of revival reflected the Welsh holiness tradition, dictating his restriction of church membership to the regenerate rather than an Erastian mixed church (Thomas 1997: 151–2). Similarly, Arthur Wallis, at the high water mark of restorationism, insisted that revival is incomplete without apostolic church government (Wallis 1979: 120).

An additional variable, in part shaped by eschatology, is our place on the optimism–pessimism continuum. Hopes for world-wide revival [R5–6] are greater among Postmillennialists than Premillennialists. Paradoxically, both reformed writer Iain Murray (Murray 1971: 39 ff.) and restorationist Arthur Wallis look to Scripture's as-yet-unfulfilled prophecies to overturn a pessimistic 'eschatology of disaster' (Wallis 1979: 6).

Optimism–pessimism also has social influences. The United Kingdom may be more pessimistic because of our experience of long-term decline; the United States' pragmatic 'can-do' attitude appears more optimistic. Hence church historian Richard Riss cites many twentieth-century North American examples of revival (including Pentecostalism, the healing and Latter Rain movements, the Jesus movement and charismatic renewal) (Riss 1988). Where the British look for R5 or R6 to reverse secularisation, Riss's acceptance of lower numbers resembles R3 and R4 (Riss 1998: 6–7). The current greying of American Boomer churchgoers will probably undermine this cultural optimism (Sine 1991: 145–70).

Conflict

Another reason Riss recognises more revivals is because, unlike reformed commentators, he welcomes Pentecostal/charismatic spirituality. 'Revival' is a contested term. Current disagreements between reformed and charismatic revivalists echo the division in attitudes toward the First and Second Awakenings.

Charles Finney is the lightning rod for this controversy. Opposing a rigid Calvinist dependence on God's sovereign decision in sending revival, he favoured an Arminian reliance on human agency to cause revival (Finney 1928). In actual fact, he mainly relied on prayer meetings as the God-appointed method of working up revival. These are still regarded as the 'secret' of revival (Dunn 1992: 218), and Michael Brown views the prayer movements of the 1980s and 1990s as precursors to the Toronto and Pensacola revivals (Brown 1996: 18).

Although Mills describes Calvinists praying as if revival depended on them and Arminians interceding as if God is sovereign (Mills 1990: 33), Calvinists generally oppose Finney's activist revivalism and its charismatic continuations. Theologian David Wells exemplifies the reformed critique of contemporary Evangelicalism, attacking Finney's surrender to human agency and emotional experientialism as a compromise with modernity and the market, and a sacrifice of transcendent depth to immanent breadth (Wells 1994: 65–8, 129).

Some charismatics are uneasy about recent revival trends. This can be seen as a generational conflict or denominational competition in an ecumenical–economic marketplace, with each renewal wave resisting the next. Hence Pentecostals were suspicious of mainstream charismatics in the 1960s, and earlier charismatics rejected restorationism, Wimber's Third Wave and the 1980s prophetic movement. Rick Joyner, a supporter of contemporary revivalism, saw prophetic conflict as territorial (Joyner 1995: 31), and predicted a 'civil war' in the church over what he saw as this new move of God (Joyner 1996: 1–8).

Phenomena

The Toronto 'phenomena' (falling, laughing, animal noises, etc.) epitomise the problem of emotionalism, so much so that in Christian bookshops the revival shelves are mostly dedicated to charismatic renewal. This led to a new apologetic for traditional revivalism, sans phenonema; hence, perhaps, the re-publication of Thomas's book. American pastor Bill Randles' polemic dismissed Toronto as a 'mystical revival' (Randles 1995: 57). In this he followed Benjamin

Warfield's attack on spiritual experientialism as a symptom of Catholic mysticism (Warfield 1988: 649 ff.).

Brian Edwards tried to be objective in his study of revivalism, acknowledging that charismatic experiences do occur. But in practice he was clearly unhappy with extremism, insisting that 'error, excess and the unusual' were not compulsory (Edwards 1990: 196). As with many reformed Christians, his discomfort expressed a restrained Apollonian emphasis on worship as liturgy, in contrast to a Dionysian stress on celebration and exuberance (Roberts 1990: 228).

Edwards' insistence on the supernatural origins of revival also explains his reluctance to acknowledge any psychological or sociological explanations (Edwards 1990: 217). By contrast, charismatics welcomed complementary perspectives. For example, Patrick Dixon (Dixon 1994: 233 ff.) and Mark Stibbe (Stibbe 1995: 71 ff.) deployed theories of altered states of consciousness to justify visions and trances.

In America, Christian apologist Hank Hanegraaff led the reaction to what he called the 'counterfeit revival'. According to Hanegraaff, the manipulation of contemporary revivalism needed to be replaced by a 'reformation' of true doctrine (Hanegraaff 1997: 17). As I heard during a discussion about Toronto L'Abri, the search for 'something more' threatens conservative Evangelicals' confidence in the finished work of Christ on the Cross.

Prophecy

With Clifford Hill the disagreement over revival turns into prophetic conflict. In 1990 the Kansas City Prophets gained prominence within John Wimber's Association of Vineyard churches. They predicted that in October 1990 there would be revival in Britain. Wimber brought them over for a conference in the London Docklands Arena, which he hoped would kick-start the revival.

Clifford Hill as a self-styled prophet warned the Kansas City Prophets against coming, and with the non-arrival of the revival he denounced them as false prophets.[1] When the Toronto Blessing spread, he condemned it as the fruition of the apostasy which the prophets had introduced (C. Hill 1995). Paradoxically, Hill

---

[1] Interview with the author 6 September 1996.

had earlier been an enthusiast of revival while he worked for the Evangelical Alliance (C. Hill 1980: 180). By the late 1990s, however, he had come to believe that, instead of revival, Britain faced divine judgement. After the death of the Princess of Wales, the dispute produced two 'Diana prophecies': one circulated by Gerald Coates predicting revival (Coates 1997), the other given by Hill threatening judgement (C. Hill 1997).

Much current revivalism is a form of prophetic Pelagianism, an oracular extension of Finney's methods. Revival predictions encourage hearers to work for revival and thence themselves to fulfil the prophecy. Prophetic revivalism is therefore popular in Arminian groups such as Gerald Coates' Pioneer network. His prayer meetings in Westminster at Marsham Street in 1997 were an attempt to spark off revival, a potential transition from R2 to R4 or R5.

Such activist revivalism, however, must sit uneasily with reformed charismatics who also seek revival. Although Clifford Hill tried to form a reformed Charismatic network to counter false revivalism, Terry Virgo's New Frontiers International has explored both Calvinist and charismatic extremes.

Dissonance

There is a danger of disappointment with prophetic revivalism if revival does not materialise. Leon Festinger has analysed the failure of prophecy in the case of the Jehovah's Witnesses, and the cognitive dissonance as they sought to explain the parousia's non-occurrence (Festinger, Riecken and Schachter 1956). Cognitive dissonance can also be seen in the key players' reactions to the 1990 Docklands debacle.

Mike Bickle, leader of the Kansas City Fellowship, saw the controversy as a sign of divine discipline (Bickle 1995: 91), but Wimber maintained that Paul Cain had predicted merely 'tokens' of revival (Wimber 1991: 27). David Pytches, who introduced the Kansas City Prophets to Britain, proffered three possible explanations: the prophets could have been wrong; the revival might have been prevented by opposition; or perhaps the Docklands conference birthed other new developments, such as the Alpha course.[2]

---

[2] Interview with the author 18 October 1996.

Patrick Dixon simply sees the 1990 failure as unimportant. For him, the positive spin-offs were more significant (Dixon 1994: 88). The issue cannot be dismissed, however, because revival prophecies are still given. Bill Bright, leader of Campus Crusade, in 1995 prophesied that America would see a national [R4–5] revival in 2000 (Bright 1995).

Cognitive dissonance raises the question again of definition. Gerald Coates is a 'glass-half-full' man, seeing the positive signs of revival rather than negative contra-indicators (Coates 1998: 4–8). In contrast, Colin Dye, leader of Kensington Temple, appears to have had a cold shower of realism. Although still advocating revival, Dye has been persuaded by statistics of freefalling church attendance that revival is a long-term prospect (Dye 2000).

Context

Contextual factors also affect revivalism. In America, church attendance rose after World War II. In part, this mild R5 revival was due to a re-establishment of societal norms after the dislocation of war. In Britain, apart from R2 revivalism associated with Billy Graham's campaigns, church growth was only a temporary and local halt to R6 secularisation.

In the 1980s Reaganism and Thatcherism coincided with a resurgence of state authoritarianism and individualistic entrepreneurialism. The consequent revival of confidence in the power of individuals to effect change and a new cold war had ecclesiastical counterparts in the popularity of church growth and church planting. By 1990 not only charismatics but also conservative Evangelicals like Brian Mills and Brian Edwards were writing optimistically about revival.

By the mid-1990s this revivalism of hope had turned into a revivalism of despair. Instead of seeing revival as a product of hopeful trends, Evangelicals reached out for revival as a solution for failure. The Toronto Blessing in 1994, therefore, was welcomed as a sovereign outpouring in contrast to disastrous human attempts at organising evangelism, such as JIM (Jesus in Me) and Minus to Plus. Like Trotsky's over-predictions of revolution, 1990s revivalism was a clutching at straws, the construction of a *deus ex cultura* to reverse secularisation's inexorable march.

Politics

Some of revivalism's confusion arises from an identification of nation and church that lends itself to right-wing politics. This is encouraged by the use of Old Testament examples of revival, such as Edwards' reference to Hezekiah, in which the restoration of Yahwism is as much political as religious. Consequently, revivalism often becomes a plea for national greatness. Applied to a nation state, such rhetoric distorts its primary application to the people of God, equated in the Old Testament with the combined nation church of Israel but in the New Testament identified with the international church of God.

This accounts for the ironic situation in which previously Nonconformist minister Clifford Hill advocates an Erastian revival of the state church and the monarchy as bastions against a multi-faith society and a Catholic plot to rule the European Community (C. Hill 1995). In America revivalism underpins civil religion. This underlies Bill Bright's call for national revival in America, based on the idea of the United States as a covenant nation under God. In the current clash of civilisations between America and Islam, this civil theology could prompt a national(ist) revival.

Even where revivalism does not directly support the political right, its anti-political quietism frequently relegates faith to a privatised sphere with little political relevance. Many of revivalism's much-vaunted social results are moral (combating drunkenness, swearing, etc.) rather than tackling structural evils. Significant changes, like abolishing slavery, were due more to long-term campaigning led by Evangelical parliamentarians and slave uprisings led by Baptist deacons than to revivalism as such.

Some Evangelicals have therefore tried to rescue revival as a symbol from the right. In the 1980s Jim Wallis, founder of the Sojourners Community in Washington DC, called for a revival to unite Evangelicals against nuclear arms and American foreign policy (Wallis 1983: 124). In Britain, Methodist minister Jack Burton advocated a revival free from fundamentalism and opposed to Thatcherism (Burton 1995). South African activist Graham Cyster talked of a 'contextual revival' in which God would send what the context needed: if justice he would send justice, if healing then healing.[3] Of obvious relevance to South Africa, this illustrates

---

[3] Personal conversation with the author.

the way in which 'revival' is an ideological construct, a terrain of conflict which opposing ecclesiastical factions try to capture.

Capitalism

Revivalism is often seen as a movement of the poor. Today, however, the chiliasm of despair has been replaced by a Millenarianism of affluence. Instead of landless peasants or dispossessed urbanites, contemporary revivalism occurs among rich middle-class Westerners (those who frequent Holy Trinity Brompton, for example). Here, experiences of the Spirit are add-ons to their affluent lifestyle. Contemporary revivalism is a cultural expression of advanced capitalism, in its internal and external effects.

Internally, revivalism is consumerist. Adherents shop around for a religious equivalent to the marketisation of experience in the wider economy, where retail outlets provide an 'experience' to encourage return custom. Charismatic revivalism provides emotional release for those who have made it up the greasy pole of techno-capitalist society at the expense of their psychic dislocation (Hervieu-Léger 1993: 144).

Externally, contemporary revivalism spreads by utilising advanced means of communication such as the Internet and television. As news is transmitted, like all advertising, it creates increased demand for the product. However, the use of technology is not wholly novel. Christian revivals always exploit the newest developments: roads under Rome, the printing press with the Reformation, international shipping during the Great Awakening.

Society

Contemporary revivalism contradicts the widespread belief, echoed by Os Guinness, that revival cannot happen in modern, technological, urban society (Guinness and Seel 1992: 10). Classical revivals are said to have occurred in the Celtic fringes (Wales, the Hebrides) or the colonial edges (East Africa, Indonesia) of modernity: the periphery, not the metropolis. But this is only true for R4–6 revivals. Certainly, Europe has not seen regional revivals, cultural awakenings or a reversal of secularisation. But R1–R3 revivals proliferate at local level.

Because of institutional differentiation and the decline of religion's role as a legitimating ideology in the West, higher levels of revival are unlikely. Laurence Singlehurst, head of Youth with a Mission in the United Kingdom, advances another reason for the absence of revival. Typically, he says, revivals occur in societies where people have many face-to-face relationships, whereas cities today promote impersonal encounters. Consequently, news of someone's conversion does not spread in the same way through a local community (Singlehurst 2001: 44).

Singlehurst therefore advocates Cell churches to overcome urban anonymity by intentionally forming smaller relationship networks. He also suggests, however, that in postmodern, multi-cultural cities revivals are likely to be restricted to sub-cultures, whether middle-class Holy Trinity Brompton members or Nigerian Pentecostal migrants. In addition, as the centres of ideological hegemonic influence become more independent of ecclesiastical control, revivals will increasingly be characteristic of the sociological and ideological margins of the *oppidus*, not its centre.

Postmodernity

Postmodernity witnesses the re-enchantment of the world, the resurgence of religion. Typically, this occurs in the aestheticism of exotic Orthodox liturgy or kitsch Catholicism, but perhaps Pentecostalism will soon become fashionable? This would not mean the end of secularisation in the West, in so far as it refers to the end of the church's dominant ideological position. It does, however, imply the reversibility of enlightenment, perhaps improving the soil for R3–R5 revivals.

Modernity excluded the transcendent and produced an iso-phrenic flattening of experience. In response, fundamentalist religion, including revivalism, seeks to precipitate a reversal through extreme means, whether religious terrorism or prophetic pronouncements (Baudrillard 1996: 17). In this, however, revival-ism risks becoming virtual, the hype of a hyper-real simulacrum of revival, where revival will not happen because it has already happened in anticipation (Baudrillard 1992) – a spectro-revival (Derrida 1994).

In this form, revivalism represents nostalgia for Christendom, a necrophiliac idolatry. Instead, we need a *neo-vival*, embracing the new thing God does. We cannot expect a return to the identification of church and nation. Revival will remain located within a hostile society. Even the supposed deprivatisation of religion amounts to little more than the absorption of Christianity into pressure group politics within pluralistic society (Casanova 1994: 5). Wiser revivalists, like Argentinean Ed Silvoso, recognise that revival should not lead to Christian political control, but will coincide with continued social disintegration as the world slips inexorably to its demise (Silvoso 1994: 71).

Pietism

Revivalism may be seen as a new social movement opposing the colonisation of the lifeworld by marketisation (Habermas 1981). Leonard Ravenhill wrote in the 1950s that revival tarried in part because of commercialism within the church (Ravenhill 1972: 13). Here, Pietism reveals its counter-cultural potential. Its anti-worldly asceticism challenges the ideology of consumption.

For example, Pensacola, originating from Pentecostalism rather than the charismatic movement, differed from Toronto largely through its emphasis on repentance. This message could undercut the pleasure principle of late capitalist religion. Not the recovery of religion's public role by the hierarchy but precisely the popular subjective experientialism slated by sophisticated intellectuals could overcome Christianity's irrelevance.

Revivalism's radical potential is more likely to be seen among the marginalised poor of the Third World or migrants in the cities of the First World. Urban theologian Ray Bakke writes that the 'Empire strikes back' as the colonised flow from the periphery to the centre (Bakke 1997: 178). The danger is of the immigrant church's passionate pre-critical naïvety becoming acculturated to the host community's cynicism.

Spiritual hunger is the main condition for experiencing revival (Smith n.d.) and this hunger is what affluence denies. In the intensity of urban experience (Brook and Pain 1999: 42), however, the recovery of ecstasy, the *ek-stasis* of those who are literally *en-theos* (enthusiastic), may be a way to break through apathy (Stibbe 1995). As Dupré notes, corporate faith needs 'intense and deliberate' personal experience to survive in pluralistic societies that undermine its legitimacy (Dupré 1998: 143).

Breakthrough

Cox has written that Pentecostalism's bodily-mediated experience of God represents the future of postmodern Christianity (Cox 1996: 64). As Mannheim observed, even in quietist mode enthusiastic religion threatens rationalistic political and ecclesiastical control (Mannheim 1936: 213). Wright dismisses revival phenomena as merely human responses to the divine (Smail, Walker and Wright 1995: 152), but we need a more nuanced approach to spiritual experience.

Rahner's theology of signs describes spiritual experience as the mediation of immediacy, whereby the transcendent is authentically communicated through the immanent while being simultaneously shaped by psychological or sociological factors (Rahner 1966: 244). As Tillich wrote, our historical experience of the New Being is ambiguous (Tillich 1978: 162–82). Hence revival is always a mixture of flesh and spirit. An unmediated revival is a docetic revival.

Revival dwells in 'excess' (Webb 1983). We need the fire. From flirting with sociological relativism, we must adopt Tertullian's intellectual impossibilism, welcoming the Montanist Spirit exploding among the marginalised. God is on the edge. He comes from Teman, the desert (Habakkuk 3:3). Revival breaks out in society's unregulated zones: its cracks, interstices and seams. The unlikeliest places – secular England, perhaps?

Unfulfilled prophecy gives us at least permission to hope that the earth will one day be full of the knowledge of the glory of the Lord. What is that other than revival? It is a question of eschatology; what Moltmann called 'expectation thinking' (Moltmann 1967: 35). And this is a matter for prophecy. Ravenhill claimed that revival waits for the prophet to declare God's purposes and awaken expectancy (Ravenhill 1972: 26). Our capacity to imagine the transcendent, to dream, to envision may be diminished in our mediatised society. But God uses the prophet to speak his word to the powers of the domination system, and to herald the new creation (Wink 1992: 7).

References

Bakke, R. (1997). *A Theology as Big as a City*. Downers Grove: IVP.

Baudrillard, J. (1992). *The Illusion of the End*. Cambridge: Cambridge University Press.

Baudrillard, J. (1996). *Cool Memories II*. Durham, North Carolina: Duke University Press.

Bickle, M. (1995). *Growing in the Prophetic*. Eastbourne: Kingsway.

Bright, B. (1995). *The Coming Revival. America's Call to Fast, Pray, and 'Seek God's Face'*. Orlando: New Life.

Brook, C. and Pain, K. (eds) (1999). *City Themes*. Milton Keynes: The Open University.

Brown, M.L. (1996). *From Holy Laughter to Holy Fire: America on the Edge of Revival*. Shippensburg: Destiny Image.

Burton, J. (1995). *England Needs a Revival*. London: SCM Press.

Casanova, J. (1994). *Public Religions in the Modern World*. Chicago/London: University of Chicago Press.

Coates, G. (1997). *A Call to Pray for the Nation*. Cobham: Pioneer.

Coates, G. (1998). Revival? Revival? What Revival? *Spread the Fire* 4.5: 4–8.

Cox, H. (1996). *Fire from Heaven: The Rise of Pentecostal Spirituality and the Reshaping of Religion in the Twenty-first Century*. London: Cassell.

Derrida, J. (1994). *Specters of Marx*. New York/London: Routledge.

Dixon, P. (1994). *Streams of Revival*. Eastbourne: Kingsway.

Dunn, R. (1992). *Don't Just Stand There ... Pray something!* Amersham-on-the-hill: Scripture Press.

Dupré, L. (1998). *Religious Mystery and Rational Reflection*. Grand Rapids: Eerdmans.

Dye, C. (2000). A Nation without God. *Revival Times* 2 (2), February.

Edwards, B.H. (1990). *Revival! A People Saturated with God*. Darlington: Evangelical Press.

Festinger, L., Riecken, H.W. and Schachter, S. (1956). *When Prophecy Fails*. Minneapolis: University of Minnesota Press.

Finney, C.G. (1928). *Revivals of Religion*. London/Edinburgh: Oliphants.

Gérest, C. (1973). Spiritual Movements and Ecclesial Institutions: An Historical Outline. *Concilium* 9.9: 37–57.

Guinness, O. and Seel, J. (eds) (1992). *No God but God: Breaking with the Idols of our Age*. Chicago: Moody Press.

Habermas, J. (1981). New Social Movements. *Telos* 49: 33–7.

Hanegraaff, H. (1997). *Counterfeit Revival*. Dallas: Word.

Hervieu-Léger, D. (1993). Present-Day Emotional Renewals: The End of Secularization or the End of Religion? In Swatos, W.H. (ed.) *A Future for Religion? New Paradigms for Social Analysis*. Newbury Park/London/Delhi: Sage.

Hill, C. (1980). *Towards the Dawn: What's Going to Happen to Britain?* Glasgow: Fount.

Hill, C. (1995). *Shaking the Nations.* Eastbourne: Kingsway.

Hill, C., Fenwick, P., Forbes, D. and Noakes, D. (1995). *Blessing the Church? A Review of the History and Direction of the Charismatic Movement.* Guildford: Eagle.

Hill, C. (1997). Diana Princess of Wales. *Prophecy Today* 13.6: 35.

Hill, M. (1973). *A Sociology of Religion.* London: Heinemann.

Hocken, P. (1995). Renewal and Revival: A Catholic Perspective on the Toronto Blessing. *Good News* 117:18–19.

Joyner, R. (1995). *Epic Battles of the Last Days.* Charlotte: MorningStar.

Joyner, R. (1996). Civil War in the Church. *The MorningStar Prophetic Bulletin* May: 1–8.

Joyner, R. (1998). A Bridge to Revival. *The MorningStar Prophetic Bulletin* January: 1–4.

Lambert, F. (2000). *Inventing the 'Great Awakening'.* Princeton/Oxford: Princeton University Press.

Mannheim, K. (1936). *Ideology and Utopia.* London: Routledge & Kegan Paul.

Mayr-Harting, H. (1990). *The Coming of Christianity to Anglo-Saxon England.* University Park: Pennsylvania State University Press.

Mills, B. (1990). *Preparing for Revival.* Bromley: STL/Eastbourne: Kingsway.

Moltmann, J. (1967). *Theology of Hope.* London: SCM.

Murray, I.H. (1971). *The Puritan Hope: Revival and the Interpretation of Prophecy.* Edinburgh: Banner of Truth.

Ortlund Jr, R.C. (2000). *Revival Sent from God: What the Bible Teaches for the Church Today.* Leicester: IVP.

Rahner, K. (1966). *Theological Investigations* Vol. 4. London: Darton, Longman & Todd.

Randles, B. (1995). *Weighed and Found Wanting: The Toronto Experience Examined in the Light of the Bible.* Cambridge: St Matthew.

Ravenhill, L. (1972). *Why Revival Tarries.* Carlisle: STL.

Riss, R. (1988). *A Survey of 20th-Century Revival Movements in North America.* Peabody: Hendrickson.

Riss, R. (1998). Renewal or Revival? *Spread the Fire* 4.1: 6–7.

Roberts, K. (1990). *Religion in Sociological Perspective.* Belmont: Wadsworth.

Silvoso, E. (1994). *That None Should Perish.* Ventura: Regal.

Sine, T. (1991). *Wild Hope.* Dallas: Word.

Singlehurst, L. (2001). *Loving the Lost: The Principles and Practice of Cell Church.* Eastbourne: Kingsway.

Smail, T., Walker, A. and Wright, N., (1995²). *Charismatic Renewal: The Search for a Theology.* London: SPCK.

Smith, O. (n.d.). *Hunger for Revival.* Carlisle: STL.

Stibbe, M. (1995). *Times of Refreshing: A Practical theology of Renewal for Today*. London: Marshall Pickering.

Thomas, I. D. E. (1997). *God's Harvest: The Nature of True Revival*. Bryntirion, Bridgend: Gwang Bryntirion Press.

Tillich, P. (1978). *Systematic Theology* Vol. 3. London: SCM.

Wallis, A. (1979). *Rain From Heaven: Revivals in Scripture and Heaven*. London: Hodder & Stoughton.

Wallis, J. (1983). *The New Radical*. Tring: Lion.

Warfield, B.B. (1988). *Studies in Theology*. Edinburgh: Banner of Truth.

Webb, S.H. (1983). *Blessed Excess: Religion and the Hyperbolic Imagination*. Albany: University of New York Press.

Wells, D.F. (1994). *God in the Wasteland. The Reality of Truth in a World of Fading Dreams*. Grand Rapids/Leicester: Eerdmans/IVP.

Wimber, J. (1991). Revival Fire. *Renewal* 184: 27.

Wink, W. (1992) *Engaging the Powers*. Minneapolis: Fortress Press.

Chapter 12

Revival: Empirical Aspects

William Kay

Introduction

This chapter describes the mainly rural Welsh Revival and the mainly urban Azusa Street Revival and then analyses their empirical aspects, subjecting them to sociological and psychological reflection.

Welsh Revival

By the end of the nineteenth century Wales had been industrialised. By 1880 between a quarter and a third of the male labour force of Wales worked in the coal industry; this number rose to about a half when those working in the railways and docks were added in. Unionism grew. From the same date, national identity was fostered, partly by the educational campaigns of Lloyd George, and produced a pressure for home rule, disestablishment of the Anglican Church and for increased use of the Welsh language (Davies 1994: 468, 473). Welsh Nonconformity, or 'chapel', was at the heart of village life and responsive to preaching, especially in the Welsh language.

The Welsh Revival of 1904–5 has been traced back to various people.[1] Evans (1987) considers that two men, Seth Joshua and Joseph Jenkins, really prepared the ground. Seth Joshua was a travelling evangelist who held missions all over Wales. His engagements

---

[1] Both Jessie Penn-Lewis and F.B. Meyer claimed credit for it (Evans 1987: 168ff.).

were usually centred on a congregation that was attempting an outreach into its community. Although in the summer of 1904 he attended a convention in Llandrindod Wells modelled on the lines of the interdenominational gatherings at Keswick, he was, as an evangelist, unimpressed by Keswick teaching on the grounds that it appeared to cultivate holiness 'at the expense of service' (Evans 1987: 52). There is no evidence that Joshua became a holiness preacher rather than an evangelistic one as a result of a single brief exposure to the Keswick doctrine of 'holiness by faith'.

Joseph Jenkins was the minister of the Calvinistic Methodist church at New Quay, on the western coast of Wales in Cardiganshire. Concerned about the spiritual state of his young people, he arranged a series of meetings to deepen their devotional life. Seth Joshua preached there on 18 September 1904, by which time there were already evidences of renewal. Soon after these meetings Joshua recorded in his diary that 'the revival is breaking out here in greater power' and that young people were 'breaking into prayer, praise, testimony and exhortation in a wonderful way ... they are entering into full assurance of faith coupled with the baptism in the Holy Spirit. The joy is intense' (Evans 1987: 59).

Joshua spoke the next week at Blaenannerch, about fifteen miles south-west and slightly inland. Among those attending was Evan Roberts, who had just started training for the Calvinistic Methodist ministry at its ministerial school in Newcastle Emlyn. Roberts (1878–1951) was a determined and single-minded young man who frequently prayed for many hours at night. He was affected and agitated by the preaching he heard and fired with determination. He returned to Newcastle Emlyn, but was unable to settle down to his studies, and so intensified his nights of prayer that by 10 October he was considering leaving his training to launch immediately into ministry. He described his experiences of prayer in this way:

> One night last spring, while praying by my bedside before retiring, I was taken up to a great expanse, without time or space. It was communion with God. Before this I had had a far off God. I was frightened that night, but never since ... from that hour I was taken into the divine fellowship for about four hours ... this went on for about three months (Bartleman 1980: 34, Evans 1987: 66).

He went home by train, a journey of fifty miles, on 31 October, after being given permission by the minister to speak (in Welsh) at the weekly prayer meeting at the Loughor Chapel where he grew up.

A youth meeting followed the prayer meeting and seventeen people attended. After protracted appeals and descriptions of what was happening in New Quay, all seventeen responded. The following night, Roberts preached again, as he also did on 1, 2, 3 and 4 November in nearby chapels, and on each occasion the congregation made confessions of faith.

Roberts taught four things: (1) past sin must be confessed; (2) any doubtful elements in the lives of Christians should be removed; (3) Christians must give themselves entirely to the Holy Spirit; (4) public confession of Christ must be made. On 4 November he received a vision of the white and red horses of the Book of Revelation during the meeting. This vision confirmed to him that the revival would triumph across the whole of Wales. He continued to preach locally each night. On 9 November the meeting, this time in a Congregational chapel, lasted eight hours and ended 'with scenes of wild jubilation' (Evans 1987: 91). By now newspapers were showing an interest, and the first report of Roberts' meetings appeared in the *Western Mail* on 12 November 1904. The account stated:

> Instead of the set order of proceedings to which we are accustomed at the orthodox religious service, everything here was left to the spontaneous impulse of the moment. The preacher, too, did not remain in his usual seat. For the most part he walked up and down the aisles, open Bible in hand, exhorting one, encouraging another, and kneeling with a third to implore a blessing from the throne of grace. A young woman rose to give out a hymn, which was sung with deep earnestness. While it was being sung several people dropped down in their seats as if they had been struck, and commenced crying for pardon. Then from another part of the chapel could be heard the resonant voice of a young man reading a portion of Scripture.

This had the effect of publicising the meetings so that when, on Saturday 12 November, a letter arrived in Loughor asking for a Sunday preacher in Aberdare, thirty-five miles to the east, Roberts replied affirmatively by telegram. Anticipation grew and excitement spread. Meanwhile, other preachers were also holding meetings, some along the informal lines established by Roberts and others with more formal preaching and teaching. Roberts had written to his friend Sidney Evans, who had remained in the New Quay area, with the instructions to 'establish revival meetings there. Call all the denominations together. Explain the "four conditions"; and at the end of the meeting let all who have confessed Christ

remain behind' where they were to pray for the sending of the Holy
Spirit 'more powerfully now' (Evans 1987: 99). Similar revivalism
occurred in Carmarthen and Ammanford (about thirty miles north
of Loughor), where Seth Joshua reported that, on 19 November
when he held meetings, 'to my surprise the chapel was filled with
people ... there is a wonderful fire burning here'.

Evan Roberts was in the Rhondda valley, about fifty miles east of
Loughor, at the end of the first week of December. The valley was
poor and 70 per cent of the male workforce were miners (Davies
1994: 471). Even before his visit, 600 people had professed conversion. Reporters from London were by now interested in the phenomenon and filed copy saying that the meetings were 'absolutely
without any human direction or leadership'. Describing the pattern,
it was said that:

> the meetings open – after any amount of preliminary singing, while the
> congregation is assembling – by the reading of a chapter or a Psalm.
> Then it is go-as-you-please for 2 hours or more ... three-fourths of the
> meeting consists of singing. No one uses a hymn book. No one gives out
> a hymn ... as a study of the psychology of crowds I have seen nothing
> like it. You feel that the thousand or 1500 persons before you have
> become merged into one myriad-headed, but single-souled personality
> (Davies 1994: 127).

Or, as *The Times* reported:

> Presently a young man pushed his way through the crowd and, kneeling
> in the rostrum, began a fervent prayer of penitence and for pardon.
> Once again, in the midst of his prayer, the whole congregation break
> forth into a hymn, repeated with amazing fervour and vigour eight
> times. A man in the gallery raises his voice to speak. The people listen,
> and meanwhile Mr Roberts has resumed his seat and watches all with a
> steady and unimpassioned gaze. The man confesses his past – he has
> been a drunkard, he has been a Sabbath-breaker, he had known
> nothing of a Saviour, but now something has entered his heart and he
> feels this new power within him compelling him to speak. While he is
> speaking the people give vent to their feelings in a hymn of
> thanksgiving, repeated as before again and again. Thus the hours creep
> on. It is long past midnight. Now here, now there, some one rises to
> make his confession and lays bare his record before the people or falls
> upon his knees where he is and in loud and fervent tones prays for
> forgiveness (3 January 1905).

So the momentum continued after Christmas. But at the very end of January 1905 criticism of Roberts appeared in correspondence columns of the *Western Mail*. This inaugurated a protracted and heated discussion, although one without any participation from Roberts himself. Peter Price, a Congregational minister, who signed himself ostentatiously '(BA hons) Mental and Moral Sciences Tripos, Cambridge (late of Queens College Cambridge)', objected to Roberts' claim to be under the immediate control of the Holy Spirit and he dismissed physical manifestations of the Holy Spirit, of whatever kind, as exhibitionism. Those who knew him agree that these attacks affected Roberts and by way of reaction he became even 'more passionately concerned about immediate revelations from the Spirit' (Evans 1987: 135, quoting Henri Bois).

Meanwhile, the revival continued as other preachers pressed forward with the work. W.S. Jones saw revival effects in the Bangor area (Jones 1995: 99) and Evan Lloyd-Jones in the Nantlle area (Evans 1987: 113). Roberts moved up to Liverpool, where there was a Welsh community, and here the strain showed. He stopped praying in one meeting because he felt 'great disobedience' was present, and in one of the largest meetings he complained that there was someone in the crowd who was trying to hypnotise him (apparently, there was). At other occasions he remained silent in the pulpit for long periods. Dramatically, he announced that the Free Church of the Welsh was not founded 'on the rock'. If this indicates that Roberts was becoming unbalanced and denunciatory, this is not how the newspapers of the time saw it. 'He himself never inveighs against specific forms of evil' (Evans 1987: 141).

He returned to North Wales in May and Anglesey in June and Bala and Caernarvon in July. By now Roberts had nearly finished his journeys. He had moved in a large circle round the outer edges of Wales in an anti-clockwise direction. By the end of the summer he was in central Wales, in Llandrindod Wells, and after that became reclusive and, despite many invitations, withdrew from public life. To all intents and purposes the revival was over. It is estimated that during that year 100,000 people had been added to the churches of Wales.

Azusa Street Revival

The mid-Pacific coast of the United States enjoys a delightful climate and, being settled long after the rest of the country, has produced a culture less staid and more adventurous than the eastern areas originally colonised by the Pilgrim Fathers. Among the jewels of the coast is Los Angeles, a city so attractive that after the railroad reached it in 1876 it doubled in size in twenty years and became a thriving, bustling multi-cultural mixture – the fastest-growing city in the United States (Nelson 1981: 183). It was to this city that W.J. Seymour (1870–1922), the son of a freed slave, arrived by railroad on 22 February 1906. He was responding to Julia Hutchins, who had invited him to be the pastor of a holiness congregation she had founded a year before.

Seymour's religious history is difficult to reconstruct, but it appears that he was converted in a black Methodist Episcopal congregation before moving to the Wesleyan holiness community, where he acted as a pastor in the Houston area, Texas, in 1905. During this period he attended the Bible School of Charles Parham. He integrated Parham's teaching that the baptism of the Holy Spirit is evidenced by speaking in other tongues with Wesleyan holiness 'second blessing' theology.

When Mrs Hutchins discovered that Seymour taught about the evidential value of speaking in tongues she locked him out of the church building. Seymour then held meetings at the home of Edward Lee, a member of the Hutchins' congregation with whom he was staying, and then a few weeks later, at Lee's suggestion, at the home of Richard and Ruth Asberry in Bonnie Brae Street. On 9 April 1906, just before he was due to leave to take the meeting at the Asberrys', Seymour prayed for Lee, who promptly spoke in tongues. The news excited the gathering at Bonnie Brae and attracted a crowd that outgrew the home. In the following week they rented 312 Azusa Street, a white wooden two-storey building that had been a church and livery stable, and began a series of meetings that transformed themselves into an urban revival.

A contemporary account of a meeting in the first week was given by the *Los Angeles Times* (18 April 1906). It was scathing in its assessment of what was going on. Under the headline 'Weird Babel of Tongues', the sub-headline read, 'New sect of fanatics is breaking loose'. Scathing or not, however, the account provided free publicity that served to attract fresh visitors. The article ended: 'Another speaker had a vision in which he saw the people of Los Angeles flocking in a mighty stream to perdition. He prophesied awful destruction to this city unless its citizens are brought to a belief in the tenets of the new faith.'

A more sympathetic and equally contemporary account was given by Frank Bartleman, who wrote:

> Brother Seymour was recognised as the nominal leader in charge. But we had no pope or hierarchy. We were brethren. We had no human programme. The Lord himself was leading ... we did not even have a platform or pulpit in the beginning ... we did not honor men for their advantage, in means or education, but rather for their God-given gifts ...
>
> Brother Seymour generally sat behind two empty shoe boxes, one on top of the other. He usually kept his head inside the top one during the meeting, in prayer. There was no pride there. The services ran almost continuously. Seeking souls could be found under the power almost any hour, night and day. The place was never closed nor empty ... in that old building, with its low rafters and bare floors, God took strong men and women to pieces, and put them together again, for his glory. It was a tremendous overhauling process. Pride and self-assertion, self-importance and self-esteem, could not survive there.
>
> Someone might be speaking. Suddenly the Spirit would fall upon the congregation. God himself would give the altar call. Men would fall all over the house, like the slain in battle or rush for the altar en masse, to seek God. The scene often resembled a forest of falling trees ... a Baptist preacher, was sitting on the chair in the middle of the floor one evening in the meeting. Suddenly the Spirit fell upon him. He sprang up from his chair, and began to praise God in a loud voice in tongues, and ran all over the place hugging all the brethren he could get hold of. He was filled with divine love (Bartleman 1980: 57–61).

According to Bartleman, the revival was persecuted when police were asked to break up the meetings. Despite all this, the congregation grew so that there were 300–350 worshippers in attendance for much of the time, and occasionally the numbers doubled. What particularly struck visitors was that the meetings were inter-racial. The leaders of the congregation were black and white. Seymour, as pastor, was black, along with the trustees Richard Asberry and James Alexander. Yet whites where also in responsible positions, together with gifted black women. According to Robeck (2002) the congregation was fully integrated in that its leadership was black and white and its membership included Hispanics and other ethnic minorities.

Within the building upstairs were rooms for several residents, including Seymour, and, when he married, his wife. It was from here that in 1906 he launched the *Apostolic Faith* with a run of

5,000 copies that, in two years, soared to 50,000. Apart from occasional and scattered asides in contemporaneous writings, signed articles in these periodicals are the only sources available for reaching the kernel of Seymour's teaching and ministry.

So, for three years Azusa Street represented a microcosm of what the global church might be – 'all races, sexes, classes and nations' (Nelson, 1981: 204) gathered there harmoniously because, as Seymour proclaimed, 'we recognise every man that honours the blood of Jesus Christ to be our brother'.[2] In this simple and humble statement of faith Seymour articulated his vision for the church. The Cross of Christ is intended to bring humanity into a new wholeness. As he put it in other words:

> the secret is: one accord, one place, one heart, one soul, one mind, one prayer. If God can get a people anywhere in one accord and in one place, and one heart, mind, and soul, believing for this great power ... Pentecostal results will follow ... the Pentecostal power, when you sum it all up, is just more of God's love. If it does not bring more of God's love it is simply a counterfeit (Nelson 1981, quoting the *Apostolic Faith*, June to September 1907, May 1908: 205).

Thus although Seymour fervently believed in the restoration of the gifts of the Spirit to the church and, indeed, that he was living in the 'last days', the essence of his message, and one which may explain why the Azusa Street Revival was so attractive to Pentecostals all over the world, was its simplicity and its sense that God was forging new moral and spiritual values among the marginalised and poor of a great modern city. Such a perception was particularly powerful for Americans brought up in the aftermath of the Civil War, and during a decade when three or four black people per week were being lynched (Nelson 1981: 32).

On 18 April 1906 the San Andreas Fault moved, and 340 miles up the coast a huge earthquake shook San Francisco, leaving three quarters of its population homeless. An apocalyptic tension raised levels of belief that the events in Azusa Street represented divine acts.

---

[2] Seymour spoke before World War I and without consciousness of subsequent contention over gender-inclusive language. It is clear from his acceptance of women (black and white) and men (black and white) in the leadership of the Azusa Street mission that his vision was of a church where racial and gender categories were irrelevant.

In October 1906 Parham visited Azusa Street at Seymour's invitation, but instead of responding warmly and sympathetically to what he saw – and what was in many respects the consequences of his own teaching about the Holy Spirit – he criticised its 'animalisms', 'trances' and 'meaningless sounds and noises', and then asserted that the revival was 'his own work but gone awry' (Robeck 2002: 1056). Seymour's people resisted Parham, so Parham left to open a rival congregation a short distance away. It was here that Seymour demonstrated his true spirituality. He neither recriminated nor faltered and when, shortly afterwards, unproved charges of immorality were laid against Parham in Texas, the immediate danger to the revival passed. Parham's days as an incipient Pentecostal leader began to come to an end.[3]

Revival continued unabated until 1908. Despite the financial panic of 1907, when the American stock market fell 45 per cent, the debt on the property at Azusa Street was cleared. On 13 May 1908 Seymour married Jenny Evans and, by so doing, released a wave of criticism, especially from Clara Lum, the main administrator of the *Apostolic Faith*, who believed that the closing days of the present age were no time for 'marrying and giving in marriage'. Lum left Azusa and took the international mailing list of the periodical with her to Portland, Oregon, and so prevented Seymour becoming a leading national or international figure in the emergent Pentecostal movement. Funds that were being sent in to Los Angeles were diverted northward to Lum, and so she effectively stole from Seymour and irreparably damaged his work. Further damage occurred when William H. Durham, a dynamic preacher, came to the city in 1911 and, in Seymour's absence, attempted to take control of the mission.

In August 1912 Alexander Boddy, the Vicar of Sunderland, England, visited Azusa and left behind a description of what he found: 'I found a large company of white and coloured people assembled. Sister Jennie (Mrs. Seymour) a coloured sister, was

---

[3] Arguments over Parham's racial views surfaced in a seminar at the World Pentecostal Conference in Los Angeles in 2000. On one side, he admitted Seymour to his Bible School, evangelised in the streets of Houston with him and paid his train fare to Los Angeles – thus indicating an enlightened view. On the other side, he was said to support aspects of the Ku Klux Klan – thus indicating a reactionary view. Further general discussions of this topic are found in Wacker (2001: 340, note 25).

leading in hymn-singing, and giving exhortations between'
(Boddy 1912: 244, 245).

Other congregations formed by new Pentecostal preachers like
Bartleman were also founded in the Los Angeles area and removed
sections of Seymour's congregation, so that by 1913 the tide of
revival was receding. Seymour had obviously been affected
personally by the setbacks he had suffered, particularly since all
those who had acted against him were white. From 1915 onwards,
after changing the constitution of the mission, he insisted that all
the officers of the church should be 'people of colour'. The congregation dwindled and his contribution to the revival was over. He
died in 1922.

Empirical Aspects of Revival

These two accounts of revival illustrate the following empirical
aspects: concern for (biblical) morality, social harmony, preaching,
public confession of sin, visions, tears, falling over, spontaneity,
newspaper reports, denominational rapprochement, unprepared
singing, collective behaviour, apocalyptic fears, humility, participation, love, prayer, continuous meetings, racial accord, penitence,
female prominence or equality, conversions and rededications to
Christ, prophecy, speaking in tongues and faith. There may be other
aspects also, but those selected here will probably subsume them.
'Spontaneity', for example, covers a huge range of behaviours.

In the sections that follow an attempt will be made to explain the
various empirical aspects of revival, and to do so from social and
psychological standpoints.

Sociological

The social aspect of revival is demonstrated by the public behaviour
of those caught up within the phenomenon. The public behaviour
may be in religious places or during religious services, or it may be
extended beyond these on to the streets and into places of work.
Within the Welsh Revival unusually gracious social behaviour of
men and women was manifested in the pits and between the different churches. The pre-shift prayer within the coal mines grew
directly out of the revival (Jones 1995: 205). The willingness of
denominations to co-operate with each other by attending each
other's meetings and by allowing Evan Roberts to preach from their

pulpits is particularly startling, considering the unyielding doctrinal differences that had been so frequently rehearsed in previous (and, unfortunately, subsequent) disputes (Morgan 1999: ch. 4). Similarly, the behaviour of drunkards who gave their money to good causes or simply brought their earnings home to their long-suffering families are also obvious social benefits that arise from the heart of the revival itself (Jones 1995: 220). Perhaps most telling, in the light of later trade union bitterness, was the willingness to resolve disputes within the workplace without rancour. In essence, these social changes may be interpreted as multiplied individual instances of extensions of Christian ethics to the home and the community, including the places of employment. They did not constitute transformations of social structures or redistributions of power or wealth: prosperous middle-class gentry could and did complain that the revival was preventing their servants keeping regular hours (Jones 1995: 248).

Church attendance rose sharply in Wales after 1904 and, as the analysis of confirmation candidate figures shows (Brown 1986), the fruits of revival were to be found in religious re-dedication, which lasted, in many instances, for a lifetime. There were in Welsh congregations for the next fifty years people who could point back to their experiences of the revival, and it was these people who were the stalwarts of church and chapel attendance (Davies 1994: 506).

The singing found in revival is an extension and intensification of that found in traditional Christian worship. The repetition of songs and hymns has two effects. Firstly, the congregations are able to think beyond the mere mechanical repetition of the words to the spiritual realities that the words signified. Secondly, the sense of empathy and of human bonding is cemented by a collective singing. Each singer is in unison or harmony with every other to form a new whole that is greater than the sum of its parts.

From a sociological point of view, what is most significant about the Welsh Revival is that it took place within a society where close family and friendship ties created a tight nexus. The generally interconnected nature of Welsh society ensured that once revival began in one town or one valley it rapidly spread within that town and within that valley.

What this means is that revivals that take place in settled and integrated rural communities are likely to follow different patterns from revivals that take place in urban areas. The rural revival spreads within communities and from community to community by word of mouth, and the news media play only a secondary role in drawing attention to events; the urban revival appears to survive by the flow of fresh visitors brought in by the news media, and word of mouth plays only a secondary role in dissemination. The rural revival in the case of Wales appears to have followed the itinerary of Evan Roberts, and he remained its chief facilitator, and when his public ministry came to an end, the revival gradually subsided. Seymour guided the Azusa Street Revival, but it continued in his occasional absences up to 1912–13. Analytic oversimplification is a danger here, however. There were certainly 1904 revival meetings in the urban centres of Swansea and Cardiff without Roberts, and their big congregations grew and engaged in a variety of mercy missions, for example, among impoverished children, and, conversely, the Azusa Street phenomena travelled to the rural settings of camp meetings outside Los Angeles.

More crucially for sociological theory is the indication that revival does not appear to conform to some of the models utilised by prominent sociologists of religion. For example, the Durkheimian view that religious concepts symbolise society or that religious representations are the work of the collective mind (Lukes 1975: 461, 242) have little or no resonance with the revivals describe here. The Welsh Revival is by no means an expression of an ideal society or situation: the preaching of Roberts concerned *personal* sin and a willingness to bend to the Spirit. Religious representations are almost entirely absent in this aniconic Protestant form of religion. Or, to take the Marxist assertion that religion functions to legitimate political and social authority (Mitchell 1966), the example of both revivals turns such an account on its head. The revival is, at least initially, counter-cultural, and rather than legitimating political and social authority, stands out against it. It would be perverse to argue that the Welsh Revival rode on the back of Welsh political aspirations, even if subsequent politicians attempted to use the fervency and community spirit generated by the revival for their own political ends, as Lloyd George's detractors would contend. More starkly, the Azusa Street Revival, by demonstrating racial integration, was a standing rebuke to segregationist attitudes and policies, and there can be no weight given to the view that its enthusiastic scenes are simply explicable in terms of a sudden desire for racial reconciliation. Rather, as the chronology indicates, the theological imperatives came first and, from these, racial reconciliation followed.

Seeking to analyse revivals through the function of charismatic leadership might provide an alternative sociological perspective.

Both Evan Roberts and W.J. Seymour were charismatic leaders in the strict meaning of that term, and the Weberian account of religion that sees its rise as growing out of the life trajectory of a charismatic leader could be employed. Yet the leaders in both cases were not seeking to establish new cults or religious communities. Rather, they took steps to deflect attention away from themselves and on to the Holy Spirit or to Christ. Perhaps if they had been unscrupulous men, they might have produced cultish results, but their concern was to renew and publicise Evangelical Christianity. So the stages that mark the emergence of a new religion, a charismatic leader followed by a consolidating bureaucratic authority, do not fit Wales in 1904 or Azusa Street after 1906. Moreover, sociological focus on charismatic leaders is purely descriptive and offers no agreed explanation as to their appeal: to say that a leader is successful because he or she has leadership qualities, even if these are charismatic, seems little more than tautology.

Psychological

Convincing psychological writing on revival is limited partly because psychology is primarily concerned with individuals rather than groups or societies and partly because revival meetings are not easily accessible to hard-edged research. The literature on psychological revival is best thought of as an amalgamation of the psychological literature on individual conversions.

The classic account of individual conversion is given by William James, who states:

> to be converted ... denotes the process, gradual or sudden, by which the self hitherto divided, and consciously wrong, inferior and unhappy, becomes unified and consciously right, superior and happy, in consequence of its firmer hold upon religious realities (James 1902: 194).

The process of conversion by this account is one of personality unification. The self is divided and fragmented and unable to bring all its energies to bear upon one style of life, one set of aims. Conversion resolves these apparently intractable subconscious contradictions and, by doing so, produces emotional release or joy.

The study of conversion has distinguished between sudden and gradual conversion, and concluded that sudden conversion occurs in middle to late adolescence, is emotional, follows a stern theology, presumes a passive role for the convert and results in release from sin and guilt. Such conversions are contrasted with the gradual kind, which began slightly later in life, are intellectual and rational, follow a compassionate theology, an active seeking role by the convert, and stem from a quest for meaning and purpose (Argyle 2000: 23 ff., Hood et al 1996: 283, Loewenthal 2000: 45 ff.). None of this precisely explains how conversion takes place and what triggers the complete reorientation that follows.

It is true that stress may precede conversion and that a personal crisis linked with low self-esteem, depression and uncertain sense of identity may all also be reported in the retrospective accounts given by converts of their pre-conversion lives. Research by Ullman indicates that converts may have experienced unhappy childhoods and less-than-warm feelings for fathers (Ullman quoted in Beit-hallahmi and Argyle 1997: 119, Hood et al 1996: 289). Such research confirms the picture of the convert as unsettled and ripe for change, ready to jettison the emotions and baggage of the past and to look for a fresh beginning. The typical gradual conversion links changes in religious identity with a search for meaning. This rational search for a purpose for existence in one's own life may, during the searching stage, traverse many philosophical and religious positions and theories. Once meaning is reached then the self is reconstructed, then this, in its simplest form, means that the individual describes him or herself differently. The religious testimony of the convert creates a narrative by which the new identity is confirmed.

Other features of the psychological literature deal with suggestibility, the factors that are associated with religious experience (Beit-hallahmi and Argyle 1997, Wulff 1991). These factors usually attempt to identify personality types or dimensions that make conversion propitious, but because of the huge number of people converted in revivals and the range of ages and kinds of people involved in such mass events, many personalities are likely to be involved. In other words, it is impossible to predict which people in some communities in Wales were likely to be affected, because practically all of them were.

Although the psychological literature has provided an analysis of conversion and, by grouping together many accounts of the process, isolated common features and factors, the essence of the experience remains elusive (Paloutzian 1996). It is impossible to predict who will and who will not be converted. It is impossible to replicate the conditions under which conversion takes place and, even if the converted personality is integrated and finds new meaning and identity, this hardly explains the phenomenon in its entirety.

In the case of the Welsh Revival it is possible to argue that the prior knowledge of the Bible that many people would have had predisposed them to conversion; that their childhood exposure to biblical stories and to the life of Christ and concepts of sin and salvation rested uneasily within their unconscious minds; and that, once the revival began to burn, these childhood concerns and memories found expression and resolution within the conversion process. This explains why some of the accounts of revival meetings report public confession of sin and anxiety and distress among those whose consciences were awakened. In the case of the Azusa Street Revival, it is arguable that the inter-racial hatred of the preceding years had created deep-seated anxieties within the unconscious minds of many Americans, both black and white, and that the revival brought these concerns to the surface and resolved them in the person of Christ, the ultimate victim and the creator of a new egalitarian community – the church.

Such psychological explanations, while interesting and potentially illuminating, cannot be verified or related directly to the experimental evidence upon which contemporary psychology largely rests. This means that the distinction between sudden and gradual conversions and between rational and emotional bases for conversion cannot be sustained during the extraordinary events that constitute revival. This is because the steps within the process of gradual conversion may take place in more rapid succession during revival, with the result that gradual conversions actually become sudden. In addition, the heightened emotion that characterises revival can also be found in other group activities, whether football matches or carnivals. Religious excitement, like other forms of excitement, is a surface phenomenon and, though it may increase receptivity to preaching, does not constitute an explanation of religion any more than sporting excitement constitutes an explanation of football.

Conclusion

I conclude that social and psychological standpoints add a range of possible understandings of revival, but that, in the nature of the case, it is not easy for these disciplines to be rigorously applied. This is a methodological limitation stemming from the fact that revivals are such undisciplined, ephemeral and various events. Psychology is not equipped to deal with multiple instances occurring in transient collective situations. Equally, sociology is not well equipped to deal with large-scale, unpredictable, historical phenomena – especially in the absence of relevant statistics. After all, Durkheim's classic work on suicide depended on an analysis of excellent cross-cultural suicide data (Durkheim 1897). No comparable data exist in relation to conversions at revivals.

Even if one attempts, as I have done, to appreciate the human networks of kinship that may facilitate revival in rural areas, this does not explain the phenomenon in urban areas. Psychological and sociological explanations may be suggestive – as they are in relation to latent moral or racial anxieties – but their power to penetrate to the centre of revival events is limited by their methodological need on the one hand to listen to the theological discourse by which the participants interpreted their own experiences and on the other by the requirement to discover non-theological causal factors, that is, variables specific to psychology and sociology, and to do this without first-hand observation.

Probably the best contemporary attempts to use sociology to assess revival are in the writings of Margaret Poloma (1996, 1998), who has distributed questionnaires to discover the 'fruit', the consequences, of the Toronto Blessing. But this method, innovative though it is, could not be applied retrospectively to the historical revivals of Wales or Azusa Street.

The emotional side of revival and the behaviours associated with it – falling down, crying, crying out, seeking reconciliation, being 'hungry for God' – which fascinate its detractors are not in themselves inexplicable (Scotland 2000: 242 ff.). Nevertheless, a secular age finds itself surprised that such intense emotion is connected with religious rather than temporal realities.

References

Argyle, M. (2000). *Psychology and Religion*. London: Routledge.

Awstin Davies, T. (1905). *The Religious Revival in Wales 1904*. Six pamphlets of collected newspaper reports, 1904–5, published by the *Western Mail*.

Bartleman, F. (1980). *Azusa Street: The Roots of Modern-day Pentecost*. South Plainfield: Bridge. First published in 1925 under the title *How 'Pentecost' came to Los Angeles – How it was at the Beginning*.

Beit-Hallahmi, B. and Argyle, M. (1997). *Religious Behaviour, Belief and Experience*. London: Routledge.

Boddy, A.A. (1912), A meeting at the Azusa Street Mission Los Angeles. *Confidence* 11.5, November: 244–5.

Brown, R.L. (1986). *The Welsh Evangelicals*. Cardiff: Tongwynlais Tair Eglwys Press.

Burn, G. (2002). Review of K. Corcoran (ed.) *Soul, Body and Survival*. In *Theology* 825 (May/June).

Cox, H. (1996). *Fire from Heaven: The Rise of Pentecostal Spirituality and the Reshaping of Religion in the Twenty-first Century*. London: Cassell.

Davies, J. (1994). *A History of Wales*. Harmondsworth: Penguin.

Durkheim, E, (1897), *Le Suicide: étude de sociology*. Paris: Alcan.

Edwards, J. (1741). *The Distinguishing Marks of a Work of the Spirit of God*. Bishop's Waltham: Revival Library DVD.

Edwards, J. (1746). *A Treatise Concerning Religious Affections*. Albany: Sage Software.

Evans, E. (1987[3]). *The Welsh Revival of 1904*. Bridgend: Bryntirion Press.

Hood Jr, R.W., Spilka, B., Hunsberger, B. and Gorsuch, R. (1996[2]). *The Psychology of Religion*. London: The Guildford Press.

James, W. (1902). *The Variety of Religious Experience*. The Gifford Lectures, given in Edinburgh 1901–2. Subsequently published variously.

Jones, B.P. (1995). *Voices from the Welsh Revival*. Bridgend: Evangelical Press of Wales.

Jones, G.E. (1997). *The Education of a Nation*. Cardiff: University of Wales Press.

Loewenthal, K.M. (2000). *The Psychology of Religion*. Oxford: Oneworld.

Lukes, S. (1975). *Émile Durkheim: His Life and Work*. Harmondsworth: Penguin.

Mitchell, G.D. (1966). *Sociology: The Study of Social Systems*. London: University Tutorial Press.

Morgan, D. (1999). *The Span of the Cross*. Cardiff: University of Wales Press.

Nelson, D.J. (1981). For Such a Time as This. Unpublished doctoral dissertation, University of Birmingham, England.

Paloutzian, R.F. (1996²). *Invitation to the Psychology of Religion.* London: Allyn & Bacon.

Poloma, M.M. (1996). *The Toronto Report.* Bradford: Terra Nova.

Poloma, M.M. (1998). Inspecting the Fruit of the 'Toronto Blessing': A Sociological Perspective. *Pneuma* 20 (1): 43–70.

Robeck, C.M. (2002). 'William Joseph Seymour'. In Burgess, S.M. and van der Maas, E.M. (eds) *International Dictionary of Pentecostal and Charismatic Movements.* Grand Rapids: Zondervan.

Scotland, N. (2000). *Charismatics and the New Millennium.* Guildford: Eagle.

Wacker, G. (2001). *Heaven Below: Early Pentecostals and American Culture.* Cambridge, Massachusetts: Harvard University Press.

Wulff, D.M. (1991). *Psychology of Religion: Classic and Contemporary Views.* New York: John Wiley.

Chapter 13

Selling Revival as Worship

Pete Ward

Revivalism was based on the ability to 'sell' evangelism. In the last twenty years, however, the market for this born-again product has declined in the United States and has all but collapsed in the United Kingdom. As evangelism as event and product has waned, it has been replaced by worship as the chief activity and emphasis for Evangelical Christians. As a result, the spiritual geography of revivalism has eroded, and we now inhabit a new experiential landscape. Encounter with Christ is now no longer located in a one-off life-changing experience at the moment of conversion. Present-day worshippers expect to be led into regular moments of intimacy and encounter with Christ. Inviting Jesus to 'come into our hearts' has been replaced by weekly fillings with the Holy Spirit. At the level of practice, rather than doctrine, revivalism is slowly changing its theological clothes.

This chapter traces the organisational and economic background to what I believe are primarily cultural and spiritual developments. The material positioning of this essay should therefore not be read as reductive in this regard. Tracing the means of cultural and theological change within the movement may lead to a more located history of ideas. (This essay will be extended into a longer work on the theology of Evangelical mission and worship).

Revivalism: Communication in the Market and Cultures of Production

Socially, economically and organisationally, revivalism is a culture that has been produced. The activism of Evangelicalism and its emphasis upon personal change through conversion has given it a particular cultural emphasis (Bebbington 1989: 2). New social forms were developed to fulfil this mission: for example, Finney's development of a technology of revivals (Bebbington 1989: 8).

> The spirit of the age – flexible, tolerant, utilitarianism – affected Evangelicals as much in practice as in thought. Field preaching, an activity that lay near the heart of the revival, was an embodiment of the pragmatic temper. If the people would not come to church, they must be won for Christ in the open air (Bebbington 1989: 65).

A basic pragmatism resulted in the willingness to co-operate across denominational boundaries in creating voluntary organisations – the London Missionary Society and the British and Foreign Bible Society are just two (Bebbington 1989: 66). The emphasis upon mission and activism can be expressed through the term 'means'. 'Means was the key word signifying the whole apparatus of human agency,' writes Bebbington (1989: 41). Embracing human agency within Evangelical mission led to the communication of the faith in the marketplace. This was particularly the case in the United States.

Following the revolution and the passing of the First Amendment to the Federal Constitution in 1791 the legal privilege of religion in the United States was removed (Butler 1990: 268). Butler argues that, as a result, churches began to compete in an open marketplace. This competition was not simply with each other; it was also against the goods and technology of the wider society (Butler 1990: 275). The significance of the market in the development of American Christianity and in particular Evangelicalism has become part of a broad consensus among religious historians (Carpenter 1997, Hatch 1989, Moore 1994, Sweet 1993, Wells 1993). Hatch argues that through market competition American Protestantism, and Evangelicalism in particular, has embraced a 'democratized populism' (Hatch 1989: 5). It is the adoption of forms of communication and religious life associated with popular culture that has brought this about. 'The democratization of Christianity, then, has less to do with the specifics of polity and governance and more with the incarnation of the faith in popular culture' (Hatch 1989: 9).

Hatch describes the innovation of those he calls religious entrepreneurs in the early nineteenth century. Competition in the marketplace led to the development of revivalistic camp meetings characterised by vernacular, popular styles of preaching, publishing and the creation of a mass religious market, and the development of new styles of spiritual songs based on folk tunes (Hatch 1989: 125 ff.). It was Evangelicals who were most successful in adapting to this new arena of innovation and competition in a religious market-place: 'Evangelical religion prospered largely because the price was right and the streets were filled with vendors' (Hatch 1989: 15).

A marketplace paradigm of mission and evangelism placed reviv-alism and other innovative religious movements close to the centre of culture in the United States (Hatch 1989: 61). The result of this competition was the development of a whole host of diverse mission agencies, educational institutions, publishing houses and organisa-tions. Power was diffused and operated primarily on the basis of popular appeal (Hatch 1989: 65). Moreover, the diversity of reli-gious pluralism that the market created meant that few Americans were left untouched by the gospel message (Hatch 1989: 68).

Moore describes the adoption of the marketplace as leading to the 'commodification of religion'. He describes this as a process whereby religion is seen as the equivalent of other cultural com-modities such as the opera, the ballet, art or literature. Like these other artistic and cultural activities, religion structures itself so that it can be 'consumed' by people wishing to be 'cultured' (or reli-gious). Moore argues that this process has meant that religion, in order to win an audience for its message (or product), has increas-ingly tended to adopt a commercialised approach for its activities (Moore 1994: 5). 'By degree religion itself took on the shape of a commodity,' he writes (Moore 1994: 6).

It was nineteenth-century industrialisation that allowed religion to make this move. The church had always, to some extent, existed in the marketplace. Indeed, according to Moore, to be excluded from the marketplace was to be excluded from cultural significance (Moore 1994: 9). As the marketplace changed, however, the nature of religious life changed with it (Moore 1994: 7).

> The transformations that market logic could effect over vast distances broke Christianity from a parochial setting. Church leaders saw the means to give reality to their humanitarian charities. Their sphere of influence went beyond local churches. Revivals became businesses because markets showed the way to evangelise the far corners of the globe. Market logic promised universal redemption (Moore 1994: 271).

Revivalism was born from the growing market for the gospel. Evan-gelical religious institutions were therefore structured around the various processes of sales and marketing. It is possible to describe these various processes of production as themselves being a 'culture'. Du Gay calls this the culture of production (du Gay et al 1997: 6). Using this idea of du Gay's we can identify three distinctive cultures of production within the movement: Revivalism as Business, Revivalism as Voluntary Organisation, and Revivalism as Student Membership Group.

Revivalism as Business

Revival sells to an international market. In particular, there has been a 'special relationship' of market and exchange between the United States and the United Kingdom. It is wrong to assume that the cultural traffic in this relationship has always been one-way. Instead, it is perhaps best to describe the relationship as being 'interdependent', even if in the last thirty years the United Kingdom has received more than it has given. 'Novelty' in Evangelicalism in the United Kingdom has very often been the result of a new development imported from the United States (Bebbington 1994: 368). Yet even such imports can be seen as a result of the 'investment' of religious culture in America in previous generations, as Rennie observes in the case of the Harringay Crusade:

> In the person of Billy Graham, Britain's conservative evangelicals were not receiving a fresh input from America, so much as they were garnering yet one more dividend from theological investments they had been making in the United States and Canada for over a century (Rennie 1994: 347).

Investment and exchange in the eighteenth and nineteenth centuries had been such that, in significant ways, Evangelicalism could be said to share in common culture. This is especially the case in the use of styles of communication and adoption of the market to spread the gospel. An example of this is the transatlantic ministry of George Whitefield.

During the eighteenth century the wider cultural context of communication and trade in the American colonies and the United Kingdom became agent of the religious cultural production of revival. Lambert suggests it was Whitefield's 'Preach and Print' strategy that separated him from his predecessors and created the Great Awakening (quoted in Sweet 1993: 15). Stout identifies this as a significant ecclesial innovation: 'Instead of building his revivals around traditional institutional supports in established and Nonconformist churches, Whitefield built his revivals around the press' (Stout 1993: 111).

The effect of the use of the press and the fact that much of his preaching took place in secular venues or in the open air meant that Whitefield managed to bypass the need to invoke ecclesiatical or educational authority to support his ministry. Instead, his authority and status relied solely on his personal popularity. Whitefield's mass revivals should not be seen as 'church' and indeed they were never bounded by the limits of local communities or congregations. The audiences, publishers and supporters should rather be regarded as 'powerful parachurches'. These were groups of 'disconnected individuals bound to voluntary religious associations based on market place organisation' (Stout 1993: 122). Following Whitefield, revivalism increasingly adopted the social patterns of the marketplace and business, but it also evolved through the spread of voluntary societies and organisations.

Revivalism as Voluntary Organisation

The voluntary society was adopted on both sides of the Atlantic as a means to structure evangelistic activity. Early examples include The London Missionary Society or the British and Foreign Bible Society (Bebbington 1989: 66). In America there was the formation of the American Tract Society, which was an imitation of the Religious Tract Society in London (Nord 1993: 243). The business of revival and these various voluntary organisations were interconnected. An example of this can be seen in the ministry of D.L. Moody and his relationship with The Young Men's Christian Association (YMCA).

Started in London by George Williams, the YMCA was introduced into America during the latter part of the 1850s (Shedd 1955: 15; for the origins of the YMCA see Binfield 1973). In 1860 Moody gave up his job as a shoe salesman in order to devote himself full-time to YMCA work and other Christian ministry. Marsden comments: 'That the YMCA rather than any denomination should be Moody's main formal contact with the Christian community was indicative of an important tendency in American evangelicalism, greatly furthered by Moody himself' (Marsden 1980: 34).

In 1872 Moody was invited by William Pennefather to speak at the Mildmay Conference (Bebbington 1989: 159). Although this was his first visit, through the YMCA, Moody was able to very quickly gain significant contacts in the United Kingdom. The next year, with the song leader Ira Sankey, he was invited to return to lead a number of evangelistic services. The success of Moody and Sankey was such that by the time they left the United Kingdom in 1875 they had become internationally renowned figures. It was through the initial support of the voluntary society the YMCA that Moody was able to establish himself. From this position he could develop the various enterprises and ventures, including colleges and schools, which have become associated with him (Marsden 1980: 34).

Revivalism as Student Membership Group

In the eighteenth, nineteenth and early twentieth century exchange between America and the United Kingdom meant that revivalism shared a common culture. After a period of decline on both sides of the Atlantic, there was a steady reversal of fortunes. The renewal of Evangelical religion in America and the United Kingdom during the 1950s and 1960s followed roughly similar and parallel trajectories (Bebbington 1994: 368). There were, however, says Bebbington, three differences between Evangelicalism in America and in the United Kingdom. Firstly, American Evangelicals tended towards ecclesiastical separation, whereas in the United Kingdom the movement has been primarily within existing denominations, in particular within the Anglican Church. Secondly, in America, fundamentalism marked a key phase in the development of the movement; this was not the case in the United Kingdom (Bebbington 1994: 371). Thirdly, he identifies what he calls a 'secular tendency' in American Evangelicalism. He describes it like this: 'A mixture of populism, individualism, democratization, and market-making has recently been defined as the essence of the American way of shaping religion ...' (Bebbington 1994: 373).

There are a number of wider social and economic reasons why these three tendencies may have been more prevalent in America than in the United Kingdom. Perhaps most significant among these is the size of the American religious market. This is not simply related to the difference in populations. It is also the fact that a significantly higher proportion of the population in America maintain church affiliations. In a Gallup poll taken in 1976, 34 per cent of Americans described themselves as being 'born again'. In 1980 the same question was answered positively by 40 per cent (Bebbington 1994: 377). Moreover, this substantial proportion of the population were in the regular habit of making significant financial donations to religious causes. Bebbington recounts: 'In the years immediately after the war American religious organisations, taken together, actually enjoyed a higher annual income than the whole budget of the British Government' (Bebbington 1994: 378).

The cultural economy of Evangelicalism in the United Kingdom relied less on market capitalism and more on voluntary organisations and student membership groups (see Ward 1996). The chief pattern of contextualisation and cultural production was the youth fellowship or student Christian Union. *Growing Up Evangelical* (Ward 1996) describes how innovative patterns of Christian evangelism, discipleship and worship were first developed in youth work and were then transported into parish life by leaders nurtured in these youth movements.

The renewal of Evangelicalism in the United Kingdom has been widely attributed to this strategy (see McGrath 1994: 35, Saward 1987: 31, Ward 1996: 6 ff.). Four distinctive factors came together to bring about the Evangelical resurgence in the United Kingdom. Firstly, the Public School Camps started by Eric Nash (or Bash as he was known by the campers). Linked to Scripture Union, it was through these camps that a whole generation of (mainly Anglican) Evangelical clergy were to be brought to faith and then trained in Christian evangelism and discipleship (see Eddison 1982). Secondly, the growing ministry of the Inter-Varsity Fellowship (IVF), the related Tyndale Fellowship for Biblical Research and the Inter-Varsity Press (IVP). The Christian Union Movement gave many young Christians their first taste of leadership and initiated them into Evangelical theology (see Johnson 1979, McGrath 1994: 35). Thirdly, the work of the Crusaders Union of Bible Classes and the spread of the Anglican Pathfinders and Churches Youth Fellowship (CYFA). Work amongst mainly middle-class young people in parishes or Bible classes provided a steady flow of committed Evangelicals into the universities (see Ward 1996: 23–62). Finally, the example of John Stott, in his steady commitment to parish ministry within the Anglican Church, was an inspiration to many (McGrath 1994: 35). On being made rector of All Souls, Langham Place in 1950 Stott set about applying the lessons he had learned in student and youth work to an Anglican parish. As Dudley-Smith recounts:

John Stott at this stage of his life knew himself to be a 'product of Iwerne and the CICCU [Cambridge Inter-Collegiate Christian Union], having learned from them whatever I knew of evangelistic and pastoral work.' Faced with this awesome opportunity, he was itching to apply their well tried principles, which he had seen God use and honour to the realities of a Church of England parish (Dudley-Smith 1999: 251).

A similar testimony is given by David Watson in his autobiography (Watson 1983: 39). He notes that involvement in the camps was the 'most formative influence on my faith', going on to say that the camps taught him the basics of evangelism, Christian nurture, prayer, Bible reading and pastoral work with individuals and with groups (Watson 1983: 39). Stott and Watson each had an international dimension to their work. At the same time, they were both rooted in parish ministry within the Anglican Church. Their careers reflect a distinctive pattern in Evangelical life in the United Kingdom. In America, itinerant evangelistic organisations routinely operated very like businesses. In the United Kingdom the 'culture of production' was very different. An Evangelical culture nurtured on public school boys' camps and at CICCU was perhaps less likely to be sympathetic to the 'vulgarities' of popular culture. At the same time, it seems clear that one of the major factors in limiting the spread of a commodified, media-orientated Evangelical religion in the United Kingdom was the size of the market, rather than any refined sensibilities.

The Business of Worship

In the 1980s the culture of production within Evangelicalism was to be fundamentally changed. Student membership groups and voluntary societies such as Scripture Union and the IVF (now known as UCCF [Universities and Colleges Christian Fellowship]) were to be eclipsed by revivalism that was more market orientated and organised along the lines of secular business. What was distinctive, however, in the United Kingdom was that these businesses were not selling evangelism, they were to sell worship. This was an elemental change within revivalism and it has come about because worship sold better than evangelism in the United Kingdom. To illustrate how worship cornered the market, we can look at the relative fortunes of three businesses: the collapse of Music Gospel Outreach (MGO), the success of *Come Together* and the impact of Spring Harvest. These three together illustrate firstly how revivalism as a market-orientated business, rather than as student membership group, was able to colonise the United Kingdom. Secondly, they show how this was only possible by a shift from evangelism to new and innovative ways of selling worship.

The Collapse of MGO

MGO was originally formed as a networking organisation for evangelistic beat groups during the 1960s. MGO promoted their activities through their magazine, *Buzz* (Payne 1966: 2). MGO was effectively a partnership between three people. The chairman of the new organisation was David Payne, Geoff Shearn was in charge of training and Peter Meadows was editor of *Buzz*. All three were to play formative roles in the development of the new paradigm of cultural production within the Evangelical sub-culture. Soon the business and entrepreneurial activities of MGO were starting to take shape. In 1972 a number of gospel artists launched out as full-time professional musicians: these included Parchment, Malcolm and Alwyn, Graham Kendrick, The Glorylanders, The Advocates, Judy MacKenzie and Dave Cooke, and Ishmael and Andy. This was a significant new development for the Christian music scene. As *Buzz* put it: 'Suddenly the Jesus music scene has exploded. A year ago there was hardly anyone in Britain operating full-time in contemporary Christian music. But from this autumn there will be at least 8 full-time soloists and groups' (*Buzz* October 1972: 10–11).

In addition to acting as music publisher through its linked company Thankyou Music, MGO was also directly involved in management of three of these artists (*Buzz* October 1972: 10–11). By 1975, however, these activities were under severe financial strain and MGO announced losses for the financial year of £47,800. The next few years were to prove very difficult financially, and in 1978 MGO sought financial and organisational refuge in a merger with the Christian book publishers Kingsway Publications, based in Eastbourne.

MGO became Kingsway Music and quickly moved from contemporary Christian music (used mainly for evangelism) to worship music. The first album of this new generation of worship songs was called *A New Song* and featured The Cobham Fellowship singing material first used at the Capel Bible Weeks. Despite success with these ventures, Kingsway Music came close to going out of business. But all this was to change when one of Shearn's colleagues, Nigel Coltman, discovered an old songbook in the Kingsway warehouse with the title *Songs of Fellowship*. According to Coltman, the book was imported from America, and it had for a while been out of print. It was a comparatively simple task to gain permission to use the title of the book for the new worship series he was at that time planning with Shearn (Cummings 1991: 31). The new Kingsway Music publication *Songs of Fellowship* included material already published by Thankyou Music. Cummings is clear that at the time there was considerable interest in the songs associated with both renewal and with the new House churches:

> Inadvertently Kingsway had stumbled across a hugely in demand product. The songs of charismatic renewal were just beginning to creep from Britain's pioneering house churches into the mainstream denominational churches and *Songs of Fellowship* quickly became the premier source book (Cummings 1991: 32).

The first edition of *Songs of Fellowship*, *Book 1*, was published in 1979. The book had just fifty-three songs and was partly financed by a large order from the charismatic organisation Crusade for World Revival, who paid for 3,000 copies in advance, a significant proportion of the original print run of 8,000. To accompany this initial book, an album, *City of God*, featuring its songs, was released. Coltman recalls that the album cost £800 to record, yet it sold over 33,000 copies: 'God gave us that album and from that time the company went from strength to strength' (quoted in Cummings 1991: 33).

Kingsway released the *City of God* and *Songs of Fellowship* albums before the original songbook. These albums were advertised in *Buzz* a year before *Songs of Fellowship Book 1* was made available. The success of *Songs of Fellowship* led to a new edition in 1981, this time featuring 159 songs. Kingsway collected material to expand the book by soliciting sample tapes and visiting churches and Christian events (Cummings 1991: 3). One of the main criteria for selecting songs for inclusion in the *Songs of Fellowship* books was that they were currently in use in churches (*Worship* [*Encore*] Winter 1992: 10). In 1983 *Songs of Fellowship Book 2* was published and in the same year *Buzz* reported that overall sales of *Songs of Fellowship* had reached 90,000. Within ten years the combined *Songs and Hymns of Fellowship* were to have sold over a million copies worldwide (Cummings 1991: 3).

The Success of Come Together

The success of Kingsway Music and their publishers Thankyou Music during the 1970s and 1980s was based on a decisive shift of emphasis from evangelism to worship. This move was driven by the need to survive, which meant sales. Negatively, it was realised that the United Kingdom was not really a viable market for Christian artists. Positively, the charismatic movement showed that a broader market had been created for worship songs. It was the success of events such as *Come Together* which first showed the way for those involved in *Buzz* and MGO.

In September 1972 Jimmy and Carol Owens' musical *Come Together* arrived in the United Kingdom. The event, featuring the American pop star Pat Boone, toured major venues in Edinburgh, Birmingham, Liverpool, Belfast, Coventry and London. Many of these were sold out and hundreds were turned away from performances (*Buzz* October 1973: 29). (I can personally vouch for this, being very disappointed to miss the performance in Bristol.) *Come Together* was brought to the United Kingdom and administered by prominent charismatics Jean Darnell, who was closely involved with the renewal movement, and Gerald Coates, from the House churches. Gerald hosted the first performance of *Come Together* in Westminster Central Hall, London (Coates 1991: 93).

Come Together made a significant impact on the Evangelical scene, but it was also a massive financial success. In three years Word Records reported that the accumulated sales of the *Come Together* album were 57,869 copies. This made the musical the all-time best-selling Christian album in the United Kingdom. Moreover, according to *Buzz*, this probably meant that it had sold double the number of its nearest rival (*Buzz* October 1976: 13). Jimmy and Carol Owens followed up their success with another musical worship event, *If my people*, which toured twenty towns and cities during 1975. The significance of *Come Together* was that it made charismatic worship much more widely available. The adoption of record releases and concert tours introduced a commodified product that people could consume. The publication of the music allowed a kind of franchising arrangement so that local groups could start to arrange their own events and concerts. *Come Together* therefore represents a significant turning point in the generation of Evangelical religious culture. Most importantly, it primarily focused upon a charismatic style of worship and spirituality, rather than upon the preaching of the gospel. The success of this articulation of mediated religious culture for charismatic worship was to be repeated throughout the following years, in particular through events and festivals. The most successful of these was Spring Harvest.

The Impact of Spring Harvest

Spring Harvest came about through a partnership between British Youth For Christ (BYFC) and *Buzz*. The key figures behind this were Clive Calver, Director of BYFC, and Pete Meadows, who was still the editor of *Buzz*. Three thousand people attended the first Spring Harvest from 7–13 April 1979 at Tower Beach Holiday Village in Prestatyn, North Wales (*Buzz* June 1979: 38). Although Graham Kendrick and Dave Pope led worship, the emphasis was placed at first upon the event as a place to receive Evangelical teaching. The event featured a number of Evangelical speakers, including Luis Palau, Clive Calver, Eric Delve, Pete Meadows, Doug Barnett and Ian Barclay. As the numbers attending increased, what became evident was that although the emphasis upon teaching was to remain, the primary impact of Spring Harvest was to be through the marketing of a particular kind of worship music.

During the 1980s the number of weeks and the venues where the event was held were to multiply. In 1987 *Buzz* reported that 50,000 people had attended (*Buzz* June 1987: 13). By 1990 this number had increased to 80,000. The impact of Spring Harvest upon the church in the United Kingdom has been deeply significant. According to Walker, Spring Harvest has been 'the greatest success of evangelical and charismatic Christianity in Great Britain since the initial Pentecostal revivals in the first half of this century' (Walker 1998: 307).

Central to the impact of Spring Harvest was the way the event spread charismatic styles of worship around a large number of churches in the United Kingdom (*Buzz* June 1983: 38). Spring Harvest was the major showcase for Graham Kendrick's worship songs. Originally a folk rock musician, Kendrick started to write worship material in the late 1970s. He was soon encouraged by Shearns to record some of this material. In 1979 his first worship album, *Jesus Stand Among Us*, was released on the Kingsway label. It was through Spring Harvest that Kendrick was able to win an accepting audience for his new material and so the focus of his own ministry began to change. As Kendrick says, this was a slow process:

Spring Harvest started fairly small, just a couple of thousand people, but as it grew and my role within it as worship leader developed, so it became a matter of course for me to present to the selection committee several songs for inclusion in the programme. And that kind of accelerated the process ... (quoted in Cummings 1990: 52).

The numbers of people attending Spring Harvest meant that it was a significant market, not only for organisations such as Kingsway, but also for Spring Harvest itself. A succession of products emerged from the event. These included live worship albums, tapes from seminars, worship books featuring the songs from each year's event and books containing the themes used in the seminars. The sales of worship materials in particular were very high. Between 1984 and 1989 Word Records sold 100,000 units linked to Spring Harvest. In addition to these sales, the Spring Harvest 1989 Celebration album sold 20,000 copies (*Worship* [*Encore*] Autumn 1989: 14). These sales figures are an indication of the impact Spring Harvest made on the church in the United Kingdom. It also points to the shift of the culture of production within revivalism from evangelism to worship.

Conclusions

The story of Spring Harvest and the success of Graham Kendrick and other United Kingdom-based worship artists were to transform the culture of production of revivalism not only in the United Kingdom but also in America. Today, worship artists such as Martin Smith and Matt Redman are developing a growing popularity in America as well as in the United Kingdom. These artists were nourished in the new climate that was generated through the activities of people such as Pete Meadows, Clive Calver, Nigel Coltman and Geoff Shearns. Some of the faces have changed, and festivals such as Soul Survivor have burst on to the scene, but the culture of production has remained the same. The one key difference, however, is that now revivalism is selling worship and not evangelism, and intimacy rather than conversion.

References

Bebbington, D.W. (1989). *Evangelicalism in Modern Britain: A History from 1730s to the 1980s.* London: Unwin Hyman.

Bebbington, D.W. (1994) 'Evangelicalism in its Settings: The British and American Movments since 1940'. In Noll, M., Bebbington, D.W. and Rawlyk, G.A. (1994). *Evangelicalism: Comparative Studies of Popular Protestantism in North America, the British Isles and Beyond.* Oxford: Oxford University Press.

Binfield, C. (1973). *George Williams and the Y.M.C.A.* London: Heinemann.

Butler, J. (1990). *Awash on a Sea of Faith: Christianizing the American People.* Cambridge, Massachusetts: Harvard University Press.

Buzz. Published monthly October 1965 – September 1987.

Carpenter, J.A. (1997). *Revive us Again: The Reawakening of American Fundamentalism.* Oxford: Oxford University Press.

Coates, G. (1991). *An Intelligent Fire.* Eastbourne: Kingsway.

Cross Rhythms. Published bi-monthly May 1990 – May 1995.

Cummings, T. (1990). Interview with Graham Kendrick. *Cross Rhythms,* September.

Cummings, T. (1991). Songs of Fellowship Story. *Cross Rhythms,* August/September.

Dudley-Smith, T. (1999). *John Stott: The Making of a Leader.* Leicester: IVP.

Du Gay, P., Hall, S., James, L., Mackay, H. and Negus, K. (1997). *Doing Cultural Studies: The Story of the Sony Walkman.* London: Sage.

Eddison, J. (ed.) (1982). *Bash: A Study in Spiritual Power.* Basingstoke: Marshalls.

Hatch, N.O. (1989). *The Democratization of American Christianity.* New Haven: Yale University Press.

Johnson, D. (1979). Contending for the Faith: A History of the Evangelical Movement in the Universities and Colleges. Leicester: IVP.

Marsden, G.M. (1980). *Fundamentalism and American Culture: The Shaping of Twentieth-century Evangelicalism 1870–1925.* Oxford: Oxford University Press.

McGrath, A. (1994). *Evangelicalism and the Future of Christianity.* London: Hodder & Stoughton.

Moore, R.L. (1994). *Selling God: American Religion in the Marketplace of Culture.* Oxford: Oxford University Press

Noll, M., Bebbington, D.W. and Rawlyk, G.A. (1994). *Evangelicalism: Comparative Studies of Popular Protestantism in North America, the British Isles and Beyond.* Oxford: Oxford University Press

Nord, D.P (1993). 'Systematic Benevolence: Religious Publishing and the Marketplace in Early Nineteenth Century Publishing'. In Sweet, L. (ed.)

Communication and Change in American Religious History. Grand Rapids: Eerdmans.

Payne, D. (1966). You Catalysts and 1966. *Buzz*, January.

Rennie, I.S. (1994). 'Fundamentalism and the Varieties of North Atlantic Pentecostalism'. In Noll, M., Bebbington, D. W. and Rawlyk, G. A. *Evangelicalism: Comparative Studies of Popular Protestantism in North America, the British Isles and Beyond*. Oxford: Oxford University Press.

Saward, M. (1987). *Evangelicals on the Move*. Oxford: Mowbray.

Shedd, C.P. (1955). *History of the World's Alliance of Young Men's Christian Associations*. London: SPCK.

Songs and Hymns of Fellowship. (1985). Eastbourne: Kingsway.

Songs of Fellowship Volume One. (1981). Eastbourne: Kingsway.

Stout, H. (1993). Religion, Communications and the Career of George Whitefield. In Sweet, L. (ed.) *Communication and Change in American Religious History*. Grand Rapids: Eerdmans.

Sweet, L. (ed.) (1993). *Communication and Change in American Religious History*. Grand Rapids: Eerdmans.

Ward, P. (1996). *Growing Up Evangelical: Youthwork and the Making of a Subculture*. London: SPCK.

Walker, A. (1998). *Restoring the Kingdom: The Radical Christianity of the House Church Movement*. Guildford: Eagle.

Watson, D. (1983). *You are my God*. London: Hodder & Stoughton.

Wells, D.F. (1993). *No Place for Truth, or Whatever Happened to Evangelical Theology?* Leicester: IVP.

Worship [Encore]. Published quarterly Spring 1987 – Autumn 1989.

Chapter 14

Ecstatic Spirituality and Entrepreneurial Revivalism: Reflections on the 'Toronto Blessing'[1]

Rob Warner

The very term 'Toronto Blessing'[2] was resisted by many English[3] participants as a misnomer, but became the only widely recognised descriptive term for the events of 1994–7. It quickly became apparent that Evangelicals, Pentecostals and charismatics, the groupings with the greatest interest in revival, were greatly divided in their evaluations, possessing no agreed framework with which to assess the unusual phenomena associated with Toronto (TTB).[4] In this paper we shall explore the following questions:

---

[1] We shall refer to the place as Toronto, the church as Toronto (TAV) – Toronto Airport Vineyard – and the phenomenon itself as Toronto (TTB).

[2] The term was first coined by a journalist on *The Times*.

[3] Reference is made to the *English* charismatic tradition because charismatic tradition has distinctive and complex nuances in Scotland, Wales and Northern Ireland. Indeed, the scale and speed of TTB adoption was much greater in England. Where a broader distinction can be made between the United Kingdom and the United States, for example with regard to the differentiation between Pentecostal and charismatic traditions, the wider term is used. The analysis of this chapter is specific to England and indirectly applicable to the rest of the United Kingdom.

[4] The only united statement, drawn up for the Evangelical Alliance, drafted by me and Stephen Sizer, preserved evangelical unity by avoiding any definitive diagnosis of Toronto. Euston Statement (Evangelical Alliance 1994).

- Does Toronto (TTB) suggest a discernible life cycle for ecstatic spirituality?
- What is the significance of spontaneous and contagious ecstatic phenomena and what is their most relevant precedent?
- What made the extravagance of Toronto (TTB) so amenable to the English?
- How did the development of Toronto (TTB) reflect the entrepreneurial charismatic quest for ultimacy?
- Does Toronto (TTB) have possible implications for the plausibility of revivalist hopes in the context of Western Europe?

The Life Cycle of Ecstatic Spirituality

Stage one entails spontaneous surrender to intense physical and emotional responses. The outbreak of the 'Toronto Blessing' was sudden and widespread. While events at Toronto (TAV) preceded outbreaks in England, several eruptions appear to have occurred without direct dependence upon the Canadians (Hilborn 2001: 158 ff.). The initial phenomena included much falling over, trembling, weeping and laughter. These were generally described as 'manifestations', usually taken to mean a direct impress of the Holy Spirit. Subsequent reflection divided those who retained this initial emphasis, and therefore continued to focus upon the phenomena (Arnott 1995, Gott and Gott 1995), from those who preferred to describe them as physiological and psychological responses, however involuntary and spontaneous (Warner 1995: 125, Smail, Walker and Wright 1995), to a perceived and overwhelming sense of the manifest presence of God.

In stage two, as time passed and news spread, initial spontaneity inevitably gave way to standardised responses. These could be imposed through manipulation due to the emotional pressure of a preacher, through physical propulsion from those offering prayer ministry,[5] through deliberately or unintentionally formalising a new set of customary responses – falling over has been more or less mandatory in some Pentecostal churches for many years, and in Toronto (TAV) respondents were in later months lined up with sufficient space between the rows to allow for normative prostrations

---

[5] Both these complaints were made to me by those sympathetic to Toronto but concerned about manipulative styles of preaching and prayer ministry.

– or through a heightened sense of expectancy that a Toronto-style (TTB) meeting was sure to lead to exotic responses.[6]

In stage three, at least in some settings, including Toronto (TAV), there was a tendency to create a hierarchy of physical and emotional phenomena (Warner 1995: 128–9). People were thus encouraged to return for further prayer not only to 'soak in God', but also to graduate to the next phase of ecstatic surrender. This was accompanied in Toronto (TAV) by an inclination to interpret phenomena (Warner 1995: 129): each reaction was given a symbolic significance that again served to encourage people to seek elevation to the next level of anointing.

Stage four was decline. Ecstatic intensity cannot long be sustained as a normative spirituality. People become bored with repeated responses, grow wearied by the physical demands of spiritual aerobics and protracted meetings, or become disillusioned when ecstatic surrender fails to deliver significant inner change or tangible progress in the mission of the church. This may then lead to the establishment of a shrine. When the fires of ecstatic spirituality have burned low, a small number of churches tend to become the self-appointed guardians of the sacred tradition, retaining their loyalty to a particular era or experience and affirming its continued relevance and authenticity when others have long since moved on.

This pattern is hardly new. Sarah Edwards' intense and recurrent physical and emotional abandonment to God in 1742, leading to sleepless nights, a heart bursting with joy, and, in her words, the frequent 'failing of bodily strength', was much cited by apologists for Toronto (TTB) as a significant precedent for an overwhelming sense of the presence of God.[7] However, while Jonathan Edwards had no doubts about the authenticity of his wife's experiences, this period of ecstatic intensity lasted a mere seventeen days. Ecstatic spontaneity is by its nature short-lived.

Significance and Precedent

While not all periods that have been called revivals have been accompanied by exotic revival phenomena, many have. The most

---

[6] Without being able to test the observation with a control group, my impression was, increasingly, that a preacher's illustrative stories tended to shape the vocabulary of normative response at a charismatic event.

[7] Published by Edwards as a chapter within his own memoir (Edwards 1974: Volume 1: lxii–lxviii).

common phenomenon is falling to the ground, known variously as
the failing of bodily strength (during the eighteenth-century Great
Awakening), falling under the power of the Spirit (for the early
nineteenth-century American Methodists), being struck (in mid-
nineteenth-century Ulster), being slain in the Spirit (according to
the twentieth-century Pentecostals), and resting in the Spirit (for
twentieth-century charismatics).[8]

Since non-Pentecostal churches do not customarily encounter
exuberant physical and emotional outbursts on a regular basis,
their infrequent eruption requires explanation. Martyn Lloyd-
Jones argued in his preaching on revival in the 1950s that, because
we are integrated beings, it is not surprising if a powerful spiritual
encounter produces emotional and physical reactions (Lloyd-Jones
1992: 145). This allows for the possibility of physical and emotional responses, without offering criteria by which to determine
their authenticity.

John Stott sought to be more selective, arguing that authentic
falling to the ground in the Bible was always forwards, in deliberate
prostration (McCloughry 1995). Given references to falling as if
dead, which suggest collapse rather than decorous adoption of a
seemly posture, Stott claims more than the biblical texts allow.
Similarly, he attempted an *a priori* exclusion of the very possibility
of animal noises – their frequent occurrence a greater part of
the legend than the actuality of Toronto (TTB) – arguing that any
identification with animals made participants less than human
(McCloughry 1995). This indiscriminate exclusion was curiously
untroubled by biblical metaphors that exalt the human spirit by
comparison with a particular excellence found within the animal
world, for example rising on wings like an eagle. Stott's conclusions
were shaped by behaviour normative within his own culture.

Charles Chauncy's catalogue of precedents for the phenomena of
the Great Awakening, decried by him as the 'great commotion', was
made with two intentions. Firstly, to demonstrate that the phenomena had both parallels and origins in non-Christian religions.
Secondly, to discredit the Great Awakening itself: the very presence
of such phenomena, according to Chauncey, was enough to demonstrate the invalidity of the entire enterprise. Some opponents of
Toronto (TTB) applied the same logic. Non-Christian instances of
various phenomena were collected, with the intention of thereby

---

[8] Warner cites many eighteenth- and nineteenth-century accounts of this
phenomenon (1995: 100–103).

invalidating every instance of such behaviour. Much was also made of the unusual character of Toronto (TAV), a unique cocktail of Vineyard and various Pentecostal influences, including some prosperity teachers (Jebb 1995, Sizer 2001). With such sources, the argument ran, no good could come out of Toronto (TAV).

Defenders of Toronto (TTB) also collated precedents, enumerating the physical and emotional phenomena of various revivals. Of course, precedents cannot prove authenticity. The most they could achieve was to demonstrate that such phenomena are not intrinsically anti-Christian. While Toronto (TTB) apologists sought to prevent the out-of-hand dismissal of phenomena that had frequent precedents in periods of revival, their identification of such similarities inevitably invited the unwarranted conclusion that, since such phenomena occur in periods of revival, Toronto (TTB) represented at least a preparation for revival (Arnott 1995: 230, Chevreau 1994: 34). A broader historical perspective would have muted such claims.

In his early writings, Jonathan Edwards had been an apologist for the Great Awakening.[9] A few years later in *The Religious Affections* (1746), his most ponderously balanced of books, Edwards turned his guns on the twin extremes of phenomeno-centricity. He dispatched with the reductionist rationalism of those like Chauncy, who despised all physical and emotional phenomena and claimed their very presence precluded an authentic work of God. But he gave equal space to refuting the enthusiasts who wanted emotional and physical phenomena thrust centre stage, because they assumed their very presence demonstrated a significant work of God. Stages two and three in our life cycle of ecstatic spirituality – standardisation and creating a hierarchy of responses – reflect this tendency to increasing phenomeno-centricity.

Edwards' analysis of the correlation between physical responses and lasting inner change also remains pertinent.[10] Some showed strong reactions and enjoyed lasting change; some, strong reactions and no significant change; some, no reactions and no change; and some, no reactions and lasting change. Edwards' observations invite

---

[9] See Edwards' works of 1736 and 1741, both contained in Edwards (1965). Edwards himself was never prepared to deliver an unreserved defence of the Great Awakening, insisting that tares inevitably grew among the wheat in his own ministry.

[10] See Edwards' work of 1743, *An Account of the Revival in Northampton in 1740–42*, in a letter to a minister of Boston (Edwards 1965: 159).

two conclusions. Firstly, the revival phenomena are neutral in themselves, neither proving nor disproving an authentic work of God. Secondly, the phenomena neither guarantee nor preclude significant inner change. In short, while revival phenomena were initially endorsed by Edwards with some enthusiasm, his later conclusions suggest that the church is wise to move beyond ecstatic spirituality as soon as pastorally appropriate. Such eruptions may be spontaneous and authentic, but placed centre stage they tend to generate inauthentic conformity, exhaustion, disillusion and unreality.

Turning to a much earlier precedent, ancient Israel was familiar with itinerant ecstatics, the prophetic bands among whom Saul was overwhelmed by the presence of God (1 Samuel 10). For someone of Saul's personality type, at least, the very proximity of such a group was sufficient to provoke a spontaneous altered state of consciousness. None the less, far from being considered a universal gateway to spiritual ultimacy, this particular prophetic tradition makes no further contribution to the shaping of Israel's religion or nationhood. Compared with the Torah and the histories, the writing prophets and the compilers of wisdom, these Old Testament ecstatics are considered authentic but marginal.

If these prophetic bands are accepted as a pre-revival instance of ecstatic spirituality in the Judaeo-Christian tradition, they reinforce the argument that there is no justification for phenomenocentricity. Even when genuine, such phenomena matter little and are of no lasting consequence. Ecstatic spirituality is a so-what spirituality, deserving neither the hysterical denunciations of Chauncy nor the hype of its indiscriminate devotees. Edwards scrupulously sought to distance himself from both polarities.

Toronto (TTB) and the English

It should not be surprising that thousands of church leaders flew to Toronto. Edwards wrote of clergy and businessmen visiting towns where revival had broken out (J. Edwards 1965: 8) and the same phenomenon occurred during the Welsh Revival (Davies 1992: 179 ff., B. Edwards 1990: 141–2). Although Stott was deeply dismissive of such journeys, emphasising divine omnipresence,[11] he failed to take account of three realities: firstly, the manifest presence of God,

---

[11] In a letter published in Dudley-Smith (2001: 413).

the possibility that God does something of particular significance in a specific place; secondly, the deep-rooted religious instinct of pilgrimage; thirdly, the natural desire of leaders to learn from churches perceived to be strategically significant, as thousands have done for several decades by visiting Stott's own church, All Souls, Langham Place in London.

While Toronto (TTB) was a global phenomenon, anecdotal evidence suggests a far higher receptiveness in English churches than anywhere else. The English who attend football matches may behave in such ways, but not generally the sort who go to church. Toronto's (TTB) flamboyant and uninhibited displays of physical eccentricities and powerful emotions seem particularly unsuited to the English Christian temperament.

Three factors within the broader cultural context may have contributed to the English assimilation of Toronto (TTB).

Firstly, Pentecostalism can be interpreted as an overthrow of Enlightenment rationalism – where fundamentalism was itself rationalistic, Pentecostal experience stood against the reductionism of the age (Cox 1995). Even so, Toronto (TTB) may in part represent a revolt against the cultural hegemony of secularisation. Western European charismatics believe in a God who can manifest his presence, bring revelation and provide healing, and yet they experience life in a culture that functions largely without reference to God. Craving for a definitive outbreak of the divine presence may have quickened the appetite for Toronto-type (TTB) experiences.

Secondly, the growth of clubbing in the early 1990s expressed the desire for self-authentication through an altered state of consciousness: clubbers only really came alive in these moments of ecstatic intensity. Toronto (TTB) may have become for some the charismatic equivalent of clubbing, ecstatic self-actualisation in the presence of God.

Thirdly, particularly since the 1960s, a growing range of alternative therapies promised self-actualisation through cathartic physical and emotional expression of deeply repressed hurts and energies. Given that Christian culture in the West follows several decades behind the prevailing culture, Toronto (TTB) may have functioned in part as the charismatic assimilation of group therapy.

Turning to the particular character of English charismatic renewal, whereas in the States 'charismatic' and 'Pentecostal' remain almost interchangeable terms, in the United Kingdom there are fundamental distinctions of pneumatology and temperament: many charismatics reject the classical Pentecostal requirement of a mandatory second blessing accompanied by tongues, and do not subscribe to an obligatory, exuberantly extrovert style of preaching and singing. In the early days of charismatic renewal, English charismatics quickly developed filters to exclude what they considered the Pentecostal excesses of North Americans. Being slain in the Spirit, as it was then called, was actively discouraged in early Fountain Trust meetings, according to Douglas McBain,[12] because 'We don't do that kind of thing in Britain.' Similarly, while some New Church networks were greatly influenced by heavy shepherding in the late 1970s, charismatics in the historic denominations promptly filtered out such Americanisms. A significant factor in English amenability to Toronto (TTB) was therefore thirty years' familiarity with filtering out the culturally unpalatable. While some Pentecostals and New Church leaders were untroubled by Toronto's (TAV) unself-critical exuberance and links to prosperity teachers, the English charismatic tradition was well practised in sifting for the authentic while declining to accept a neo-Pentecostal package deal.

This distinction can be clarified by the observation that the two most familiar motifs for contemporary Americans are the entrepreneur and the therapist (Bellah et al 1985). This has resulted in many churches recasting themselves in entrepreneurial or therapeutic categories. On the whole, Pentecostals and New churches are not only more extrovert, but more entrepreneurial in their ethos. Charismatics in the historic denominations are more inclined to emphasise therapeutic categories.[13]

A further critical factor in Toronto's (TTB) accessibility was the Vineyard connection. John Wimber had served as a bridge in England between the historic denominations and the New churches. Originally invited to the United Kingdom by a Baptist, his closest links subsequently were with Anglicans. Indeed, the Vineyard movement in the United Kingdom was largely staffed in its early days by former Anglican curates. After the death of David Watson, Wimber was probably more influential than any indigenous leader among British charismatics in the historic denominations.

---

[12] In personal conversation.

[13] For example, Mary Pytches represents the Anglican charismatic tendency to develop counselling teams alongside prayer ministry teams. The Pentecostal methodology was more inclined to focus healing ministry as a crisis event at the hands of the anointed thaumaturgist.

In his church planting, Wimber was unmistakably an entrepreneur.[14] When church planting in the United Kingdom, some Vineyard leaders spoke of 'realising Vineyard capital' in a town, by which they meant actively pursuing transfer growth among Christians who had attended Vineyard conferences and bought Vineyard worship CDs. In his conferences, however, Wimber functioned as a charismatic therapist. There was no necessary connection between the content of his teaching on the Kingdom of God – largely drawn from George Eldon Ladd – and the method of his ministry sessions. Moreover, while the logic of power evangelism would suggest a ministry session out on the streets, the actual ministry times were specifically for delegates and intensely therapeutic, often dealing with such issues as rejection, addiction and low self-esteem.

If Toronto (TAV) had not been part of the Vineyard, it is doubtful that it could have made such an impact in the United Kingdom. If its provenance had been essentially Pentecostal, many English charismatics would have been more wary. The connection with Wimber lent credibility and allowed the charismatic filters to be applied to specific aspects of Toronto (TTB) rather than eliciting a more widespread and immediate instinct to avoid the entire package. Toronto-style (TTB) prayer ministry was interpreted as an intensification of the Wimberism already widely accepted among English charismatics.

Toronto (TTB) and the Quest for Ultimacy

By the 1980s, many entrepreneurial Evangelicals had shifted their emphasis from the truth that endures to success that is guaranteed.[15] Future hope was often displaced from the parousia to the triumph of the church. The roots of this optimism can be traced in American pragmatism and Finney's revivalist theory. Late modernity produced a breeding ground for mechanical theories that appeared to guarantee results, from church growth to prosperity teaching, from power evangelism to seeker services, from Cell Church to the purpose-driven church. To suggest there is no value in any such

---

[14] New Frontiers International were at pains to emphasise the proximity between Wimber and their own Terry Virgo in their network magazine at the time of Wimber's death.

[15] This argument is developed in my unpublished work in progress, *Reconstructing English Evangelicalism 1980–2000*.

approaches would be intemperate, but many English churches had become particularly susceptible to the quest for the quick fix, the instant solution. There has been a persistent failure to take account of the cultural specifics of Western Europe that render the unreconstructed importation of the latest North American model of a successful church deeply implausible. We should note a curious reversal of Evangelicals' late-nineteenth-century response to diminishing influence, when many withdrew into Premillennial pessimism. In the late twentieth century many embraced a gospel of assured success and promised ever-greater imminent advance, even as church attendance and influence continued to slide.

This quest for ultimacy tends to be heightened among charismatics and Pentecostals. The common assumption is that Pentecost represents the normative condition of the church. This may even have been Luke's own perspective in the early chapters of Acts. However, later in that book, the dominant motif for Paul's ministry is no longer apostolic wonder-working equivalence with Peter, but rather the parallel between Paul's journey to Rome and Jesus' to Jerusalem. Luke can hardly be said to dismiss the outpouring of the Spirit, but his determinative pivot for the missionary church remained Calvary, not Pentecost. Among some Pentecostals and charismatics can be detected a conviction that the church ought permanently to inhabit Acts 2, turning a blind eye to Luke's later chapters of slower growth, imprisonments and martyrdoms.

In the 1980s entrepreneurial optimism seemed vindicated when Evangelical Alliance personal membership and Spring Harvest attendance rocketed, Wimber's conferences became extremely popular, and the New churches enjoyed significant growth. In the 1990s the Evangelical boom was over: renewal and restorationism failed to deliver the promised goods, the decade of evangelism was a flop – excepting Alpha – and the national church planting initiative proved a false dawn. Far from enjoying burgeoning growth, Evangelical and charismatic churches were showing signs of late onset decline, albeit not as rapid as other sectors of the church, and the post-Christian trajectories of Western European culture were accelerating apace.

Wimber's power evangelism similarly failed to deliver the promised ultimacy: there were not enough healings, nor enough resultant conversions. The fact that David Watson, an early admirer of Wimber, and John Wimber himself, both died young might have served as a stark warning that rhetoric had lost touch with reality. Then Toronto (TTB) intensified Wimberism. If the world could not be turned to Christ by mass healings, surely widespread experiences of the manifest presence of God would turn the tide. When the short-lived eruption of Toronto (TTB) caused many charismatics' thoughts to turn to revival, the late-modern gospel of imminent success may have been drinking in the last chance saloon.

When Toronto (TTB) began to wane, golden fillings and dust emerged, interpreted as tangible evidence of divine presence and favour. The fillings were not a new phenomenon: similar claims were made among some poor communities in Latin America in the 1970s. However, claims of golden favour now appeared among rich Western charismatics, not obviously in need of divine dentistry. After the fillings came Pensacola, a traditional North American, localised, Pentecostal revival. Two prominent aspects of Pensacola were notably non-transferable: the evangelist urged the congregation to hurry to the front while the doors of heaven were temporarily open; and they were instructed to repent of such grievous sins as beer in the fridge. English charismatic filters rejected the former as shameless manipulation, the latter as obsolete teetotalism.

With each intensification of the quest for ultimacy, support diminished. Some who bought Wimber couldn't buy Toronto (TTB). Some who accepted Toronto (TTB), at least in part, had no time for the golden claims. Many concluded that Pensacola represented a culturally specific expression of traditional, Pentecostal and legalistic revivalism, relevant neither to non-Pentecostal churches nor to Western European culture. The quest for ultimacy continued to drive enthusiasts towards the next great hope for revival, including a Diana prophecy[16] and two New Church networks announcing prophecies that scheduled national revival to coincide with their imminent major events.[17] Increasingly Toronto (TTB) and attendant expectations of imminent revival faded from the moderate charismatic majority, not with a bang but a whimper.[18]

Toronto (TTB) and the Plausibility of Revival Hopes

The heightened expectancy aroused by Toronto (TTB) begs the question whether revival is a plausible hope for twenty-first-century

---

[16] Promulgated mainly by Gerald Coates.
[17] Pioneer and New Frontiers International.
[18] A phrase I used in my own epitaph on Toronto for *Renewal* magazine (January 2001).

Western Europe. The problems of definition are acute. The term 'revival' is used in three ways. Firstly, the bringing back of spiritual life to the church. Secondly, the bringing to conversion of many beyond the church, which more literally would be termed an awakening, but customarily in the United Kingdom is subsumed within the category of revival. Thirdly, a well-organised evangelistic campaign, according to Finney's mechanical theory. Even if we reject the hyperbolic third use of the term, there is little clarity about what constitutes revival. For example, Whitefield eventually concluded that much of his own revival ministry had been a rope of sand, that is, almost worthless, since he had failed to organise discipleship classes like the Wesleys; and Spurgeon claimed to have experienced continuous revival at his church, choosing to redefine the term to signify church growth and vitality without the attendant intensity or phenomena usually associated with revival. The term has been used to describe events so diverse in duration, theology, and geographical spread that there is no standardised usage, no established framework of objective criteria by which to determine whether a particular period constitutes a genuine revival. The term is too elastic, too subjective, to function as a clearly defined category.

This imprecision is further distorted in popular usage by unrealistic expectations about the numbers converted. In the Great Awakening, 1730–45, there may have been 25,000–50,000 professions of faith from a New England population of 340,000. In 1830 in America, 100,000 converts. In 1857–9, 500,000 in America, 200,000 in Sweden, 100,000 in Ulster and 50,000 in Wales. These numbers are certainly substantial, but still represent a minority within the general population.

Popular usage also often assumes that revival brings unity within and beyond Evangelicalism, and that authentic revival is an unambiguous event. In reality, existing divisions tend to be exacerbated: some strict Calvinists repudiated the meetings of the Wesleys as inauthentic; Evan Roberts' withdrawal from the Welsh Revival and subsequent breakdown may have been precipitated by Peter Price, a Congregational minister and rival revivalist, who repudiated Roberts' meetings as bogus exhibitionism. I have elsewhere argued that a desire for revival is an additional Evangelical characteristic to add to Bebbington's quadrilateral (Calver and Warner 1996: 99–100). It would be more precise to identify as an Evangelical distinctive vigorous disputes about revival, typified by dogmatic claims and counter-claims.

Even when not specifically speaking about revival, extravagant hopes are the common currency of late modern entrepreneurial Evangelicals. For example, Joel Edwards, writing about his Movement for Change:

> The nation will hear our biblical voice, and acknowledge the role of Christianity in its midst. Many will turn to Jesus through our witness in words and deeds. Policy-makers will take account of our values, rather than increasingly attack them. The door to the Gospel will swing open as people are forced to notice 'the evangelical factor'.[19]

Similarly, Nicky Gumbel's aspirations for the 'reconversion of England and the British Isles' through Alpha include the hope of 'prisons emptying', 'the divorce rate coming down', and 'many young people in full churches'.[20] The quintessential late-modern Evangelical entrepreneur Clive Calver typified this enthusiasm: 'I believe he's going to use us to change this nation in a way that we haven't seen since Wesley and Whitefield.'[21] This tendency to vision inflation among entrepreneurial Evangelicals coheres conveniently with exaggerated assumptions about the impact of past revivals, thus giving ostensible precedent to aspirations that disregard both the present alienation of Western European culture from Christianity and the perceived irrelevance and impotence of the Western European church.

Toronto (TTB) exhibited two factors common in periods of revival, namely an openness to intense spiritual experiences that result in fresh surrender to God, and a new awareness of sin, resulting in confession and repentance. However, this intensification of God awareness and conviction of sin showed little sign of extending beyond the sub-culture of some charismatic churches. For those who decline to conclude that this demonstrates the wholesale invalidity of Toronto (TTB), this suggests that further consideration is needed of the cultural prerequisites for revival. Much of the ministry of Wesley and Edwards addressed those who presumed nominal churchgoing to be sufficient, without any experiential assurance derived from personal, saving faith. It may be that revival, in the broader sense of an awakening that extends beyond the church,

---

[19] Joel Edwards, Evangelical Alliance, September appeal letter 2000: 4.
[20] Alpha UK Strategy Day, March 2001.
[21] Preaching at the Holy Trinity Brompton (HTB) Conference, Focus 1994.

despite usually being conceived as a potential privilege of the church universal, is better understood as a phenomenon that requires a specific context, namely a Christianised and broadly Protestant culture in which churched and unchurched share a common framework of assumptions concerning the existence of God, absolute morality, and the last judgement. This may explain the lack of any widespread revival in England since the mid-nineteenth century and the absence of Evangelical revivals from southern Europe.

In Western Europe today, increased spiritual awareness would not automatically be associated with the Christian God – the new spiritual quest is generally characterised by the assumption that Buddhism, Hinduism and syncretistic paganism are far more likely to provide spiritual sustenance and wisdom than Christianity. Similarly, acute feelings of guilt resulting in weeping, agonies of spirit or broken sleep would more likely precipitate not a prayer of confession but a visit to a counsellor or a request for Valium. Given the twenty-first-century context of secularisation and pluralism, when Christian influences are far from pervasive and appear to be receding fast, cultural constraints may mean that a traditional Evangelical revival has become a culturally obsolete aspiration, only capable of shooting blanks.

Conclusions

As an eruption of ecstatic spirituality, Toronto (TTB) combined irrelevance, absurdity, extravagance and highly significant personal spiritual experiences. It exposed among Evangelicals and charismatics, notwithstanding their general approval of revival in principle, a singular lack of agreed criteria with which to evaluate or provide pastoral supervision to such phenomena and events.

If Toronto (TTB) can be interpreted as a contemporary equivalent to the early Hebrew ecstatic tradition, inasmuch as it was authentic, it signified little. Perhaps Samuel's assessment of the wandering ecstatics is an apposite epitaph for Toronto (TTB). He commended them to Saul for a momentary and genuine divine encounter, but saw neither need nor reason to travel with them long term.

As Toronto (TTB) faded, the Evangelical entrepreneurs continued their quest for ultimacy, longing to secure the triumph of the church and immunity from both postmodernity and the way of the Cross. Faced with prospects for the church in Western Europe that resembled more the time of Jeremiah than Nehemiah, closer to survival than revival, theirs was the rhetoric of defiant optimism – or denial born of cognitive dissonance. Meanwhile, charismatics with a more therapeutic orientation inevitably detached themselves from Toronto's (TTB) intense, crisis-driven methodology. The English charismatic tradition of filtering perceived North American excesses progressively filtered out Toronto (TTB) itself.

References

Arnott, J. (1995). *The Father's Blessing*. Orlando: Creation House.

Bellah, R., Madsen, R., Sullivan, W., Swidler, A. and Tipton, S. (1985). *Habits of the Heart: Individualism and Commitment in American Life*. Berkeley: University of California Press.

Bebbington, D. (1989). *Evangelicalism in Modern Britain: A History from 1730s to the 1980s*. London: Unwin Hyman.

Boulton, W. (ed.) (1995). *The Impact of Toronto*. Crowborough: Monarch.

Calver, C. and Warner, R. (1996). *Together We Stand*. London: Hodder & Stoughton.

Chevreau, G. (1994). *Catch the Fire*. London: Marshall Pickering.

Cox, H. (1995). *Fire from Heaven: The Rise of Pentecostal Spirituality and the Reshaping of Religion in the Twenty-first Century*. New York: Da Capo Press.

Davies, R. (1992). *I Will Pour Out My Spirit: A History and Theology of Revivals and Evangelical Awakenings*. Tunbridge Wells: Monarch.

Deere, J. (1993). *Surprised by the Power of the Spirit*. Grand Rapids: Zondervan.

Dudley-Smith, T. (2001). *John Stott – A Global Ministry*. Leicester: IVP.

Dixon, P. (1994). *Signs of Revival*. Eastbourne: Kingsway.

Edwards, B.H. (1990). *Revival! A People Saturated with God*. Darlington: Evangelical Press.

Edwards, J. (1961 [1746]). *The Religious Affections*. Edinburgh: Banner of Truth.

Edwards, J. (1965). *Jonathan Edwards on Revival*. Edinburgh: Banner of Truth. Comprising: *A Narrative of Surprising Conversions* (1736); *Distinguishing Marks of a Work of the Spirit of God* (1741); *An Account of the Revival of Religion in Northampton in 1740–42* (1743).

Edwards, J. (1974 [1834]). *The Works of Jonathan Edwards* Vols 1, 2. Edinburgh: Banner of Truth.

Evangelical Alliance (1994). *Euston Statement on the Toronto Blessing*. Reprinted in Calver, C. and Warner, R. (1996). *Together We Stand*. London: Hodder & Stoughton and Hilborn, D. (ed.) (2001). *'Toronto' in Perspective: Papers on the New Charismatic Wave of the Mid 1990s*. Carlisle: Paternoster.

Evans, E. (1969). *The Welsh Revival of 1904*. Bridgend: Evangelical Press of Wales.

Finney, C. (1978 [1835]). *Lectures on Revivals of Religion*. Virginia Beach: CBN University Press

Finney, J. (2000). *Fading Splendour*. London: Darton, Longman & Todd.

Glover, P. (ed.) (1997). *The Signs and Wonders Movement: Exposed*. Epson: Day One.

Gott, K. and Gott, L. (1995). *The Sunderland Refreshing.* London: Hodder & Stoughton.

Heelas, P., Martin, D. and Morris, P. (eds) (1998). *Religion, Modernity and Postmodernity.* Oxford: Blackwell.

Hilborn, D. (ed.) 2001). *'Toronto' in Perspective: Papers on the New Charismatic Wave of the Mid 1990s.* Carlisle: Paternoster.

Hill, C., Fenwick, P., Forbes, D. and Noakes, D. (1995). *Blessing the Church.* Guildford: Eagle.

Hocken, P. (1994). *The Glory and the Shame.* Guildford: Eagle.

Jebb, S. (1995). *No Laughing Matter.* Bromley: Day One.

Kay, W. (2000). *Pentecostals in Britain.* Carlisle: Paternoster.

Lloyd-Jones, D.M. (1992²). *Revival.* London: Marshall Pickering.

Martin, B. (1998). From Pre- to Postmodernity in Latin America: The Case of Pentecostalism. In Heelas, P., Martin, D. and Morris, P. (eds) *Religion, Modernity and Postmodernity.* Oxford: Blackwell

Martin, D. (2002). *Pentecostalism: The World their Parish.* Oxford: Blackwell.

McCloughry, R. (1995). Interview with John Stott. *Third Way,* October.

Murray, I. (1994). *Revival and Revivalism.* Edinburgh: Banner of Truth.

Noll, M., Bebbington, D.W. and Rawlyk, G. (1994). *Evangelicalism: Comparative Studies of Popular Protestantism in North America, the British Isles and Beyond, 1700–1990.* Oxford: Oxford University Press.

Pawson, D. (1995). *Is the Blessing Biblical?* London: Hodder & Stoughton.

Pietersen, L. (ed.) (1998). *The Mark of the Spirit?* Carlisle: Paternoster.

Poloma, M. (2001). *A Reconfiguration of Pentecostalism.* In Hilborn, D. (ed.) *'Toronto' in Perspective: Papers on the New Charismatic Wave of the Mid 1990s.* Carlisle: Paternoster.

Roberts, D. (1994). *The 'Toronto' Blessing.* Eastbourne: Kingsway

Scotland, N. (2000²). *Charismatics and the New Millennium.* Guildford: Eagle.

Sizer, S. (2001). *A Sub-Christian Movement.* In Hilborn, D. (ed.) *'Toronto' in Perspective: Papers on the New Charismatic Wave of the Mid 1990s.* Carlisle: Paternoster.

Smail, T., Walker, A. and Wright, N. (1995²). *Charismatic Renewal: The Search for a Theology.* London: SPCK.

Spurgeon, C. (1996). *Spurgeon on Revival* ed. R. Backhouse. Eastbourne: Kingsway.

Stibbe, M. (1995). *Times of Refreshing.* London: Marshall Pickering.

Virgo, T. (1996). *A People Prepared.* Eastbourne: Kingsway.

Warner, R. (1995). *Prepare for Revival.* London: Hodder & Stoughton.

Weber, M. (1991 [ET 1948]). *From Max Weber: Essays in Sociology* eds H.H. Gerth and C. Wright Mills. London: Routledge.

Wesley, C. (1906–16). *The Journal of the Rev. John Wesley, A.M.* 8 Vols
ed. N. Curnock. London: Robert Culley.
Whitefield, G. (1960). *Journals.* Edinburgh: Banner of Truth.
Wimber, J. (1985). *Power Evangelism.* London: Hodder & Stoughton.

Chapter 15

Revivalism, Faddism and the Gospel

Ian Stackhouse

Linguistic showmanship, what we might even call grammatical gnosticism, is a particular temptation for preachers of the gospel. There is nothing like a few aorist tenses or Greek word studies to impress a congregation, though in many cases it amounts to nothing more than exegetical fallacy. Etymology and tenses, we have since discovered, are not nearly as significant as some preachers might have us believe. However, the common usage of the noun 'revival', reflected in the title of our conference, is significant, for it represents a spirituality all of its own, and is the root, I shall argue, of the present malaise in the Evangelical–charismatic movement.

Biblically, the theme of revival appears as a verb: the cry in Psalms 80 and 85 for God to revive his people, the work of his hands. This cry is elemental, visceral, and, given the propensity of the contemporary church to fade into mediocrity, an entirely legitimate one to adopt. Nothing is more common in the Christian church than spiritual atrophy, against which the prayer for the Spirit to revive his church is not only apt, but necessary. Once the verb becomes a noun, however, an important shift takes place in the collective consciousness. By dismissing a decent, robust and dynamic verb for a noun, which is what we do when we deploy the term revival, we enter a particular religious psychology, and arguably a consumer package, that has at its centre the hope and expectation of large-scale evangelistic impact and church growth. We enter the world of altar calls, the anxious seat, and mood-inducing music. We enter the world not just of revival but revivalism.

For a time, in the mid-1990s, certain quarters of the charismatic movement embraced this revivalism as the sole rationale of its existence. In the wake of the Toronto Blessing, the connection was quickly made between the refreshing and the revival, which, it was believed, would quickly follow on (Warner 1995). It is a hope that has been present from the very earliest days of the charismatic movement, and after Toronto it manifested intensely. But the fact that we are still waiting for revival has had massive theological and pastoral repercussions. Not least of these is the old biblical adage that 'hope deferred makes the heart grow sick' – a sickness compounded by the fact that in so many other places in the world the church is experiencing unprecedented growth. Hence what charismatic Evangelicals have done in that 'hope deferred' waiting time is obvious. Faced with the surprising and unexpected reality of numerical plateau – a trend inconceivable twenty years ago – combined at the same time with old eschatological convictions of triumph and success, charismatic revivalists have despaired and lost patience, deciding that if the sovereign Lord is not going to send revival, then something will need to be done to make it happen.

Looking at the history of what has been tried in order to facilitate this revival, the list is impressive. Territorial spirits, identificational repentance, signs and wonders, Kansas City Prophets, seeker-sensitive services, power evangelism, Alpha and Cell Church are just a few of the things that have been promoted as the key strategy for revival, each one of them designed to gather in the promised harvest. New initiatives have appeared on the horizon, argues Percy (1995: 152), about every two years, heralding themselves as panaceas. But in reality, given the speed by which they become obsolete, they are nothing more than fads. And it is this faddism, which has thrived in the context of revivalism, that is the pathology we are seeking here to locate. For what it has contributed to is the overall demise of ecclesial identity, coupled to a general loss of nerve about the power of the gospel itself to create its own hearing: in short, a crisis of confidence about the central tenets of Christian mission.

Christian Faddism

Fad may seem a harsh description for an initiative such as prophecy and the prophetic or even power evangelism. They have, after all, biblical echoes, and in the case of Wimber's kingdom theology – the theological matrix out of which power evangelism arose – a much-needed critique of traditional atonement theology was offered to the charismatic movement in the mid-1980s (Wimber 1985).

Wimber's emphasis on 'kingdom now' questioned the practical deism of a good deal of Evangelical theology, and took seriously the often-neglected atonement metaphor of *Christus victor*. Arguably, the same applies to the teaching surrounding prayer warfare, where the emphasis on territorial spirits has caused, at the very least, a revision of the largely ahistorical and apolitical nature of the church's prayer life. This much one surely must concede to those particular emphases.

Unfortunately, however, these theological rationales do not explain their popularity. If the architects of these various initiatives are theologically adept, theological concerns are not always at the forefront of those who employ these strategies, as evidenced by the theological incoherence of these initiatives when they sit alongside one another in a church. Given the high degree of pragmatism that currently exists in the Evangelical–charismatic constituency, a seeker-sensitive approach to evangelism, coupled to spiritual prayer mapping, and supplemented by some version of holiness piety, can often be found operating at the same time in the same place. Their popularity lies not in their theological compatibility, for indeed they derive from very differing theological stables, but in the promise they offer of numerical growth and increasing influence. The obsession with growth, of a numerical kind, is the common theme that runs throughout. Behind each new strategy, whether it be Alpha, Cell Church, power evangelism, praise marching, identificational repentance, is the search for that elusive key to unlock the harvest. And ever since Gladstone's flirting with single-interest groups to try to maximise his electoral popularity in the late nineteenth century (Pugh 1980: 22–40), we call this faddism: politics based on pragmatic concerns rather than conviction, or, in the case of the charismatic – Evangelical stream of Christianity, praxis rather than theology. It is a faddism that shows no signs of abating.

The most recent form it has taken is the G12 initiative, adopted by Kensington Temple and the Sunderland revival churches. Essentially, G12 is an attempt, through trickle-down discipleship, to cause a multiplier effect, leading to revival. Like many growth strategies tried in the United Kingdom, including prayer warfare, G12 takes its cue from the South American experience of church growth, and seeks to replicate the phenomenal growth of Protestant Christianity in countries such as Argentina and Bolivia, in the West. But the logic of this approach fails on a number of counts. Firstly, it confuses cause and effect. The success of cells and discipleship in these countries is a consequence of revival, not a cause. And secondly, the uncritical replication of these methods fails to take into account the vastly different missiological scene of South America. The same applies to the way South Korea used to be held up and courted as the paradigmatic growth scenario. To think that the cultural and missiological setting of South Korea would easily translate into a Western church coming to terms with its lost Christendom was to be guilty of naïvety. Yet repeatedly various places of revival phenomena are celebrated as the answer to the declining church in the United Kingdom.

For more overtly charismatic reasons, Brownsville, as a peculiarly American phenomenon, and even Toronto, as an oddly non-Canadian phenomenon, have been, and still are to some extent, upheld as the precursors of revival in the United Kingdom. Both epicentres of revival power display, in their own settings no doubt, a good deal of spiritual authenticity. And clearly one can learn a great deal from what happens elsewhere. One can even be affected by it in a way that represents genuine and lasting transformation. It would not be the first time in the history of revival that large numbers have travelled to a place in the hope of 'catching the fire', and, positively, many return profoundly changed. What is disturbing, however, is the way places like Brownsville and Toronto, themselves representing very different theological and spiritual motifs, are mimicked uncritically. Susceptibility to only the latest and the sensational demonstrates an adolescent spirituality; one that is demonstrably ill prepared for the vagaries and mundanities of normal Christian living. Moreover, it encourages a fascination with the novel that weakens the tenacity and perseverance required for the challenging missiological setting the charismatic–Evangelical church finds itself in.

Having stated the problem of faddism thus, we must be careful not to overly insist on theological precision or purity before engaging in the task of mission. Pragmatism is not necessarily as pernicious as some reformed theologians portray it. Being pragmatic is an inevitable, indeed sometimes wise, way to proceed. Pragmatism and theological integrity are not mutually exclusive, for there is no such thing, as Bebbington has reminded us, as pure, undistilled religion. Indeed, it would be churlish to suggest that there is nothing at all to be gained from recent evangelistic initiatives. But the seriousness of the situation is that, in the widespread hankering for the latest and the novel with which to effect revival, the church's ascetical life has been attenuated and the gospel itself has been eclipsed as the primary resource of the church's spirituality and mission. It is to this we now turn.

The Loss of the Gospel

With the emphasis on cells, prayer warfare, church planting, power evangelism, prophecy and the like, what is strangely absent from current thinking on mission is an understanding of, and confidence in, the gospel itself as Paul describes it: the power of God unto salvation. The absence of proclamatory discourse can partly be explained by the general disdain for classical preaching. In the overall development of contemporary models of ministry, preaching, as with most traditional means of grace, has suffered at the hands of spiritual immediacy that is the hallmark of charismatic worship. Moreover, the emphasis on the visual, the dialogical, the testimonial and the dramatic has contributed to what Ellul so vividly describes as 'the humiliation of the word' (1985). A more important factor than this, however, in explaining the overall lack of confidence in the gospel's efficacy for mission, is the way so many of the initiatives undertaken in the last twenty years have introduced extraneous agendas to the task of mission that ultimately question the power of the gospel to create its own hearing.

A good example of this is the way seeker-sensitive evangelism, which attracted many charismatic and Evangelical churches in the early 1990s, required the churches to be inductive in its communication. According to the first principles of homiletics, the inductive approach is, of course, essential, but seeker sensitivity goes beyond this to the point that something of the scandal of the Cross is lost to the churches' proclamation. This may not be true for those originators of the idea of seeker-sensitive evangelism. Generally, the feeling is that Willow Creek preaches a traditional gospel of repentance and faith in Jesus Christ. But the way seeker sensitivity translates into the vastly different scene of post Evangelical, if not post Christian, Britain, where despair about numbers is often the primary impetus for evangelism, has aroused concern that it is the felt needs of the listener and not the crisis of the gospel upon which evangelistic communication is predicated. The same charge has been levelled at Alpha; namely that the note of repentance, which is the first note of the gospel, has been diluted for the sake of an audience and a brand of Christianity that has some striking resonance with modern consumer living (Ward 1998).

When we look at other fads that have been embraced over the years we discover further erosions of confidence and belief in the gospel's self-sufficiency. Prayer warfare is of particular note, for here there is an implicit, if not explicit, understanding that without the insights and revelation offered by techniques such as prayer mapping, or without the unity made possible through identificational repentance, successful evangelism is just not possible. How else does one interpret the message of popular videos such as *Transformations*, with its focus on the way church unity brings revival? Not only is this simple causality, namely unity equals revival, unhistorical as far as the history of revivals is concerned, but it is also detrimental to the gospel, for it suggests that the efficacy of the gospel is ultimately contingent upon the right conditions. More seriously, it suggests that the gospel is unable to overcome the principalities and powers of a given area, until they have been demolished by the specific technology of prayer warfare.

For a gospel that has at its centre an authentic note of triumph, expressive of that disarming of the principalities and powers by the Cross and resurrection, this is a strange posture to be sure; a posture made more ironic by the fact that charismatic eschatology is for the most part over-realised. Yet here is a prayer method that seriously understates the triumph and the power of the gospel. Ultimately, the gospel is not sufficient in itself to create faith (Lowe 1998). To be fair, proponents of prayer warfare argue that they are merely implementing the victory of the Cross through their prayers. There is some validity in this claim. Certainly, their enthusiasm and passion for the lost is laudable. But what they fail to recognise is that in the hands of those who see in these strategies something of a panacea for a movement that is in decline, such methods as spiritual mapping and prayer marching are one more way in which the gospel, as the primary resource of all evangelism, is undermined. Uncritical and unreflective of the finer nuances that these strategies represent, the way they are employed in the church is often nothing less than a theological clutching at straws.

The Loss of Ecclesial Identity

Perhaps the most insidious effect of faddism, be it programme or place, is the way it has fostered an exhortatory mode of discourse in the church, at the expense of doctrinal and doxological language. It is inevitably the case. Once the church becomes simply a means to an end – in the parlance of revivalist churches, to gather in the harvest – then it is no surprise that the primary language of the church is motivational rather than revelatory. And in so far as charismatic churches, and surprisingly restoration-style churches, have aspired to the revival dream, it is this language that has come to the fore.

The language of exhortation can be expressed in two ways: exhortation to be the pure community whose holiness elicits revival power from on high (classic revivalism along the lines of 2 Chron. 7:14) (Murray 1998: 8–13); or, alternatively, exhortation with the intent of mobilising the saints to evangelistic action. Curiously, it is this latter theme – equipping the saints for militant evangelism – that has been the particular way contemporary revivalists have perceived their mission. Apart from the influence of Brownsville (Brown 1995), the classical revival language of tarrying and repentance has been relatively weak. Indeed, one perceives among a good many contemporary revivalists a distancing from the classical spirituality of revival, precisely because it holds the church in suspense (Singlehurst 1995). Either way, whether one is observing a church that is on its knees praying, or out there evangelising, the crisis perceived is one of declining numbers, to which revival is the answer. In the process what is lost to the church is the indicative mood of faith, whereby the church is continually reminded of her Christocentric identity; the indicative out of which all imperatives, be it the command to holiness or evangelism, ought to flow. In the dialectic that has emerged in recent years between mission and maintenance, such a pastoral mode of discourse, which is what the indicatives of faith represent, has been criticised as hopelessly outdated. Edification of the saints in the doctrines of faith is one of those practices that has been daubed irrelevant in the general scheme of things: growth is everything. Thus the idea that the ministry of the church should be employed in catechising the saints is regarded as something of an indulgence.

A cursory glance shows that most critiques that have been offered in the last decade implicitly, if not explicitly, make this point (Drane 1994: 165–73). Once again, the reason for this lies in the way revival is understood at the grass roots as something to do with the popularity and growth of the church. There is simply no time, or inclination, to set about the arduous task of catechesis. But what if revival was conceived in another way? What if revival was more a prophetic critique of popular religion than a promoter of it? What if revival was less about the success of evangelism and more about the awakening of the church's memory to the gospel itself, both in its promise and its demands? According to this paradigm of revival, which has equal historical and biblical precedence to the technique approach of Charles Finney, the continual conversion of the church to the language of her own gospel is the essential task of revival, and indeed mission (Guder 2000). Indeed, without such awareness on the part of the church of the contours of faith, evangelism is nothing more than recruitment (Abraham 1989).

This, we suggest, is the direction that the present interest in revival should take: a concern to evangelise the church in her own gospel. For the most part, the focus is upon evangelism and attraction of the unbaptised, and the underlying fear is extinction, as Peter Brierley's latest statistics on church decline frighten us into yet further innovations. And innovations there will undoubtedly need to be, for there is no excuse for inertia. But what is often overlooked is the fact that revival, or indeed renewal, is as much to do with retrieval of the old as it is a celebration of the new. The call to sing a new song, as Westermeyer (1998) points out, is not so much the discovery of new and unprecedented lyrics for the sake of a new wave of Spirit activity as it is the recovery of the lost memory of the church, so that the songs we sing are infused with new energy and life. There has been a gradual, albeit grudging, acceptance in the charismatic movement that this is in fact the case. Mission churches are possible only if they themselves are immersed in and sustained by the energy of the gospel itself. We are created and habituated beings that respond to repetition and, in so far as this is the case, the gospel itself remains the primary resource of the church both for its mission and for its own interior life.

The form that this might take in revival churches ought to be many and varied. The announcement of the gospel can be as much a sacramental act around the table as it is a sacramental act from the pulpit. Indeed, the connection between communion and revival is a strong one historically. Moreover, songs are an important way revivalists of the past have sought to catechise their converts, the most obvious example, of course, being the Methodists. Central to all is the notion of mediation, namely grace as revealed through means. In contemporary revivalism – the Vineyard being a case in point – the impression is given that spiritual intensity is synonymous with immediacy, and in this instance songs are not so much vehicles of didactic as carriers in themselves of spiritual encounter. Our proposal moves in the opposite direction: freedom in the Spirit necessitates means of grace.

Whatever form it takes, it is important to state here that being evangelised in the gospel – what we are arguing is the urgent task at the present time – is not a case of the church getting saved again and again. This has been the mistake of fundamentalist revivalism, with its repeated altar calls and crisis moments, and it has led to a deep insecurity on the part of the church as to its status and identity. Rather, what is being described here is the celebration and recollection of the gospel by the church, out of which, and only after which, activity can take place. Costly discipleship and effective evangelism can only emerge out of a reawakening to the gospel itself. The radicality of Christian living, as Ricoeur reminds us (Reagan and Stewart 1979), begins in the imagination rather than exhortation.

It is as the imagination is able to trace the contours of the Christian gospel – the indicatives of death and resurrection in Christ Jesus – that it is also able to grasp the revolutionary nature of discipleship. The imperatives to put off the old and put on the new flow from the indicatives of faith in Christ, not vice versa. Revivalists have tended, in their frustration, to put the imperative cart before the indicative horse, and thereby have lost sight of the gospel. Holiness revivalism, with its repeated calls for a more sanctified life, has encouraged, as David Peterson has shown (1995), a perfectionism that is not only unrealistic, thus opening the door to a dualistic anthropology, but also unbiblical, in that it fails to do justice to the understanding of holiness as that which is given in the gospel – every bit as positional as other biblical metaphors for salvation such as justification and redemption. The loss of instinct for these positional, and indeed relational, metaphors of life in Christ is perhaps what is most disturbing about the present scene. The obsession that we observe, in certain quarters, with a particular level of intimacy as the basis of revival conditions, has meant the displacement of the scandalous, yet robust, language of the gospel. This has meant not only the impoverishment of the church's articles of faith, but also, ironically, a betrayal of historic revivalism, which regarded one of its main tasks as didactic, instructing the church in her own gospel.

Present revivalists would do better, therefore, to recover the Christian imagination, recovering the drama and the wonder of what it means to be saved, and from that to articulate the shape that life might take within such a mindset. Imperatives, after all, are as much descriptors of faith in Christ as they are raw exhortation. They presuppose that a transfer of a most radical kind has taken place. Thus the call to obedience should be seen not as a precondition of revival, but as a logical consequence of a life that has grasped the significance of conversion, the significance of baptism as the essential shape of life in Christ. Careful attention to the creation of communities in which this distinctive life might be witnessed to, is, we argue, what the present crisis of the church in the West requires;

a task that is both theological and practical. Instead of focusing on numbers, which at times has diluted the radicality of the message in the name of relevance, at other times displaced the revelation of God in Christ by sheer activity, or, conversely, created a false radicality by stressing too much the need for spiritual fervour as the precursor of revival, the church would do better to suspend its talk of revival and concentrate instead on articulating the faith to the saints.

The essential task, as Thornton (1956: 36) reminds us concerning the ministry of Jesus, is not so much to cast the gospel loose upon the world, but to ensure it has a home. To this end, the idea of numbers hardly comes into it. To be sure, the growth of the church numerically is never far from the horizon. It would be an odd church indeed that did not rejoice at the expansion of the gospel. The Evangelical impulse towards populism is a right one at this point. But when this is at the expense of the worshipping and ascetical life of the church, we need to remember that the only 'hermeneutic of the gospel' (Newbiggin 1989: 222) is a community that lives by it, and lives by it because it is true rendering of our humanity, rather than because it is popular.

Whether the charismatic movement has time and patience for such lengthy spiritual formation is a moot point. Alpha and Cell Church contain seeds of catechesis and spiritual formation, but are too geared towards getting the numbers in to be of any long-term use. Spiritual formation requires time and perseverance: what Eugene Peterson calls 'long obedience in the same direction' (Peterson 1989). Within this understanding of discipleship, the journey is every bit as important as the goal. Therefore to arrest the lengthy and often unpredictable trajectories of spiritual growth by simple answers or by programmed responses, as one might find on an Alpha course, or to assume that by virtue of belonging one is believing, is to seriously attenuate the spiritual life of the church. Conversely, to shame the church for its lack of power, intimacy and the supernatural, as so often happens in the more overtly Pentecostal revivalist settings, and to assume that power equals growth, is to introduce an unwelcome machismo into Christian spirituality. Discipleship, as Bonhoeffer (1959: 139–61) so often reminded his students, thrives best when it is secret, as does Christian growth in general, and to insist that everything needs to be measured in terms of numbers and effect is to be guilty of hubris.

Holy living, of a kind that will stand the test of time, demands organic, not mechanic, images of growth. It cares little for the immediate and short-term gain, and focuses instead on the task at hand, which is, as Jesus said, to abide. Ironically, we discover, growth occurs not by adopting the latest cure-all from somewhere around the world, but by relinquishing the numbers game altogether and attending to the larger frame of God in Christ ruling and saving.

A Church in Exile

The hype surrounding contemporary revivalism is not the first or the last time the people of God have sought to alleviate the pain of living in exile by resorting to romantic visions of the future. The exiles of Jeremiah's day are prototypical of the revival mentality, in which their prophets, in their refusal to take seriously the judgement of exile, end up denying its reality altogether (Brueggemann 1998). And what is left is an escapist message and a spirituality that is unequal to the task at hand. Exile, which we suggest is a more appropriate metaphor for the current cultural context in which the church in the United Kingdom finds herself, requires not revivalist triumphalism but brutal realism and long-term faithfulness to the primary task of bedding in authentic Christian communities, in actual locations, with actual people. It requires, moreover, the creation of gospel communities that are familiar with the somewhat messy, and often erratic, business of spiritual formation.

Beyond revival, and indeed restorationist, ideology lies a better way of conceiving Christian mission. It is a way that finds its impetus and sustenance in the gospel, is expressed in cruciformity when it come to discipleship, both individually and corporately, and is finally, by virtue of this cruciformity, outward in its movement towards the world. Added to that is a good deal of praying, as that activity which the Spirit himself inspires in us, thereby including us in his will. But apart from this, there is little more one can do. For all the planting and watering, only God can cause it to grow. But until the church makes peace with the sovereignty of God in this regard, and learns that the Spirit blows where he wills, one suspects that fads will continue to appeal to church leaderships. Each one of them will have something to say. Each one will highlight, as they have done thus far, something lacking in the church. Each one, moreover, has something to contribute, which means, for this church leader at least, they will continue to arouse interest. Approached in a particular way, however, each one can underestimate and, more importantly, undermine the significance of the institution we call the church, which, to be sure, has faced worse crises than this one, but which under the ministry of the word, sacraments and prayer and fellowship has refused to panic, trusting that through such ordinary means of grace, and through such inauspicious communities, God is bringing his kingdom in.

References

Abraham, W. (1989). *The Logic of Evangelism*. London: Hodder & Stoughton.

Brueggemann, W. (1998). *A Commentary on Jeremiah: Exile and Home-coming*. Grand Rapids: Eerdmans.

Brown, M. (1995). *High Voltage Christianity*. Lafayette: Huntington House.

Bonhoeffer, D. (1959). *The Cost of Discipleship*. London: SCM.

Drane, J. (1994). *Evangelism for a New Age*. London: Marshall Pickering.

Ellul, J. (1985). *The Humiliation of the Word*. Grand Rapids: Eerdmans.

Guder, D.L. (2000). *The Continuing Conversion of the Church*. Grand Rapids: Eerdmans.

Lowe, C. (1998). *Territorial Spirits and World Evangelisation?* Fearn: OMF/Mentor.

Murray, I.H. (1998). *Pentecost Today? The Biblical Basis for Understanding Revival*. Edinburgh: Banner of Truth.

Newbiggin, L. (1989). *The Gospel in a Pluralist Society*. Grand Rapids, Michigan: Eerdmans.

Percy, M. (1995). *Words, Wonders and Power: Understanding Contemporary Christian Fundamentalism and Revivalism*. London: SPCK.

Peterson, D. (1995). *Possessed by God: A New Testament Theology of Sanctification and Holiness*. Leicester: Apollos

Peterson, E. (1989). *A Long Obedience in the Same Direction*. London: Marshall Pickering.

Pugh, M. (1980). *The Making of Modern British Politics, 1867–1939*. Oxford: Blackwell.

Reagan, C.E. and Stewart, D. (eds) (1979). *The Philosophy of Paul Ricoeur*. Boston: Beacon Press.

Singlehurst, L. (1995). *Sowing, Reaping, Keeping*. London: Crossway.

Thornton, M. (1956). *Pastoral Theology: A Reorientation*. London: SPCK.

Ward, P. (1998). Alpha, The McDonaldization of Religion. *Anvil* 5 (4): 279–86.

Warner, R. (1995). *Prepare for Revival*. London: Hodder & Stoughton.

Westermeyer, P. (1998). *Let Justice Sing: Hymnody and Justice*. Collegeville: The Liturgical Press.

Wimber, J. (1985). *Power Evangelism: Signs and Wonders for Today*. London: Hodder and Stoughton.